THE MARATHON DES SA

Seven Days in the Sahara

ENDURING THE TOUGHEST FOOTRACE ON EARTH

The healthy body company

Healthy Body Publishing
www.thehealthybodyco.com

Logo by Leonardo Solano:
www.leonardosolano.com
New Media & Communications

Photographs by Mark Hines and John Quinn

Copyright © 2007 by Mark Hines

A Healthy Body Publishing Book
ISBN: 0-9553800-1-4

Printed in China through AlbionAsia Publishing,
Hong Kong. albionasia@hongkong.com

First published in 2007 as a Health Body Publishing paperback
London, United Kingdom

ISBN: 978-0-9553800-1-3

For information regarding permission to reproduce any material from this
book, contact www.thehealthybodyco.com

Other books by Mark Hines:

Built to Last: A New Perspective on Fitness Training for Life
Published by Healthy Body Publishing

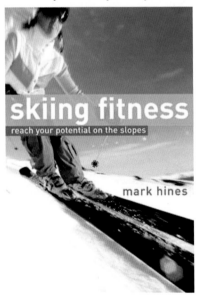

Skiing Fitness: Reach your potential on the slopes
Published by A & C Black

Signed copies of both books are available from: www.thehealthybodyco.com

The Author

Mark Hines has worked in the fitness industry for over a dozen years. He is an exercise scientist, and is currently working towards his PhD in biomedical science at King's College London. Mark has been interested in all things outdoors for as long as he can remember, something that he thanks his father and grandfather for. Mark enjoys writing and researching, and publishes a number of articles for various websites, including:

www.thehealthybodyco.com
www.ineedfitness.co.uk
www.ptonthenet.com
www.newbornfitness.co.uk

Mark began The Healthy Body Company and Healthy Body Publishing in response to a growing trend for the health and fitness industry to be lead by fad and fashion, rather than science and understanding. Over the coming years, Mark intends to publish more books and articles on exercise and health, and plans to further realise his ambitions for adventure and exploration.

Disclaimer

This book is a report of my training for, and completion of, an ultra endurance race across the desert. It is not an exercise guide by any means, and it is not an instruction manual on how to prepare for the same, or similar events, for other people. No one should ever embark on a new exercise programme or lifestyle habit without the guidance of an appropriate health-care professional. The reports included in this book should not be taken as personal advice.

It is always the responsibility of the individual to assess his or her own capacity to undertake a new exercise or lifestyle behaviour. Advice should always be sought from a G.P. before embarking on a new exercise programme. The fact that the Marathon des Sables is regarded as the toughest footrace on Earth should not be taken lightly. Anyone wishing to compete in this event should seek professional advice and ensure that they follow an appropriate and adequate training regime prior to doing so. The author and publishing house accepts no responsibility for any adverse effects that result from anyone taking anything from this book as guidance, advice or instruction, as it is not the intention of this book to fulfil such roles.

Finally, the author wishes to apologise in advance for the inclusion of some rather strong language, which was kept in the text in keeping with the nature of relationships with certain individuals. No offence is intended.

Acknowledgements

This book has been produced thanks to the help of my closest friends. I would particularly like to thank Bianca, for being a great support to me in the couple of months leading up to the event, and to Stuart, although I cannot quite remember why. I would also like to thank Emily, Sam, Mark, Johann, and all of my friends and family that encouraged me and wished me well for the journey.

Finally, I must say a huge thank you to the friends that I made during the race. Thank you to the other inhabitants of *Tente 99*: John, Mark, Carl, Richard and Selwyn, who were superb companions throughout the event. Likewise, Lee, Owen, Tom, Graham, Ed and all the other competitors that finished the race with me; the event means all the more for the friendships that were made along the way.

This book is dedicated to my father and to
the lasting memory of my grandfather.

Introduction

The *Marathon des Sables* is the most extreme and arduous foot challenge on Earth. It consists of six continuous stages of marathons across the Sahara desert in searing temperatures of up to 50 degrees Celsius. As well as facing the challenge of the distance, and being physically drained by the softness of the sand, the hot dry air and the 150-metre high sand dunes, each runner also needs to carry their food and equipment for the duration of the race. A security deposit covers the costs of a signal flare and helicopter extraction in the event of an emergency. Each runner is required to carry an anti-venom pump, to be used should they be bitten by a desert nasty.

The Inspiration

The week of the 7th March 2005

It was during this week that I watched the televised programme of Ben Fogle competing in, and completing, the *Marathon des Sables*. He often mentioned a slogan that has become synonymous with the race: 'The toughest foot challenge on Earth'. That would make many people distance themselves from the reality of the event. It would put them in awe of the fact that such a race could even exist. However, in some, the small minority of those that hear of this event, it invokes some other type of awe. It is both awe and respect and something else. Something deeper.

It is a desire to be wrapped up in the will and determination to be a part of something such as this; the feeling of already being amongst the competitors; the camaraderie experienced by everyone just wanting to get to the finish line. It really is not about winning. The primary goal is *not* to be able to run the entire distance or even to get a respectable time. It is about making it through the event, *somehow*. The reward can only be in successfully seeing it through to the end of such a challenge, along with the memories that should last a lifetime. If nothing else, it should be something to bore the kids with in years to come.

Planning Phase

Saturday, 12th March 2005

When it comes to participation in any kind of activity or event, it is always necessary to keep in mind the seven Ps:

Proper Planning and Preparation Prevents Piss-Poor Performance

With this in mind, I realise that I have to think of everything appropriate to performance, and prepare for all eventualities on the way. This means more than just how far I have to run. This means what will I be wearing? How will that feel? What happens if something breaks or becomes useless? What will I eat? What will I eat it with? How will I prepare it? How will I carry it? Will I have sufficient nutrients for the event? What medication will I need? Will I need injections before I travel? How much water will I be given and how much must I carry at any one time? Where will I sleep? What will I sleep on? What will I sleep under?(!) What if I get an injury? What if I get diarrhoea? What if I get an infection? What if I'm not fit enough? What if

I get heatstroke? Is there anybody that will want to go through this fun and adventure with me?

Before any of that I also had to think about how I would train; what I would wear for training; what surface I would be training on. Everything is about producing a similar environment to that which I will be competing in. Every detail has to be taken into account. All of the 'hows', 'whys', 'whens' and 'what ifs' have to be considered and judged. There is always a balance to be achieved between what is perfect for one thing and what is practical for the event as a whole. What provides the best nutrition unfortunately does not match with what is the lightest to carry.

There was one person that I thought might be interested in training with me and competing in this event at some point. I phoned Stuart up last week to ask if he had heard of the race. Without hesitation, or even being asked, he told me to sign him up. Excellent. This was more than I had imagined; I had phoned up to get an idea of his thoughts and yet there he was; it was as if it struck a chord with him immediately. As if there was a button in his mind that read 'in event of desert race challenge press here'. So I went onto the Internet and printed out some details from the French website www.darbaroud.com, and requested the application forms. My task for today was to design a preliminary training programme for the following year.

Designing training programmes for anything from muscle building to fat loss, from programmes for professional athletes to marathon runners, has been my bread and butter for more than ten years. The key issue with designing long-term training programmes is that they have to be designed to be 'living' documents. They need to be written as the best possible programme and then tailored according to the individual's own progress during the course of the training. Sometimes people have 'off' days, sometimes they have better days; sometimes they need to go away on business or on holiday; sometimes they become ill or there are family commitments. In a particularly hard-core training programme there is a real risk of over-training.

In order to become fitter or to develop from any type of training, the body needs to be pushed harder than it is used to. This causes discomfort and even damage that the body must respond to. The training response involves repairing damage and improving the body to prevent similar damage and discomfort at that level of work in the future. In order to improve, each training session needs to be at least slightly more challenging than the previous session. Because the adaptations occur during recovery time, improvements are dependent upon total rest time, sleep and nutrition. If you exercise before you have recovered then you will cause more damage than you might be able to recover from. If this continues over time, you become fatigued and lethargic, more susceptive to illness and injury, and training gains slow down and then reverse so you become progressively weaker and less fit. This is the over-training syndrome. When this is recognised it is necessary to take a rest from training and re-evaluate the programme.

These setbacks are expected with any long-term training programme, and especially with such a demanding training programme as one for marathon running. This is particularly so for me, because for the last ten years I have been involved primarily in strength training and martial arts and kick-boxing. When you have trained in a particular way for a significant length of time the body becomes adapted to it. This adaptation involves the very fibres of the exercising muscles. If you predominantly train for strength and power, then the muscle fibres will become better adapted for this type of work, and therefore, less efficient at aerobic and endurance work.

The reverse is also true. This means that I have spent ten years changing my body to make it useless for running a marathon. In real terms, although many people might say that I 'look' fit, I am only fit for what I do. In terms of my cardiovascular system, I might be good at explosive work such as a sprint, but for long-distance work, I am dreadful. Coupled with the fact that I used to suffer from a mild form of extrinsic asthma - I can barely run for a bus over a few hundred yards – forget covering 150 miles of the desert.

But, like those other competitors, something deep inside me was triggered by the enormity of the very existence of this event. I can cover long distances walking, although the last time that I walked a particularly long distance (over 100 miles) was when I was 15 years old and on a 9-day expedition in the French Pyrenees. Now I am 26 and I still enjoy walking for miles on end. A couple of years ago I also needed to improve my cardiovascular system for an aerobic fitness test and managed to cover three to five miles without too much trouble, on the basis of a couple of months of training. I say 'too much trouble' because it was a couple of years ago, and memory tends to hold on to the good thoughts and expel those of pain. I have forgotten about how much I struggled as I ran up and down the hills in the countryside where I used to live. I know that I have the ability to train myself to do this event. As an exercise scientist working on his Ph.D., I would be a very sorry excuse for my profession if I could not get myself in shape for the race.

I picked up some paper and began putting a template together of the days of each month that I would be running, and what distances I wanted to cover. Very few people actually run the entire race, so my attitude was that I would run when I could and walk fast when I could not. This would be the plan both for the event and my training as well. This is particularly useful, because over time I would be able to run further and need to walk less in training, whilst all the time becoming better at covering the distances required for the race itself. Additionally, I wanted to get a feel for the distances that I would be covering, rather than simply try to increase my running fitness and/or speed.

One key problem is specificity. If you want to get fitter for running then that is what you need to do. Cycling, rowing and swimming will all improve cardiovascular fitness, but they are not particularly useful for improving running-specific fitness. Treadmills require a slightly different running pattern to running over the ground. On a treadmill you do not need to push off your toes as much, nor stride as far forward. The breathing is also different if you are on a treadmill from when you are moving outside. On a treadmill the air is static and easy to take in, as opposed to when you are outside trying to gulp in air as it moves around your face; it is even more difficult if the wind is blowing any way other than straight in your mouth. So it is necessary to apply the programme to running outside.

The next issue is the environment. I will be participating in a race across the Sahara desert. My feet will be sinking into the sand, meaning that it takes longer for the foot to stabilise before I can push myself forward. This will make running not just slower but also more demanding on the leg muscles as well. Couple this with the occasional sand dune, some as high as 150 metres, and the drain on the body becomes even higher. Distance covered in a race is usually calculated as the distance over flat ground, and does not include the extra hundred or so yards thrown in for the pleasure of the dunes. This means that training should take this into account.

I need to be able to run more than a marathon a day in order to have a realistic chance of being fit enough to run a marathon in the desert. I also need to train to run up and down hills, as again the running pattern is different to running on the flat. The air is also very dry, unlike the air that I am accustomed to here in England. The hot weather and dry air mean that I will be losing a huge amount of water in the form of sweat. A one per cent loss of hydration leads to a significant decrease in performance. At around five per cent dehydration, the body's co-ordination decreases and there is a marked increase in the risk of falling and/or receiving an injury. At seven per cent dehydration, there is a serious risk to health with the possibility of passing out and even becoming comatose.

In a perfect world, all my training would take place in the Moroccan Sahara desert in hot weather, because this is the most similar environment to that of the race. I have Cambridge. So, without the desert as a realistic possibility, training will have to involve running longer distances over flat ground; running on sandy beaches elsewhere, or on any other terrain where the feet sink into the ground (such as pebble beaches and wet mud); and hill training. At this time I cannot schedule those into the training programme because I cannot judge what I will be doing or where I will be at any particular point in the future. I will also need to get out to the desert when I can, just to get an idea of what I will be doing.

Preferably I will also be in the desert for a while before the beginning of the race to get my body used to the environment. This may be possible because I have good friends in Cairo and there is a stud farm where I can stay directly next to the Egyptian Sahara. I will be there whenever possible, but due to work commitments and a lack of funds, that will be very rarely indeed.

A feature of my training is that I need to develop fitness to be able to run long distances day after day. This means that unlike training for a single marathon, whereby I would be building up to run a single bout of 26 miles, this training requires that I build up to have the capacity to run marathons one day after another. The concern here is the increasing risk of injury and overtraining, so I need to make sure that I fully recover on my days off, and reduce mileage following long runs. The important point in my training is that it must closely match the demands of the event itself.

A marathon runner, or anyone wanting to complete a marathon, might only aim to run shorter distances in training. This is fine if you only want to complete the marathon, but if you really want to improve your time, then you need to integrate running marathon distances into your training. Otherwise, the first marathon that you complete will be a shock to the body and a very tiring experience. If you are trained to run this distance then it should feel more manageable on the day of competition. An overly conservative approach is not realistic for the sand marathon, in particular, because such long distances need to be completed again and again over six days. On the other hand, in the amount of time that I have before the event, it is not realistic to suppose that I will be fit enough to manage entire marathons day after day. My goal is also only to complete the event, not to complete it fast. Being able to manage the total distances, whether or not that has to rely on a combination of running and walking, will be useful for strengthening both my connective tissues and my mind for the rigours of the actual event. I need to find a middle ground.

Change always has to be a part of the plan. If there is a line between training to prevent injury, and training that results in injury, then it can be a very fine line indeed. If you wrap yourself in cotton wool, then you might not get injured in training, but when you step out to compete you might be injured very early on, and then months or years of cardiovascular training are all for nothing. In my view it is better to train with the intention of reducing risk of injury in the event, than it is to train with the intention of keeping the body entirely within its safe limits. If you do the latter, then you are not giving your joints and connective tissue cause to become stronger, and they are therefore being left susceptible to injury.

I have trained people with similar fitness levels to myself to complete the London marathon in less than three and a half hours and with less than twelve weeks of training. The training was not pretty, but the guys made it through without dropping out of a jog, and they found the event quite comfortable.

Another feature of the race is, of course, the necessity to carry a rucksack. In order to be fit for carrying a rucksack during the *Marathon des Sables*, I will obviously need to carry one during training. In addition to the standard training for improving running fitness, there are other aspects that need to be included in the total programme. First of all I need to introduce runs on more appropriate terrain than footpaths and fields (although the soft mud in some fields will be very useful). Secondly, there needs to be strength and flexibility training integrated into the programme. At this stage I intend to complete functional flexibility exercises at the beginning and end of each training session as required. I will also begin each session with mobility work; moving my legs and body around through a similar but slightly greater range of motion than I will during the run. Stretching at the end will concentrate on particular areas that are tight and might threaten the possibility of an injury occurring over the long-term (see my book 'Built to Last: A New Perspective on Fitness Training for Life, for details on this type of training).

The strength training will be included once or twice a week only, as I do not want to encourage my muscle fibres to adapt to strength work, when I am trying to train them for endurance. The strength work will involve stability training for my ankle, knee and hip joints to help prevent running injuries, such as strains or sprains. This means single-legged squatting movements, lunges and balance work.

Sunday, 13th March 2005

This morning my thoughts were less on the training itself and more on the event. My concerns include everything from being put out of the race because of a nasty little spider or scorpion, to worst of all having to visit the dreaded French doctors for treatments. My primary concern for the race is developing foot problems. I intend to wear a few pairs of socks to limit rubbing, but even so some blisters will no doubt develop due to my feet becoming sweaty and developing frictions within my socks. The French doctors are also known to remove all the skin of the blister in their treatments. This is to help prevent the blister from becoming infected. Personally I am concerned that this might simply be an act of aggression purely aimed at the British for offending their country as our national pastime (but let's face it, it's mutual).

If all the skin is removed from the blister, then I will be left with an open sore. That, one would expect, would cause even more rubbing. I do not imagine that any injuries will be able to heal until after the race, so encouraging sores to develop seems somewhat impractical. I could be wrong about all of this, but I will no doubt stick to what I am used to. I accept that there is a greater risk of infection, but if that happens I will know about it, and after all, a blister is created for a reason. I would expect that if I cause a blister to develop during the first day, on the subsequent days the same area will become aggravated. Without any skin there, I suppose that the area would become even sorer. I think that I will just cut open the blisters to remove all the gunk, then clean them with some iodine or something equally painful, and then seal the skin back in place with a plaster. This principle has worked for me in the past, and if I take a party pack of ibuprofen, then I should be able to offset any great need to have my feet cut off until after the race is completed. Which will be fine.

I would rather that than participate in the race with open sores all over whatever mess is left of my feet. Iodine and plasters are good, whilst gaping great wholes in my feet are bad. At the moment this is the principle that I am working on. I reserve the right to change this approach during the race if I so choose. I am also only using this approach with regards to foot care – bites and stings may require some medical assistance. Additionally, if a slight sand storm happens to turn my legs bright red and sore to the touch, then I am more than grateful if some gorgeous French female doctor wants to rub moisturiser between my thighs. I will be bloody lucky to find one, as Murphy has probably already given Jean-Pierre my number, but still I can but live in hope.

Another concern is which footwear to use. Whatever I decide to wear, I should aim to use as much as possible during training as well. Most people I saw in Ben Fogle's television race were wearing trainers, but how practical are they on sand and over such a vast distance in the heat? Everyone was apparently wearing gaiters as well, which are recommended to help prevent sand getting into the shoes. Whenever I have been in the desert, I have worn boots. I bought a pair of Hi-Tec desert Magnums ahead of a trip to Cairo when I went walking for a day out in the Sahara (the walk was actually during Ramadan, and as my friends were not going to eat or drink anything, I also chose to go the day without food or water).

Being used to drinking a lot of water on any day anywhere, I particularly struggled, and felt as if someone had shoved a vacuum cleaner down my throat and extracted all the moisture from it. The thought of competing in the sand marathon *with* water made the whole event look almost *too* easy. The boots that I wore for this day were superb, and as they were a size 13, I probably sank into the sand less than if I had been wearing slightly smaller trainers. This size also allowed me to wear an extra pair of socks, which is important because the feet swell up in the heat, anyway. It is also recommended that footwear is a size or two bigger than usual because there could be an inflammatory response due to the workload, the heat, and probably an inch or two of plasters. The boots are comfortable over distances and they keep my feet safe from spiders and scorpions, as they cannot get past the thick leather uppers (I have had a horse try to eat them before, unsuccessfully, which was particularly fortunate as I was wearing them at the time).

They will also have better grip and offer my ankles more stability than trainers. For actually running in though, trainers should be more breathable for my feet, but I am not convinced that this will be the case if I am wearing a few pairs of socks. I am also not convinced that they would refrain from melting to my feet on the first day, thus giving me 'shrink-to-fit' Levi's-style trainers. One definite advantage of trainers is that they are significantly lighter than boots. I think that the key is some good trail running shoes. As an unseasoned runner, I have no idea what they are or what they do, but I think they should marry the stability benefits of boots with the comfort, lightness and breathability of trainers.

A third key issue is that of having to drop out of the race due to dehydration. It was with some of my Egyptian friends that I designed some sports drinks a few years ago. Due to economic problems, the development of the drinks has been put on hold (some swines seem to enjoy causing mischief in the Middle East and consequently the entire region's economy has been suffering for years. Not that I am being political about this obviously, but I would probably have a yacht by now and never even heard of this daft race if the powers that be behaved themselves for a change). Anyway, when the drinks were being developed, there were problems with keeping them stable in the fluid without using standard preservatives. As health-care professionals, none of us involved wanted to use anything artificial, particularly if it had adverse effects on health. What I require now, however, is a powdered product that I can simply pour into my water bottle. This is possible, so I sent an email to my friend to see what he could do. (For updates on the development of the drinks, see my website, www.thehealthybodyco.com).

A high-quality sports drink is important because the glucose and electrolytes allow water to be absorbed better than it is when drinking water on its own. The glucose also offers some carbohydrates that are crucial for energy. Proteins and fats take too long to be digested on the move, and carbohydrates are required to burn fat stores as a secondary energy source. Glucose in particular is the only fuel that the brain uses for energy – remembering that I need to combat a loss of co-ordination should I become dehydrated – and glucose can also be absorbed and used quicker than anything else. This is not good for everyday life when you want to digest foods slowly, but during exercise, you need energy available as quickly as possible, and having pure glucose is the quickest way. My drink uses some other sources of carbohydrates to ensure that after the initial burst of glucose, there is still some more energy on its way for prolonged availability. I would say that it is the best there is, but I would not have designed it to be dog food (although if you wanted something like Nitrous for your dog then buy the stuff – keep a check on www.thehealthybodyco.com).

If it is not ready for the time of the race, then I will make my own at home. I am just not looking forward to the idea of taking plastic bags of white powder through airport security. Ideally, I need my own product ready for practice. Even if you want to risk just drinking water, you still need to practise drinking high volumes in training, to help prevent stomach discomfort during the event. Water, taken on its own, can actually dilute the cells' electrolytes and this can be very dangerous in high amounts. A sports drink is better than water, provided that it is well made.

So, I now have a training structure, a partner to train with and compete with, a sports drink on the way to keep me alive, and a healthy fear of the French and the West in general. My final consideration is how I will afford to do all of this. The equipment, registration, supplies and so on all cost money. I would also like to go to Egypt to practise and take time away from work to train. Going out for a run for a couple of miles is not a problem but when I want to be walking or running much bigger distances a couple of days a week, then I am going to struggle to fit it in. The best way of affording all of this is to get as much sponsorship as possible. For this reason I need to write out a standard letter, detailing how I intend to market myself (and them) during the event and after it, and all the ways that they will get their name put about. And running this event dressed up like a camel might get me noticed but is hardly going to get me to the finish line.

This is the point when I thought that writing a book might help re-pay any debts incurred, and also provide a platform to display marketing material in photographs taken during the event. Maybe I would be lucky and have a newspaper agree to publish some of my work and thereby throw a bit of money at me and help to promote the book. The only other thing that I could do would be to ensure that I was wearing sponsor's information on my clothing and be a media monkey whenever a camera was out during the race. Great, that means that I am going to be doing even more running around. Perhaps I should write in training days involving agility work and shuttle runs just for that eventuality.

Monday, 14th March 2005

Now that I had had the weekend to think about this, the time came to phone the organisers in Great Britain (The Best of Morocco: www.realmorocco.com) and arrange to be sent the registration form. I also had the pleasure of confirming that stage four of the event would be a run of about 50 miles, stage five being a standard 26-mile marathon to follow that up, and a shorter run on the final day. At this point I am thinking that if I can run 26 miles then I can manage 50, albeit at a struggle. That sort of distance, practically a double-marathon, is something that I will think about working in to the latter stages of my training, but it will probably be more practical to envisage walking most of it rather than running it. 50 miles is an impressive distance, and I might find that I half-kill myself during training if I try it. It is also true that during the actual event there will be checkpoints where I can stop to refuel and re-hydrate myself, thus offering the opportunity of a brief respite.

I might also be walking more on that day of the race, which will make it far more manageable than if I try to commit to running the entire distance. Some of that stage will also be at night, meaning that it will be particularly cold. The sand does not hold heat very well, and there are unlikely to be any clouds, so once the sun has gone down, the warmth disappears and the temperature plummets. This will at least make the fourth day's run more comfortable than if it were all completed during the day. My new concern is that the April 2006 race is now fully booked and I must go onto a waiting list. Regardless of whether or not it is 2006 or 2007 that I race, I must still ensure that my plans are in place and that I am ready to begin training when I know. One year of *specific* training is what I believe is appropriate and I will not begin that training early if I have the extra year to prepare. I will be more active in general, making the point of doing more running, hill walking and walking out in the desert, and that should be sufficient until I am ready to begin training proper.

Another piece of disappointing information that I received from my telephone call was that the route of the race and its location changes every year. This means that I cannot realistically prepare as well as I would like for the exact distances to checkpoints, the number of checkpoints, or the location and height of sand dunes. Splendid. As a control freak, I am duly annoyed that there is an aspect of training specificity that I cannot realise, but nevertheless I am excited by the prospect of the surprise nearer the time.

The only other key issue for my preparation is food. I am used to eating predominantly organic meat, fruits and vegetables. I have a good knowledge of nutrition and sports nutrition, and although my diet is not *perfect* on a day-to-day basis, it is remarkably well balanced and healthy. During the six days of the race, I have to carry all my food. Fresh food is too heavy and bulky, and would soon decompose in the desert heat. The best food to survive the environment, as well as best for size and weight, is the foil-packed processed rubbish that is made for outdoor adventurers, the military, and campers. I never eat processed or refined foods and I know that my body works best with the organic, healthily prepared home cooking. The thought of undertaking the most arduous physical challenge of my life with the worst food available is not endearing.

On a normal day I eat in excess of 3000 kcals. On an exercising day that figure goes up to more than 4000 kcals. If I were to be highly active for the duration of an entire day, then I would calculate that in excess of 5000 kcals would be appropriate to cover losses. People in hotter climates tend to eat less than those in more temperate regions. Although I expect to lose weight from the event, I want to limit weight loss as much as possible, because if I am losing stored energy then I am in an energy deficit, and possibly limiting my performance in the process. Therefore, I would want to base my plans on consuming well above the minimum recommended 2000 kcals a day – in fact, probably much closer to 4000 kcals.

Taking too much food would increase the weight that I have to carry and place a greater demand on my performance. There is, therefore, a balance, and I have to judge what is the least amount of food that I can consume and still perform well with, against carrying too much, so that I can have everything that I need but am not weighed down by a surplus of food.

If I am carrying dehydrated processed foods, then I need to use some of my 9-litre ration of water in preparing it. This means that I need to balance my need for food with my need for water. One final concern as regards the dehydrated foods is that they are typically too low in calories for what I want; many of them are less than 550 kcals. The feeling of a hot meal is important, and I will make up the deficit by eating more than one meal at a time, including dehydrated desserts, taking milk powder to use with muesli or similar for breakfast, and continuously snacking on cereal bars and sports bars during the day. These foods are usually low in absorbable vitamins and minerals, so I might need to take along some multivitamins and oil-based fat-soluble vitamin capsules. Despite the fact that exercise increases the body's nutrient requirements, eating healthy meals between events typically rectifies this. As I will not have that luxury, I might have to make do with supplements, although this would usually go very much against the grain.

My main energy source during the event will be body fat, sparked off with carbohydrates. The luxury of actually designing a precise diet according to my needs is impossible, because I can only go with whatever is available of the foods that I can take with me, most of which will have been processed to the point of having little real nutritional value. I will also need protein to help support my body's chemical reactions and running repairs (excuse the pun) during the event. The problem with protein is that it can cause dehydration, so I should aim for a low intake of proteins compared to the other energy nutrients. But really, it is going to be whatever comes in the bag.

Thursday, 17th March 2005

This was the morning that I received the registration forms in the post. I found that I was to be around the 60th person on the waiting list, which meant that I was far beyond any guarantee of participation in 2006. The recommendation from the British organisers was to go ahead with preparation, anyway, whilst they were in the process of applying for more places in the race, and with any luck I would see myself suffering in the desert in a little over a year's time. It would be necessary to make the initial payment along with my registration, and so with no guarantees of participation, I made a tentative phone call to my brother-in-training, Stuart. Stuart told me to jog on. I was gutted.

More specifically, with Stuart embarking on a new career and looking to begin an intensive postgraduate degree in the February of next year, he just could not conceivably risk the time off or the investment. As mentioned, I was gutted. I understood completely, but the thought of doing the 'lonely runner' routine was not really what I was after. So it would just be down to the two of us then; the desert and me. No other thought entered my mind.

I set to work on completing my sponsorship letter and looking through the local Yellow Pages to find the first few companies to contact. Along with the registration form was a brochure of provisional guidelines for participation in the *Marathon des Sables*. The exact details of the course, including distances to be covered on each day and distances to checkpoints, and the type of terrain to be covered each day, will not be made available until the day before the race. Nice. There will not be any real navigation skills required during the event, as markers are clearly visible along the route, although a compass is still recommended just in case. In the event of a sandstorm, participants are expected to sit tight and not move on regardless, which will be a fun way to spend a couple of hours.

In 2003, the total distance of the race was divided up as follows: 15.6 miles on stage one, 21.3 miles on stage two, 23.8 miles on stage three, 51.3 miles on stage four, 26.3 miles on stage five and 13.8 miles on stage six. With that in mind, it is tempting to update my training plan, but though stages four, five and six are easy to judge, the first three days are a bit of a lottery. For the record, the fastest runner in 2003 had an average pace of 8 miles per hour; the fastest British male had an average pace of 5.3 miles per hour, and the fastest British woman had an average pace of 4.3 miles per hour. The slowest person had an average pace of about two miles per hour. Even so, in every race there is a 'slowest' person, and the point is that when it comes to the sand marathon, there are a lot of people in this world who will never be anywhere good enough to even make the first checkpoint of the first stage. As I said, completing the race is the primary goal, and the time is really not that important.

The brochure contains a section devoted to frequently asked questions. There is one that I find particularly amusing:

Q – How will I keep clean?

A – The short answer is that you won't. You will probably wear the same clothes throughout the race, there are no showers and the loos are not worth using – you will find a dune or a palm tree to hide behind. Women should rearrange their cycle.

The concern here is that I really want to keep my feet clean, especially if I am going to be opening up cuts and blisters. I could probably do that by rubbing in water from my rations at the end of the day, or maybe by splashing out and buying some talc to do a half-decent job. Whatever happens, I am going to be one smelly individual at the end of the race, carrying over the finish line with me quite an original perfume. From the experience of being amongst others on expeditions of varying lengths of time, no one knows that they smell. Or rather, everybody is convinced that they, and everybody else, must absolutely stink. The problem is that nobody can actually smell the body odour because they have become accustomed to it. Oh, the pleasures of this sort of thing. The situation could be worse. At least I am not a woman, and therefore, I do not have to worry about bleeding all over the place.

Contained within the brochure was an equipment list (as shown below). With some experience, I can see what I do not need, what I can make do with, and what I will be taking that is not on the list. I noticed that they did not include gaiters on the list of recommended items. The gaiters are to prevent sand getting into footwear, but most available gaiters are to prevent rain getting into boots. Hence, they are more robust, and no doubt warmer and less breathable than what I want. The photographs of past competitors show that they are wearing gaiters made from plastic materials. This seems particularly bad, because they are likely to fall apart, and although they are lighter than standard gaiters, they are going to be really good at heating up the lower legs and feet. So, in the spirit of *Blue Peter*, I may have to *make* some.

Essential Equipment List

The essential equipment list is as follows:

Backpack or equivalent

Sleeping bag (as light and compact as possible)

Small torch with batteries or head torch

10 safety pins

Lighter (not matches)

Penknife

Tropical disinfectant (Savlon, TCP or similar)

Anti-venom pump

Compass – A whistle – A small reflector mirror

One aluminium survival sheet

The 3 items that are supplied by the organisers:

A distress flare

Salt tablets

Luminous signal stick (for non-stop stage)

The items that are recommended:

Lightweight multi-terrain running shoes or a good pair of trainers

Sun glasses (100% light restricted, lightweight)

Lightweight, high carbohydrate food rations for 6/7 days

Protective head gear with neck flap

Running shorts and vest

Marathon runners water carriers with lightweight drinking tube

Compact camera and film (optional)

First Aid pack with foot-care and heat-stress medicines

Insect repellent

Green Heat cooking fuel for 6/7 days

Sew-on flags for T-shirt indicating nationality and sponsors

Passport

Spending money

Massage oils

Isotonic drinks

Ibuprofen

Multi-vitamins

Water purification tablets

Deep heat/analgesic spray

Lightweight wash kit with lip balm

Anti-diarrhoea medicine

Sweat bands (head and wrist)

Stop watch (optional)

Mess tin, knife, fork, spoon.

Each competitor must carry and consume a minimum 2,000 calories on each day of the event. Checks will be made throughout the event. The compulsory equipment and the belongings of each participant (food, survival kit...) should weigh between 5-15 kg. This minimum/maximum weight does not include your daily water supply.

The problem with going somewhere exotic is that there are always myths and legends about what you could expect to find. In desert environments the legend is that of the camel spider. The first time that I heard of the camel spider was actually from an RAF sergeant. He gave me the story of these huge things the circumference of a coffee table. The problem with telling me anything is that I am a magnet for otherwise useless information. And telling me about a spider that is bigger than the biggest in history (which can be seen in the Segdewick Museum of Geology in Cambridge) is pushing it.

I did not hear anything else about the camel spider until Ben Fogle's television coverage of his attempt at this race, and so decided to investigate. It seems that the camel spiders have gained quite a reputation from the Coalition forces in Iraq. American soldiers have reported being attacked by these things that have run after them. With a top speed of ten miles per hour, the spiders are fast, and with the understanding that they can inject awesome venom and then feast on human flesh, you could imagine running pretty fast yourself. The idea that these desert nasties were attacking the soldiers is fortunately not true. In fact, the spiders were simply running for the newly arrived shade (it was only once they got there that they presumably became peckish and started eating them).

The truth is, that there are no reported incidences of camel spiders, also known as wind scorpions, attacking humans. They do not have intoxicating venom, and they do not run around trying to eat people. In fact, the camel spider, although an arachnid, is not even a spider.

Camel spiders are by no means the only little beasties in the desert. There are all sorts of beauties out there. I recall that pleasant day's walk in the Sahara desert not far from the Giza pyramids in Egypt. It was a hot day, especially for the time of year, and without food and water, I was gasping, following my efforts against the midday sun. It was autumn at the time and the sun was to set early in the evening. At about four thirty in the afternoon I felt a change in the temperature. It was a cool feeling that told me, despite the sun still being above the horizon, that the surrounding air temperature had dropped by a couple of degrees. At this precise moment the sand became alive. Beetles, just like the scarabs from the recent *Mummy* re-make, began scrambling out of the ground. In the daytime we will all be on the move in the desert and everything will be hiding from the sun. In the evening, we will all be collapsing on the ground and lying back, just when all those little blighters want to come out and play. Happy days.

Friday, 18th March 2005

Today was a classic in the field of preparation. I posted my registration form and about thirty sponsorship letters. The real favourite of the day was going through the catalogues and finding all the equipment that I needed. Now, being a bloke, I tend to have a set means of shopping. There is simply no possibility that I will endlessly compare articles of clothing and go in and out of shops to look at prices. First shop, first thing I like, and I am set. It is unlikely that my shopping ever takes much more time or energy than that. But shopping for technical equipment is different. I enjoy anything related to problem solving, and in this case I have a huge selection of equipment to choose from, and I have to do a little research to find out what is the best for my needs. When it comes to clothing, I need to consider the fabric, the breathability, the ability to wick away moisture, how well it dries, what it feels like next to the skin and so on. The sleeping bag needs to be the smallest and lightest. The desert will not get cooler than about $+5^{\circ}$C, so I do not need a spectacular sleeping bag. I already have three of the things for various environments, including one that is good down to beyond -40°C. The problem is that they are ridiculously bulky and weigh too much.

The rucksack needs to be padded away from the body, to allow for ventilation, and it needs to have a fixed hip belt with adjustable shoulder straps. It also needs to be thin to keep the centre of gravity close to the body, and there need to be large side pockets to hold my water bottles. I have one of those and I could not find anything better in the catalogues, so I will probably use that one for the race. There are a few possibilities for T-shirts, so I will probably buy the three of them and use them in training, then make my decision once I have a preference. The footwear is still an issue. Boots are far too heavy, too restrictive and too hot. Trainers are too soft, without sufficient grip and not robust enough. There are a few possibilities from the catalogues; active footwear designed for running over tough terrain. It is just down to which ones have the most grip, the most support and feel the most comfortable. And the decision might have to be re-evaluated if the footwear that I am after does not come in a size 13.

Preparation Phase

Monday, 4th April 2005

Today is the first training day on the running programme. Having met a former student for lunch and a business meeting (Mark, from newbornfitness.co.uk), I headed home to prepare for the run. I decided that I would probably be getting muddy, and that due to the uneven surfaces I hoped to find, it would be best if I wore my boots rather than workout trainers. They offer the extra support, and I can wear two or three pairs of socks inside them, and they are heavy enough to make me work harder than I will have to in the desert. I threw a couple of 5-kg dumbbells into my rucksack, along with some clothes for padding, and decided that I was absolutely stupid. The thing weighed about 12 kgs (~26.5 lbs). I thought about this one. What I thought was that as tough as it would be compared with a lighter weight, whatever happens on this first run will hurt anyway, because I am not used to any of this, so I might as well go the whole hog and see what I find out. I put on my heart rate monitor and watch, and sorted out my MP3 player.

I calibrated my pedometer, planning to cover a couple of miles, and went out for my twenty-minute run. I returned home an hour and a half later. Two things happened. The first was that I had not properly calibrated the pedometer. I severely underestimated my stride length and so I travelled a lot further than I had intended to (well over 6 miles in all). I decided to do an interval session of five minutes running and five minutes walking. I realised that the calibration was out when I passed a signpost that told me that the nearest town was 1.5 miles behind me. That was not the town that I had started from.

The second reason that I was out so long was that I decided to keep going and do the distance before returning home. I ran for five bouts of five minutes, interspersed with five-minute walks. I switched off the heart rate monitor at one hour, following ten-minutes of walking to cool down, and then continued to walk home for another half an hour. The reason that I did this with the monitor is because after one hour it does not record information as accurately. The graph showed that my heart rate increased and decreased rapidly depending on which phase of the interval I was at, suggesting that my fitness levels are quite pathetic. Over time one would expect to see the maximal values of each peak come down, showing that my heart does not have to beat as many times per minute to achieve the same level of performance. My heart rate should also rise more gradually, reflecting an 'easing in' of my body into exercise, as opposed to the sheer panic that struck it today.

For those with knowledge of exercise physiology; I am 26 years old and my maximum possible heart rate should, therefore, be 194 beats per minute (bpm) (calculated by the controversial 220-age method). The graph showed that I was running *sub-maximally* at up to 198 beats per minute, so I still had more left if I wanted to work harder - yet more support for the idea that this method of calculating maximal heart rate is quite inaccurate. The only precise way of finding it out is to actually perform cardiovascular exercise to failure. I am not that interested, however, as I do not use any target heart rate ranges. 198 bpm was far too high though for training, but I did work myself hard when I wanted to, just for the experience of it all.

To find out the distance that I actually travelled I need to measure the route on a map. I will do this as soon as possible and then plan future routes on the map to ensure accuracy of distances. I also discovered that the rucksack is pretty useless because the hip strap is too high and, therefore, the rucksack bounces up and down, pounding my shoulders. The extra benefit of this is that the shoulder straps then loosen and pound my shoulders even more. I will ensure that I buy a much more suitable rucksack for the marathon at a later date, and strive to limit equipment to less than 10 kgs in the meantime.

During the evening it became evident that my adductors (inner thighs) and hip flexors (front of hip muscles) were particularly tight, and would need to be well stretched before the next run. The extra stress on these muscles came from supporting the extra weight and from the altered body position due to the rucksack. The rucksack also placed a repetitive stress on the upper back and neck muscles, so those will be nice and sore tomorrow. Ideally, a rucksack rests on the hips so that the shoulders are involved only to keep the rucksack against the back, rather than to support the weight.

The really good news for me is that I am preparing to fly out to Cairo on Thursday evening, apparently to help prepare a rider and her horse for an endurance race out in the Sahara, in a couple of weeks' time (although possibly just making a few guiding comments and pointing). As well as the pleasure of spending time with a good friend of mine in Egypt (Mahmoud), and the possibility of a fishing trip or just relaxing out by the Red Sea, I will also have the pleasure of training in the Sahara for my own endurance race. Before I fly out I can make the most of the next few days of training with weights, as I can use my time in Egypt to concentrate more on the desert conditions and the heat. To improve on today's run, the progression is to increase the duration of the running intervals, and decrease the time of the walks. The precise timings of each will be quite flexible, as it is difficult to know how I will respond and recover from previous running sessions until I have actually started running. I will probably have to alter the weight that I carry as well if my shoulders become too sore, otherwise I will risk injury that could set back my training. It just so happens that I tend spend a lot of my time in Cairo running impromptu clinics for friends and their relatives, so I would rather not turn up injured myself. The other goal of the training, of course, is to get away from intervals and into continuous running, but I am just not fit enough for that at the moment.

Wednesday, 6th April 2005

Following on from Monday's 6-mile overshoot, I decided to keep things simple yesterday, partly because I did not want to do too much too soon, and partly because my legs were particularly sore. If you train a muscle that has not recovered then you will cause more damage and risk becoming weaker rather than stronger. What I did do on Tuesday was go out for a brisk 6-mile walk and stop off to purchase a map of the local area. I then looked at the route that I had covered the previous day, and set about looking for areas to run for the remainder of the month. Or more precisely, I looked for where I could run for the periods of the month that I would be in Cambridge. I spoke briefly with my Egyptian friend today and he invited me to stay a further month and do some work out there. In putting forward reasons as to why this would be a good idea, he cited the fact that my other half would enjoy the break from putting up with me, and that the most condemned require a break more than any other. This is certainly true. What is also true, however, is that such a break would result in my instant demise upon returning to the country, having missed her birthday.

Today's run was kept nice, short and simple. I had already marked out a route from my house into Teversham and up to the church. That is a distance of about one mile so it was a perfect 'there and back again' route. I was tempted to reduce the weight that I was carrying, but decided to put up with it, especially as I would be without the luxury of carrying weights around for impromptu runs out into the desert. I also decided to change the intervals, so as to run for more than five minutes and walk for less than five. During the run, this translated to six and half minutes of running to three and a half minutes of recovery. My maximum heart rate was a touch lower than on Monday's run, but because of the change in intervals, my average heart rate was much higher. This suggests that although I was not working as hard at any one point in the run, over the duration of the whole thing I was actually working a lot harder than on Monday. This is the good thing about using intervals: it is very easy to make progressions. I finished the run outside my home, and switched the heart rate monitor off, as I am not overly keen on monitoring warm-ups or cool-downs. Overall, I felt better; I felt that I could have continued. And my stride length had increased along with my running pace. All in all it was a very good day in the country.

Friday, 8th April 2005

Having spent yesterday travelling out to Cairo, I was met by one of my friend's daughters, and driven through Cairo to their home. This was where I would stay for my time in town. My trip to Egypt would consist of spending time with friends, training when the chance was there, and working. Today was more of a working day, spending time with my friend and going to his stud farm.

Saturday, 9th April 2005

This was my first day of training in the desert. I took a 5-kg pack out with me, including plenty of isotonic drink, and kept my body covered to absorb sweat, protect me from the sun, and out of a general respect for the well-being of the locals. Today's training consisted of a combination of running and fast walking, using the available inclines to attack the uphills and then recover on the way down. At about 13:30 the midday sun strikes with a vengeance. It is hot and desperately dry. This was the time that I realised the American isotonic drink that I was using was awful. It was difficult to consume, made of the wrong type of carbohydrates, and did an awful job of keeping me hydrated. I ran and walked from the farm out towards Saqqara and back again. After two hours, I was hungry and thirsty. Although I had food, I avoided it because it would dehydrate me further. I was relieved to get back to the farm, but I was by no means exhausted. This was good news.

The Egyptian Sahara west of Cairo varies from flat and barren plains to gentle inclines and undulating hills. The ground is peppered with rocks, shells and bone remains. In the midday sun, there is absolutely no shelter.

Monday, 11th April 2005

Sunday was a recovery day, made up of walking around town and the farm, and not a great deal of very much else. Today was an intermediate day. I spent an hour and a quarter training my friend's other daughter around a running track at the local sporting ground. It made a huge difference to train somebody else for a change, especially carrying a lighter pack and on a solid surface. I still managed to get myself working hard, but it felt so much more pleasant than the previous day.

Tuesday, 12th April 2005

This was to be the next step in the training progression. Five hours in the Sahara desert, with kit, and carrying a heavier pack. An adaptation that I noticed from the previous run was that despite the conditions, with the heavier pack, my running pattern still improved and I was running faster, and consequently still keeping the intensity at the same level. I managed a much greater distance this time, and found myself just before the pyramids at Saqqara. These look similar to the famous pyramids of Giza, but only at first glance. As my friend Mahmoud once explained, the Saqqara area is surrounded by progressions in pyramid building. The pyramids start off with the original step design, and finally culminate in the two huge Saqqara pyramids. The difference is that they are not perfect pyramids like the ones at Giza.

The run was hard going, and I kept to the high ground on the way out, and used the lower ground on the way back. The lower ground was just as much of a challenge, because it was a longer way around, and the sand was softer. Psychologically, I prefer the more direct route over the higher ground, because I would rather dig deep and get through it, rather than take longer on a more draining route.

The view of the distant Giza pyramids was always a welcome sight. From here it is only about an hour's walk back to the stud farm.

Wednesday, 13th April 2005

Today's exercise was limited to an hour and a quarter on the running track. This time it was my friend's wife that I had the pleasure of training. It was an early start, and we were on the track before 7 am. It made a huge change to be running in the cooler, morning air, rather than the midday heat of the desert. Nihal was actually very impressive, despite my attempts at killing her off, and for me without a rucksack, I found the run an enjoyable relief. The distances that I have covered in training have been greater than what I had intended in my original planning. All this makes me feel reassured about my chances of completing the sand marathon in a year's time. It is more a question of *how* I will complete it, rather than if I will or not.

Thursday, 14th April 2005

Today's stint in the desert sands was yet another few hours of absolute joy. The bag was easier to bear, but at the same time, it is also getting lighter each time that I go out. I was informed when we set out that it would just be three hours, and so I set myself a reasonable halfway point for the turn-around. When I got there, I decided to take a seat on a rocky outcrop and get some food and water on board. Whilst there I was happy to discover which way the wind was blowing. This was accomplished by having to brace myself as an unexpected gust of wind almost took my food and kit away. I was wrestling with my water bottle and food bars to try to prevent sand getting into them. As my face was not being ripped to pieces by sand, I made the outrageous judgement that the wind was probably blowing from behind me. This gave me the added joy of appreciating in advance the fact that I would be facing into the wind on the way back. Mmm, dry-cleaned lungs please, and make it a double. I stuck to the higher ground on the way back, giving me a more undulating navigation to work with. I cannot deny that I was enjoying myself, despite the workload.

I did not seem to be leaking as badly as before and this might be because the bag is lighter, or because I am only wearing a shirt without a T-shirt underneath. It is also possible that the wind is wicking the moisture away from my skin and clothing more effectively, which can lead to false judgements regarding estimates of sweat rate. Taking water and licks of salt was far more effective than the isotonic drink that I had used previously. I still wish that I had the stuff that I had designed during my postgraduate university days, which would do the trick better still, as it would give me the energy that I required as well as the water.

As an outside possibility, there is always the argument that I am feeling better because I might just be getting fitter, but I am not convinced. The bag is definitely lighter but the uphills did seem exponentially easier than before. Yet another possibility is the fact that I was not wearing my heart rate monitor for today's journey. The strap is quite tight to prevent it falling down to my knees, and consequently my breathing muscles have to work harder. Hence, without the strap, it is easier to breath and I have improved the strength of the breathing muscles as an effect of training with the strap. Awesome.

My legs were feeling good for the run (and looking marvellous, by the way), but my feet were somewhat less convincing. I had six blisters on my feet, two on each foot were symmetrical with the other, and there were two in the centre of my right foot. I deduced that the two matching pairs on my toes were caused by rubbing against my socks, and too much movement in the front of my boots. The two on the underside were a reoccurring theme that I thought was less to do with exercise and more to do with gopping feet. A short while, a penknife blade held in the flame of a match, some iodine and half a dozen plasters later and I was as sound as a pound. This at least gave me something else to think about and fix, as the state of my guts was a subject definitely not worth writing home about at this point. Not if I wanted to be allowed back there, anyway.

Ready for another day's walk: A quick picture before turning around and heading off for what would be my last day of real desert training this spring.

Friday, 15th April 2005

Today was very much a recovery day. I ran only a mile in the morning to keep my joints moving. In the evening I went to a friend's Taekwondo class where I spent a couple of hours stretching and kick-boxing in a corner.

Another aim of my trip here was to view horses with my friend. We drove to the Nile Delta, where we had food with a local peasant, before dragging the poor man around in the car to the local stables. We then travelled up north towards Alexandria to view another few horses and the world's most environmentally uncomfortable Shetland pony.

My use is that I can recognise signs of injuries (present, past and possible future), and make a judgement as to whether or not the horse's biomechanics will affect its running ability and capacity. The first horse I viewed had an imbalance in the front right leg. This was evident from the fact that the right leg travelled too far forwards, not far enough backwards, and did not generate as much power as the front left leg. This suggests an imbalance between the shoulder flexor and extensor muscles, and a possible injury within the shoulder capsule. What this means is that the horse might fatigue early in a race and be more prone to injury (through repetition of movement or through a single impact stress).

The second horse that I viewed was a different story. In terms of the movement pattern, the horse was all over the place. It ran like a bunny rabbit on amphetamines. The hind legs came too far forward and were rotated laterally in a standing stance. What was also evident was that because of this the horse generated a huge amount of power. Basically, the muscles of the butt were long but fired quickly and powerfully, allowing a huge range of motion through the biggest muscles in the body. It was a horse that I would bet on, although a few years down the road there would probably be some joint problems occurring, and it would not do so well on endurance work. The last horse that I saw was only a year and a half old. There were a number of comments that I could have made. I could have said that whilst the forelegs were almost touching, the hind legs were almost touching either side of the paddock. Viewed running from the side, it was clear that whilst the front right leg had a good range of motion and was powerful, the other three did not have a clue and were just trying their best to follow on and not to look embarrassed. Sometimes people do not need to be baffled with information when a clear point sorts everything out: 'I know that he's young, but he runs like a tosser.' Point made.

Sunday, 17th April 2005

I spent Saturday just walking for a couple of miles. This was useful because I was still a little sore from Thursday's five hours in the desert. Today, following an early start (and a late night before), we set out just after 7am. We headed south, into Suez, and through their equivalent of the Dartford Tunnel, to the Sinai Peninsula. From there we continued south a couple of hundred miles, passing through Sharm El Sheikh before finally arriving in Dahab. The scenery on the journey was striking. The landscape varied from flat desert plains with palm trees and farmland, to dramatic and aggressive rocky hills and mountains. When we arrived in Dahab we checked into a hotel on the seafront, with views out across the blue seas of the Aqaba Gulf to Saudi.

The view from the restaurant above my bedroom

The evening was one to be remembered. We were to have dinner with a few local friends. We drove out to a pebbled area on the perimeter of a lagoon. There we relaxed on rugs by the sea, looking at the night sky and listening to the sound of the water. I ate barbecued seafood with my hands as if I had never experienced food before in my life; it was gorgeous, and all washed down with litres of sweet tea. I laid back and spoke with the guys, warmed by the fire, and drinking tea. It reminded me of my youth when I used to go out into the countryside around the town where I lived, with a few or a lot of friends; we spent the evening around a fire, talking to each other, listening to the wind, and looking at the sky. This was heaven to me.

My mother will be so ashamed that I have worn out another pair of socks.
These are the problems with having big feet.

Monday, 18th April 2005

Training went well today. It started with a 2-mile gentle stroll along the seafront. This was then closely followed by a strenuous bout of lounging by the side of the pool whilst drinking a fruit cocktail. Every now and then I fired some facial and neck muscles to raise my gaze above the pool and check that Saudi was still where it ought to be.

Having had lunch in a Bedouin-style café, all alone but for the sound of the sea, I succeeded in developing splendid sunburn on my arms and legs. I returned to the room and changed into more suitable clothing. In the afternoon we went out on a boat to view the coast, the coral and the marine life. The sea was filled with purple jellyfish (which do not sting, by the way), and we were fortunate enough to see a hoard of dolphins. On the way back they were swimming at speed by the front of the boat. I was hanging off the bow and getting soaked trying to take some close-up photographs. When they were gone, we stopped a few times to fish and made quite a collection by the time we reached the shore (dolphin-free, obviously).

Just leaving Dahab for an evening relaxing.

 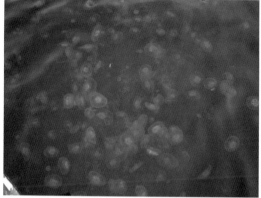

The views over the side of the boat, with coral on one side and purple
jellyfish on the other.

In the evening we drove up a wadi into the mountains, courtesy of Land
Rover, and ate a lamb that had been slaughtered for us earlier. It had been
cooked along with some vegetables in an underground oven. I am not usually
one for eating quantities of animal fat, but I was not going to be so rude as to
leave any soft tissue whatsoever (I would have eaten the bones if I could). It
was another hands only affair; I made an absolute disgrace of myself, yet again
being too busy eliminating everything in sight to notice that the others were
finished and packing everything away. We were there because we knew this
old man who had taken to living in the rocky hills. It was his way of avoiding
the distractions of strangers, and developing himself in the beautiful, secluded,
and serene surroundings.

Tuesday, 19th April 2005

Three things struck me when I woke up this morning. The first was a fly, which I promptly disposed of. The other two were also related facts and were as follows: My legs were burnt and stinging like buggery and my face was as red as a baboon's arse. As the day persisted, the burns got worse, as even my robust clothing could not keep the sun out completely.

In the morning I went for a short walk and then spent the evening deep in a mountain pass with some of our friends. It was the first place we went to where none of us had reception on our mobiles. The Sinai Peninsula has some wonderfully harsh rocks for climbing. We stopped at the end of the track to prepare for dinner (the fish that we had caught the previous night).

Anyone that has spent some time with me outside of town usually recognises that I have a bizarre fascination with climbing things. I climb anything that I can. If you cannot see me when we go out for a walk, then start looking upwards. The rock that I sent myself up was a swine. Granite and coarse rocks were coming away all over the place. I had noted three possible routes up, all challenging but each one a little easier than the one before.

An oasis amongst the barren hills.

On my second attempt at the first route, I had to give up about thirty feet from the top. It was bad to start with, and there were too many vertical climbs and too few places to rest, and the further I went up the more rocks were coming away around my hands and feet. Accepting that I am not a technical climber, that I am climbing alone and without equipment, and that the place was falling apart, I decided to make my descent and charge up another route whilst I still had some daylight left. The second route I had seen was not much better. I decided that it was getting too dark to risk it so I charged up the third route instead. There was less climbing and more scrambling, and I made the ascent in no time at all.

Having arrived at the site where we would being having dinner, the others went off for an evening's stroll, whilst I busied myself with the task of some gentle climbing.

I had the chance to take a few photos and then proceeded to part run, part fall, and part throw myself to the bottom of the rock. It was dark by the time that I got there, and I was glad that I had not spent any longer at the top than I did. It was a satisfying climb but I was annoyed at not persevering with the first route – I probably would have killed myself (many times) – but that did not mean that I liked calling it a day. I am happy to view mental challenges as an important part of my training for the sand marathon, as there will doubtless be many occasions when mental toughness is more important than physical fitness.

Views from the summit following my final attempt, the jagged ridges disappearing into the night as the sun sets. The race is then on to beat the darkness down to the bottom.

Dinner was fantastic, and I managed to devour half my bodyweight in fish, salads and vegetables. The food that I had been eating in the evening here was actually far healthier than the other food that I had eaten in Egypt. It was basic food; nothing processed and nothing cooked in fat. We only let ourselves down with the soft drinks, but that is classed as the norm for all self-respecting and hospitable Egyptians.

Thursday, 21st April 2005

This was to be my second from last day in Egypt on this trip. Having got back from Dahab on Wednesday, I spent today with my friend's two daughters, and some of their friends, on a beach near Ain Sokhna by the Suez Gulf, about 65 miles or so south-east of Cairo. We went swimming, and played football and such like on the beach. The fact that we made it at all was no easy feat, as a severe sandstorm slowed down the roads. When you are driving, a sandstorm is like an Egyptian version of our fog – just a more orange tone of pea soup. Incidentally, when walking in a sandstorm, it is like walking in fog that has nails in it. I was glad to be in the car. It stopped after about half an hour and the sky was back to its usual blue self. At the beach it was nice to get the swimming in, as I have not swum in the sea for a long time, and it has a huge effect on stamina.

It was late on Thursday night that I received a devastating blow to my training. When I removed my left sock, I realised that the ankle was almost unrecognisable. When I removed my right sock, the left looked even worse. I must have damaged some connective tissues when climbing, or at least stretched them beyond their normal elastic range, and then made it all worse running around and playing silly buggers on the beach. I was devastated. Any serious soft tissue damage would put me out of hard training with loads for at least three weeks.

Friday, 22nd April 2005

Today was the last day of my trip. I spent some time with my friends, visited the farm, and went along to Taekwondo that evening. The last time that I went along, I spent a couple of hours kick-boxing in a corner. This time I could only sit and watch, and stretch out and mobilise my damaged ankle, and I was in no state to participate in anything. Later on I discovered that the soft tissue damage extended up into the soleus and medial gastrocnemius of my left calf muscles. I have no recollection of being in any pain other than that due to the sunburn. I am absolutely gutted. The only good news is that I have learnt an important lesson. When training for a competition, don't play silly buggers at anything else. I had avoided horse riding, and even refused to walk a horse in the desert, because I knew that dragging it along for hours could have a negative impact on my biomechanics. I am glad that this happened now, and with a year of training ahead of me, I have plenty of time to rehabilitate the ankle, and get properly focussed on the task in hand.

My time in the desert at least showed me that I have the capacity to carry the equipment and make the distances. I know that the desert is tough, and the soft sand and midday heat are a huge drain, but I have still gone out there with the mindset to reach my goals. Now I need to adapt my training to make a better job of it. For anybody interested in my personal health, there have been two developments. The first is that, in fact, I did not develop two blisters on the sole of my right foot through abrasion. They were just a part of some fungal event that has since covered the area in about a dozen of the things. So that is nice. The second development is that after the first week my guts were back on track. Splendid.

Sunday, 24th April 2005

The next phase in my training is a full rehabilitation of my lower leg and ankle injury. This will be three weeks of strength, stability, mobility and proprioception (sense of awareness) training (adapted from my other book, 'Built to Last'). I had intended to introduce one or two days of this training into my programme anyway, with the aim of using it to improve my running pattern, and to prevent injuries. Better late than never.

Tuesday, 17th May 2005

Three and a half weeks have passed since the ankle injury. During the first few days of rehabilitation back in the U.K., I was struggling to walk more than a mile 'pain-free'. Over the subsequent days, I was able to increase my walking distance and managed to get by without pain quite effectively. Whilst walking across fields in the first week, it became apparent that there were issues with soft-tissue strength and stability that would need to be addressed.

In the second week of rehabilitation, I began introducing kick-boxing into my training programme. The reason for this is that I have done a lot of kick-boxing and martial arts in the past and I enjoy it. Rehabilitating an injury could just be about performing specific stretches and stability exercises, but personally, I prefer to integrate it into an exercise session that I enjoy, anyway. So, my kick-boxing sessions would consist of various static lower body stretches, combined with dynamic and ballistic stretches, and finally performing full-speed kicks and punches. Initially I used a makiwara, a wooden, sprung unit that sits on the wall and is supposed to absorb a great deal of the stress going through it.

After the third session, I noticed that the wall was cracking so I thought it best to just beat up the air instead. Probably for the best. Ordinarily, ballistic stretches (fast movements beyond a normal static range of motion) should be avoided because of the risk of injury. With martial arts it is very appropriate because it is an intermediate phase between a warm-up and the full-speed/power kicks. The trick is to warm up first, then perform any required

69

static stretches on problem areas, then go into slow and controlled dynamic stretches, before proceeding into the faster, ballistic movements.

The benefits of this style of training include improved stability, mobility and proprioception on the supporting leg; a greater functional muscle length and range of motion to reduce the risk of injuries when moving fast; and the peace of mind of knowing that if a homicidal maniac decides to have a set-to with me when I am running outside, I stand a good chance of getting away with just giving him a slap and carrying on.

I am now in week four after the injury and should be preparing to get back into running again. I am confident that my ankle is in good enough condition. The only problem now is the original goal...

...I received a letter a couple of weeks ago confirming my registration for the 2007 sand marathon. This, I thought, was just an administrative error. I phoned up to clarify and it transpired that there was confusion regarding the application forms. I then had to fill in another form and re-send it to put me back on the waiting list for the 2006 event. The problem is that I have gone from around the 50th place to the 82nd. Considering that about 50 people on the waiting list made it through to compete in the race last year, I had been rather confident about competing in the 2006 marathon. The chances of my making it now have been reduced to somewhere between slim and none. And Slim just broke his legs training.

I am therefore undecided as to whether or not I should continue with my aggressive training programme, and find myself super fit a year too early (hah!), or carry on doing my usual exercise and just add a moderate amount of running. Decisions, decisions. Really I doubt very much that I will make it onto the 2006 marathon. There are two sensible possibilities for me now:

1. I can continue on with my original training programme. If I cannot compete in the 2006 race, then I will have to change to a maintenance

programme for a while and bring my fitness back up to par before the 2007 event. My main problem with this is that it will make the marathon almost too easy and I will be too well prepared (ha-ha!). There is less of an element of danger and the unknown. This possibility is vastly less sexy than the single-year of training approach.

2. Alternatively, I can just do my own training for the time being. That would mean continuing with the kick-boxing and the walking. I would also get back into strength training when I find myself a good enough gym (I am a fussy bugger and I need to have adequate dumbbells, and a squat rack – which are more difficult to find than you might imagine). I would get back into running but probably stick to the shorter distances and without as much weight. When I have my place confirmed on the 2007 race, I would just increase the weight and run greater distances. In effect I am looking to make smaller gains rather than go all out now and then calm it all down come the spring of next year.

On the other hand, if I find out that I am going to be entering the 2006 race, then I have to pull my finger out and get into some very hardcore training for whatever period of time that I have. From my training in Egypt I know what I am capable of and I know that I could survive the race if I went tomorrow. But I am becoming an ambitious bastard now and I would rather complete it well; achieving a respectable time whilst looking good and having not a hair out of place – that sort of thing (even if I do smell like a lumberjack's armpit).

...Decisions, decisions...

Thursday, 2nd June 2005

I can now say without fear of contradiction that my foot is well and truly healed (there is probably a pun in that statement but I refuse to entertain it). However, I am still reluctant to go out running again, but this is nothing to do with the threat of injury. This is almost entirely due to another factor that has an influence on everyone's life, and that is stress. For those that are familiar with Professor Stephen Covey's work on 'Seven Habits of Highly Effective People' and so on will know where I am going with this. I have not detailed the many stressors in my life because this is a training diary and not my autobiography. Nor do I feel that you have committed enough sins to warrant knowing what is going on in my immediate world. My immediate world should be a nice and fluffy place, full of rolling hills, the most perfect grass and flowers, blue skies and lots of rabbits. It is a pleasant place where I spend my time when I am ignoring whoever happens to be talking at me.

Stress is a nasty thing that was very useful once. Back in an age long ago, it was useful to become so angry that you could tear the head off a rhinoceros - when being charged by a rhinoceros is one such example. Nowadays we have some sort of stress response to the most ridiculous things. Reading a credit card statement or the phone bill causes a stress response. Bearing in mind that this is just a piece of paper, I dread to think how people would really react if they were confronted by anything really life threatening. What I can say, also without fear of contradiction, is that health, wealth and happiness are three things within as easy reach of me as the dark side of the moon at the moment.

There are a number of reasons for this, but really everywhere that I look there are problems. Some problems are small and some are much bigger. The key to stress is knowing how to deal with it. I tend not to worry about the small problems because they are insignificant in comparison with the big problems. Once the big problems have been sorted out then it is okay to turn attention to the smaller things. I cannot sort out some of the big problems personally. Normally those problems would also be excluded, but in the cases affecting me I do care enough about the people involved for it to cause me stress.

Other problems are down to me to solve. That is something that I have to do, and worrying about the solutions is a very definite cause of stress. The relevance of this is that there is a limit to how much stress you can take. Too much stress makes a person become sullen, easily fatigued, lethargic and prone to illness. Exercise 'training', whereby you are pushing your body both physically and mentally, is also a stress and can, in fact, be rather a big one. People should not exercise too much, in terms of the combined effects of frequency and intensity, and nor should they begin *strenuous* exercise if they are already very much aware of the existence of too much stress in their lives. Deal with stress before taking on more.

At the moment I have more stress in my life than you could shake a stick at. I have been able to increase miles travelled by walking because I do not perceive that as much of a stress. I have also been able to progress well with my kick-boxing since I started training again about five weeks ago. I even started some martial arts classes four weeks ago, as this particular style complements the various martial arts and combat styles that I have practised in the past. Again, I do not perceive this as a stress, because anaerobically I am rather fit and I find this sort of training quite easy-going. As I have suggested before, I am about as good at running as a beached whale. So, until I get other things in my life sorted, it is necessary to keep active but on a lesser scale than is perhaps appropriate for my goals. This in itself is not a huge issue, as it is looking more and more like I will not be able to make it onto the list for 2006, and instead have to transfer over to the 2007 list. This is not what I want, but if I do not make the decision then there is the possibility that I will not be able to make the list for 2007 either, and then I will have died of old age before I get to have a stab at the race.

In the meantime, I have decided that the best thing for me to do is to get away from it all for a weekend. I need to get away from my distractions and stress and just relax and be content for a few days. So, I have decided to walk to Thetford forest, stay over for a night or two, and then come back home either walking or by train. A couple of days in the forest will do wonders to chill me out and bring me down to some level of normality. The plan is to head off tomorrow and then return on Sunday. This will be useful, because the forest is about 30 miles away, and therefore, I will get the chance to feel what it is like to cover a marathon distance. Planning only involves writing out my route and packing some kit to take with me.

The rucksack is just shy of 20 kg, which is significantly heavier than the bag that I will be carrying around during the race. The forecast is also for a bit of rain, which is also unlikely to be a threat during the actual event, which is nice.

Saturday, 4th June 2005

Two important things happened today. The most important thing that happened was the wedding of one of my best friends, Russell, to his American love, Ashley. If I had some of that money stuff that has been all the rage then I would have flown out to the States to be with him. Fortunately for him I was unable to go because I would have gotten him absolutely ruined the night before. But, I was certainly with him in spirit, and I would like to take this opportunity to wish them both all the best for their future here in England. I know that their future is in England because Russ is a shady looking bastard and he was deported a few weeks ago never to return. Now he has been let back in just for the wedding, but after that he has to pack his bags, bring his wife over here to jolly old England, and never again stick his big nose in the U.S.

The second important thing that happened today was that I returned home. I actually travelled home rather late last night, arriving in the wee early hours of today. Yesterday's walk was wonderful. I visited some beautiful villages on the way to Thetford forest, and I passed through a few manky ones as well. The rain started at about four o'clock. The thunder started very shortly thereafter. I am not the sort of person that is unduly concerned by thunderstorms. On this occasion, however, there was a very good reason to be very concerned indeed. That reason was the fact that I was walking between Cambridgeshire and Suffolk at the time. Open farmland surrounded me and there was barely a tree in sight. In fact, my head was clearly the highest point for many miles around. When lightning strikes there is first a charge that goes upwards from a point on the ground. The lightning bolt that comes from the clouds then meets this one and goes along that line into the earth.

What this means, essentially, is that you get a fraction of a second's warning before the main bolt hits you. Another key point is that the safest place to receive the aforementioned lightning bolt is the anus. This is with the understanding that this orifice offers less importance than any orifice around the head. An ice-cold colonic is probably the only pleasant thought that came into my mind at that time, as my posture became just a touch more stooped, just in case.

When the rain eventually stopped, it was not long before I dried out. This was a good thing, because I had been walking for a few hours and I was getting a little tired with the weight of the rucksack, and did not really want to be spending the weekend wet. Which was a shame, because the rain started back again about an hour and a half later. This time the end was not in sight. After about thirty miles of walking, I set up a shelter in the forest, promptly packed it away, no doubt muttering something along the lines of 'bugger this', and got back onto the roadside and headed for Brandon. A weekend of relaxation was not going to be a weekend of being cold and wet. Another problem was the blisters. When I was out in Egypt I managed to earn a few blisters because of my socks, but this time it was purely because of the impact forces affecting the skin just on the balls of my feet between the great and second toes.

What made this worse was that my boots were letting in all the water. Three pairs of socks were saturated. This made the blisters feel worse, and on my right foot I was starting to experience pain on the outside of the foot and just beneath the ankle. This became progressively worse and I was almost developing a limp. More than the sensation of pain was the fear of developing stress fractures. I was not sure exactly why the outside of my foot was hurting so much. I did not know if it was caused directly by the stress of impact as I was walking, or if it was due to muscles pulling on the bones.

Stress fractures can also be caused when the muscles become too fatigued to work properly. One of the functions of muscles is to distribute stress around the body. Consequently, when muscles become tired, the bones have to absorb more stress that they should, and this can result in stress fractures. By the time I made it to Brandon station, at a quarter past ten in the rain, my foot was in bits and I had only walked about 40 miles.

I managed to thaw out on the train (although I certainly did not manage to dry out) and I dreamt of a nice hot brew. When I got home, three pairs of soaking wet socks came off to reveal what appeared to be the biggest, flattest and whitest prunes that I have seen in my life. My feet were so wrinkled I could not see the blisters, although I was very sure indeed that they were there. I had also almost lost the toenail from my fourth toe on the right foot. What was left was a purple nail surrounded by blood, which was nice.

The outside of my right foot was swollen just below the ankle. This was caused by my changing my walking pattern slightly to take the stress away from the blisters. What must have made this worse was that my boots were probably a touch too small and my leg was restricted just above the ankle. This would limit the ability of the muscles of the lower leg to work properly and they would have fatigued sooner. Fortunately this was not as bad as it could have been. I put on my towelling robe and had one of the nicest brews of my life.

I was a little disappointed that I had come back, but I knew that I could have a much better time of it in nicer weather. In the meantime, I had buggered up another foot and that would need some work to get it back to normal. The good thing was the distance: 40 miles carrying 20 kg of kit over predominantly paved roads. The desert is so much softer that my feet would fare much better. In addition, I would be carrying less weight and I would not have to put up with driving rain soaking me through. I was walking at a constant speed of just under 4 miles per hour, even with a couple of stops to fill up on food and to mess about with the shelter.

I know that I can do 50 miles in a day now, even though I can only be sure of making it by walking. What I need to do now is to be able to do 50 miles in the middle of a week when I am covering marathon and sub-marathon distances as well. Then I need to do it all running most of the way. And now with what looks like a year and a half of training before the event? This is getting better and better.

Friday, 17th June 2005

Following my epic stroll in the Great British countryside, my feet have yet to recover completely. The damage was actually the same on both feet, despite my only feeling pain, and having swelling, on the right side. I have inflammation and pain along the tendons of the peroneals (the muscle itself runs down along the outside of the lower leg). The initial swelling lasted two days, but pain on the underside of the foot was persistent for about a week and a half. Then I walked about 10 miles and it came back again. The problem with tendon damage is that is takes a lot longer to heal than muscular damage. Tendons (and ligaments) generally have a much lower blood supply than muscles and are far less elastic. This means that they do not stretch easily and when they are damaged, it takes a lot longer for the tissues to heal because there are fewer nutrients travelling to the area.

Today, following a few miles of walking, I decided to cycle to nearby Biggleswade for my martial arts grading. The journey there was about a marathon's distance, but I decided to shorten it on the return by taking the train. In all I cycled approximately 35 miles. The ride itself was hellish, mainly because I had not had the chance to recuperate my energy stores following three hours of kick-boxing the previous day. This meant that many of the hills were particularly punishing, because my carbohydrate energy stores were depleted, and my body was struggling to convert fat for energy in the absence of the glycogen (stored glucose) that it prefers for higher intensity exercise. Being the pool of wisdom that I am as regards sports nutrition, I

THE MARATHON DES SABLES

could not help myself from dreaming about a chip shop. My body had a deficit of a couple of thousand calories to make up and my water bottle was most definitely found wanting.

What is also important to note is that there are very few carry-overs of cycle training to marathon training. Yes: Cardiovascular fitness improves, but the fitness of the muscles themselves is improving primarily for cycling rather than running. So, although it was nice to have a cycle ride in the countryside, I was not doing it specifically to assist in my marathon training. Conversely, becoming more active in general does help in motivation and in the adherence to a healthier lifestyle, so there are some benefits to be had at the very least. Mentally, the cycling was quite tough because of some steep hills and strong winds, which meant that there were benefits for training my attitude, if not my running fitness.

Saturday, 25th June 2005

A decision had to be reached regarding which year I would compete in the MDS. I had delayed for a couple of weeks to see if I would move any further along the waiting list, but it was not enough to give me any confidence. It was agreed that my best chance would be for 2007, and to change the registration now, rather than wait and risk losing out on both 2006 and 2007. This is a real shame, because I am just ready now to throw the rucksack on and get back into some good running. Now I am left in a sort of lull; a no man's land where there is no point aiming to be prepared for the event next April, but where I have too much training and motivation to make me want to start again from the beginning next year.

What I will do is abandon the training plan for a while and see how I go without it. I have been unable to get into the strength training as much as I had wanted, because I have not had access to a gym. I have been out of work since the spring and have not wanted to join a gym whilst I was expecting to find work in one. I also struggle to be motivated to do strength training at home, because I need access to heavy weights and a good floor.

However, I am now expecting to start work managing a corporate fitness facility at Canary Wharf in a couple of weeks' time. This will give me the access to equipment that I need and all the time that is required to use it. I will develop an appropriate training plan when I get the chance. I am doing quite a bit of kick-boxing at the moment. I am stretching lots and working on stability, both of which are useful for reducing the risk of injury from running.

And I enjoy kicking people in the head, so there is a key motivation factor there as well.

Sunday, 10th July 2005

Today marks the end of what will prove to be one of the most eventful and obscure weeks in our country's recent history. A huge focus has been on raising awareness of poverty in Africa for the world leaders at the G8 summit in Edinburgh. We also received the announcement that London would be hosting the Olympics in 2012. On Thursday, a series of attacks on London transport marked the first major terrorist action since the days of the IRA.

When I finished work on that Thursday I decided to walk to a friend's house in north London. I could not travel home because I needed to be at work outrageously early in the morning to ensure that everything was okay. Having walked the first two hours, passing predominantly static traffic, I managed to get through to my friend to find that he was not staying at home that night either. I had managed to get from Canary Wharf to halfway along Oxford Street. I did a left turn and walked down, through Soho, to Leicester Square. I had a friend that worked at one of the hotels there, where I used to work, and thought that I should at least check up on the outside possibility of a room.

No luck and no surprise, so I wandered off through Covent Garden and then over the Strand to the Thames. I managed to get through to another friend of mine who was shopping at Bluewater at the time. He was happy for me to stay at his place but would not be able to meet up with me until later on. I made the sensible decision of finding a pub; having walked along the South Bank and then back and over to St. Katherine's docks, I sat down with a pint of London Pride, and made a start on getting myself slowly pissed. I am not sure if I needed it because of the start of the day or because of the last four hours of walking around London. Probably equal measures of both.

Monday, 12th July 2005

As I am currently working as the fitness manager in a corporate health and well-being centre, I am in a position to get my training on track. I can run, stretch and do kick-boxing, and get back into strength training as well. At the moment the club is without a squat rack, which is outrageous, but in time I should be able to negotiate getting one in. Another issue with working in London is that I walk to and from the station each day. This means that I am walking at least 6 miles in travel to and from work alone, that is, from my flat to the gym. I am also on my feet all day, and from time to time will walk a little further if I have anywhere else to go in the evenings.

Friday, 12th August 2005

One month on and things are going 'alright' at work. The travelling is getting annoying because I have to wake up at the sort of hours generally only known to hospital staff and criminals. Getting home in the evening is not much better either. I find myself plugging my head into my MP3 player to drown out the noise of the train and get some sleep in. There is nothing more reassuring to your existence than waking to find your sweatshirt covered in dribble and everybody staring at you as if you were a loony.

I have made a clear point in the past that I am no longer to venture into the realms of silly buggers. More precisely, I am not to do anything that might result in injury and thereby limit my ability to train for the MdS. It seems that I did not believe it was relevant to pass this information on to my manager. She is an adorable Irish woman who refrains from saying 'feck' far too much in my opinion. So there I was, standing on an over-inflated 75 cm Swiss ball. This, I hasten to add, is not playing silly buggers. I was having a perfectly reasonable conversation with one of my staff at the time. She was concerned that kneeling or standing on a Swiss ball was dangerous, with which I emphatically disagreed, and instead pointed out that these activities were perfectly safe (although not by any means useful), and that it was only falling off a Swiss ball that could be deemed dangerous. This is similar logic to the idea that vertigo is ridiculous. Nobody dies when falling from heights. It is the ground that kills people. The falling itself is usually quite harmless.

I actually disagree with the idea that standing on a Swiss ball is a good thing to do. Some claim that it is good for stability, but for one reason, due to the shape of the thing, some muscles are being stretched and others shortened, and this does not represent normal activity on a flat ground. But it just so happened that I wanted to stretch those particular muscles, and so there I was. It was also the case that I felt that I should be doing more than just standing there, so I decided to check my proprioception by bouncing a little, then bouncing a lot, and then dancing, badly. It was at this point that my munchkin of a boss thought that it would be hilarious if she were to run up behind me and kick the ball as hard as she could. The first that I knew about this was when the ball starting deforming and my feet left the surface. My left foot then made contact with the top of the ball and my whole body collapsed over the left foot, bringing my butt down hard on my heel with an unreassuringly horrible crunching sound in my left knee, before I fell to the floor.

I lay there for some time, generally surprised at what had just happened, and a little bit angry (actually very angry, and if my boss had been a bloke, then laying on the floor whilst I calmed down would not have been an option). I knew that my knee was damaged, and I knew that I would still be able to walk on it, but I also knew that I would not be running or kicking anything for a little while. For every step of the 3-mile walk from the station to my home, I was cursing my boss. It just seemed like such a malicious thing to do. I know that I have done stuff like that to people in the past, and I always felt bad about it, but it did not mean that I would be thinking any happy fluffy thoughts about her for a week or two. These sorts of things happen in everyday life, and it is ridiculous to think that we should be wrapping ourselves up in cotton wool so that we never get hurt. We need to have fun, and when something like this happens, it would usually be forgotten about in a week or two, so it does not really matter. I just think about every little thing nowadays because it might affect my training. I will be alright again in no time, I am just concerned about myself for a change. Bit of a big girl's blouse really. I need to look into that.

Saturday, 20th August 2005

The damage amounted to soft tissue injuries to my calves and around the back and outside of the knee and leg, and some cartilage damage to the top of the shinbone. Ever since the accident, by which I mean the malicious act of kicking me off the Swiss ball (sorry Ailbhe, I am over it now!), I have been unable to kick off my left leg, run, or even kneel so that my butt rests on my ankles. The area is improving, slowly, but I cannot say that I am a happy bunny. It no longer hurts to walk, but it certainly does if I try putting any more stress through the area than that. I should be able to run a little and kick a bit by the end of this week, which is good, because I intend to start running again. The body does heal itself in time, and some areas more efficiently than others, so I can put this behind me as another interesting little challenge, and then carry on with it.

One of the main problems with working in London is the hours that I have to do. I am okay at working, but training leaves me completely knackered. I am now trying to work out how I can perform half an hour of strength workouts, stretching and kicking, and run, as well as doing my 6 miles of walking, all on a daily basis. There is the option of running to and from the station, but that means that I sit on the train and get to work smelling like a bricklayer's vest on a hot summer's day. Which personally is not my idea of a good time.

I have not been able to do much in the way of strength training over the past three weeks, on account of feeling too drained from the work hours, and finding that I have little time to fit in my own training between training other people. I have a couple of clients that are interested in kick-boxing, so I am able to do a little bit with them, but it is not enough. On Tuesday of this coming week I have a meeting with a prospective publisher. He is interested in a book I wrote about exercise to improve fitness for life (hence the original title 'Fit for Life', which I later had to change to the current 'Built to Last', which can be found at www.thehealthybodyco.com), and wants me to write a sports-specific book on exercise training for skiing as well ('Skiing Fitness', also available from the same site). What I am hoping is that he will tell me that I can get a nice juicy advance for my work, and then concentrate on writing full-time instead, and be in a much better position to do my own training. Two months into my new job that might upset a few people, but I think that the advance is unlikely to be the case, so I will no doubt have to stay put and write the book whenever I get a few minutes. What I would really like to do is ditch the flat and drive around the kingdom for a few months, so that I can eye up potential places to set my roots, and spend some good time working on my books and Ph.D. That would be too good to be true.

One other piece of interesting information for me is that one of my clients wants to run in the *Marathon des Sables* as well. She saw the madness in a recent television programme, *Into the Danger Zone: Hell on Earth* (I particularly liked the shot of the chap with what appeared to be blood all down the front of his vest), and she decided that if I was going to do it, then she would rather like to give it a go too. I told her all the glamorous stuff about it being the toughest footrace on earth; the 40 to 50 degrees of searing desert heat; the feet giving way in the sand making every mile feel like three; and the outrageous distances covered whilst carrying seven days' worth of kit (the race is six stages, but one stage is a double marathon across two days, hence the seven days). What I omitted to tell her, and what might possibly have changed her mind, is the fact that there are no real wet facilities. As a bloke, I relish the idea of being expected to be filthy for a week, but some people really fail to appreciate a thing like that.

Monday, September 12th 2005

Well, as the publisher put my mind at rest regarding the advance I was after, I am now safe in the knowledge that I am not in a position to leave work just yet. For the sort of books that I want to publish, I can expect advances in the region of several hundreds of pounds, maybe even a thousand. The royalties could reach the sort of staggering amounts sufficient to pay for a half-decent holiday. And by that I mean a holiday for myself, not 'her indoors' as well. She will have to write a book of her own apparently.

Today I went out for the first proper run in months. Up until now I have just been doing very short distances interspersed with periods of walking. This time my boss and I went for a 4-mile run around the Isle of Dogs. I recorded my heart rate and it managed to get very high towards the end. My boss is a good runner and I would class myself as a rank beginner. The 4 miles was about all that I could manage and I was very happy to get back to the club. The reason for the run is to check a route for an intermediate running club that I will be taking every Monday from next week on.

Saturday, October 22nd 2005

The running club has been going for five weeks now. There is a floor manager, Richard, who came out with me for the previous couple of weeks, but he was away on holiday last week. His plan is to manage 8 miles by January, which is possible for him, but he has a few biomechanical issues, and in addition, has had to stop and walk just short of the full distance due to his current level of cardiovascular fitness. It means that my runs have been quite comfortable, which is nice. I actually quite missed not running this week and I am looking forward to Monday's run. Another thing about the running is that my fitness is obviously improving. I feel that when I do run to or from the station that I can run further, faster, and easier than previously.

I also feel that the once-a-week running club is not enough and that I need to put in at least another day. The reason that I have been reluctant is because I have been experiencing pain in my left knee. I thought that this was still due to the Swiss ball incident, but now I can recall a kick-boxing strain to the same area one evening a while ago. As mentioned, these things happen, and the body heals. There is so much time before the race that this all pales into insignificance, anyway.

I am going through some rehabilitation exercises to correct the injury, as well as other biomechanical imbalances, and to improve my stability and proprioception. I have also had the physiotherapist assess my walking pattern using a gait scanner. It gives a printout of the pressures going through my feet, which can then be interpreted to diagnose further imbalances and stress issues.

This is important for my preparation for the MdS, because stress problems could manifest into injuries as the mileage builds up. I am currently travelling between 30 and 50 miles a week by foot, and I am already aware of feelings of discomfort in certain areas of my feet, ankles and knees. The feelings are not painful, but I know that these are areas that may become injured in the future. Orthotics could be manufactured based on the results of the gait scan, in order to support my feet in the correct position, and allow me to learn how to walk and run correctly.

The problem that I have at the moment is that my left foot does not strike the ground uniformly across a number of trials. I therefore need to work harder on the stability work and try again in a few weeks' time. I also need to buy some better trainers, to help absorb some of the stress of running. I will avoid orthotics as a matter of principle. That book 'Built to Last' is all about correcting movement problems to develop strength across the whole body, and allow joints to function properly and without being unduly stressed or imbalanced. If I can write a book like that, then I can certainly practise what it preaches, and sort out my own issues.

Whilst I now appear to be in a position to get everything in order for my training, and I have come a long way in the last few months, there is now a huge problem on the horizon that will interrupt all my good work. On the 10th of January I have an operation in Ely on my inguinal hernia. I have to have a hole cut into my left groin and then a plastic disk put inside to stop my intestines from persisting with their dream of vacating the premises (ooh, sausages…). I will be out of work for a couple of weeks, and out of training for at least four. It only takes a week of bed rest to lose all cardiovascular gains achieved. Although I will be mobile around the house, I have to be very careful not to break the stitches early. I remember training the week after a small tumour was cut out of my left shin and all the stitches went. I really do not want to see that happening again around my groin. It is bad enough that the physio told me that when he had the same operation the bruising turned his penis black. That would turn a few heads at the public urinals.

Wednesday, 14th to Thursday, 15th December 2005

I finished working in London a couple of weeks ago, and without the running club to lead, I have found it difficult to keep running on my own. Winter was upon us from the middle of November, and although the weather has since become milder, it is still difficult to think about running outside. I have kept the walking up, in fact, increasing my daily and weekly totals, but I am looking forward to running again. Another mental barrier is the upcoming operation. I know that it is going to put me out of action for a couple of weeks and I will lose most of the progress that I have made. I expect that I will be out walking as soon as possible after the operation, but the impact of running is going to put a lot of stress on the area. I am almost looking forward to the pressure of only having one true year of training. My base fitness level has improved, and I will no doubt get back there soon enough, but I doubt that I will be making any further progress until March or April, between six and ten weeks after the operation.

On Tuesday I travelled by train to Manchester to observe a lecture on osteoporosis. On the last part of the train journey, I was looking out at the Peak District and thinking about how nice it would be to go walking out there. One particular landscape looked beautiful, and I made a mental note of the station name: Edale. That evening I had it in my mind that I should walk up the hill that I saw and then back again. As the evening progressed, I began contemplating walking a little further, with the idea of getting off the train at Edale, and then walking up into the hills, and coming back to a station further along the line. On Wednesday morning my mind was made up, and I set about arranging my kit accordingly. I had attended the lecture in what I would refer to as 'smart-casual'. This consisted of my Hi-Tec Magnums (Black Jungle version) and black combat trousers, with a T-shirt and fleece. I also had gloves, my Kangol cap, and a scarf with me, as well as a thick wool-lined jacket. The jacket was not waterproof, but because of the wool it would not lose its heat-retaining properties if it got wet.

I had the right clothing, and on Wednesday morning I set off on my journey, stopping along the way to buy supplies of food, a knife (which I could use to strip wet bark away from fallen branches if I needed to make a fire), matches (which I wrapped in a plastic bag to help prevent them from getting damp or wet), the Ordnance Survey Landranger map of that area of the Peak District, and some tissues (in case of a call of nature or the need for something else to get a fire going). The food was sufficient to last the night if I happened to be out that long. Somewhere in the back of my mind was a voice telling me: 'One of us is going to forget about meeting up with a smaller station on the way to Sheffield, and just walk the whole lot.' Nevertheless, whilst waiting for the train to Edale, I sat down and began working out the route. I then texted the map details and grid references to three of my friends with a note that if I failed to call them by the evening of the 15th, then I had been eaten by the locals. The plan was that this should cover all the details necessary for a rescue if something happened to me out on the moors.

Satisfied with the route, I then made a start on reading the map properly. Regardless of whether I am walking at night or during the day, I always try to learn my route as completely as possible before I go. This means creating a 3-D image in my mind of what I would be seeing as I pass along each part of the walk. The idea is that I know where the rivers and streams are; I know when I should be on flat ground and when I should be on a hillside, and what the rest of the landscape should look like when I am there. I also need to know about specific features, such as high peaks, waterfalls, rock outcrops, woodland, footpaths, roads and villages. In this case, there was a reservoir and main road that I could expect to see from some points on the journey, as well as a coniferous tree plantation. Because Edale is such a small village, the trains were only running every two hours, and it was 15:30 by the time that I arrived.

I made a start at walking, and even broke into a run for some points, as I wanted to make it to a particular waterfall on the Kinder Scout before nightfall. I was running along a footpath, on one side of a wide stream, knowing that the best route would be to cross and attack the steeper hill, face on. I did so and clambered and scrambled my way to the top. I turned around to see Edale in the distance below me, and the moon shining above the hill that I had just left. As I faced back to the direction that I needed to be going in, I saw the sunset. Bugger! Well, I still intended to go on to the waterfall, even though it would be dark by the time that I got there, and then I would be coming back across the Kinder Scout to head off eastwards for the rest of the journey.

Twenty minutes later night fell with a thump. I stood there in the chill of the night air as white clouds swept past me at an incredible rate. I could make out about 200 metres around me and got the map out to check on direction. Ten minutes later I checked again. It was too dark to study the map, so I was grateful that I had tried to remember as much as I could. Without a torch or compass, and no real fix on anything nearby, as everything was now engulfed in clouds and the night, I could only go on a general heading, and rely on my sense of direction. Although it was only 17:30, I knew that people died

Some of the photographs that I managed to take in the hour or so
before night fell.

out here from exposure, and a level-headed person would not have put a plan
like this together at such short notice, in the middle of December.

I was happy with myself for sending the texts to my friends, and knew that I would never be giving up even under the most extreme circumstances. I have suffered from the initial stages of hypothermia once before; whilst waiting overnight in Germany for the first train back to my hotel. When your core temperature begins to drop you feel devastatingly cold, and it seems that the body loses its ability to warm itself normally. I never really appreciated until then how the body does stay warm; the way that your body gives off heat, which is then trapped by your clothes, and in turn, creates a cushion of warm air against your skin. When hypothermia begins, it seems that the body stops giving off heat in an attempt to keep the core warm, but it feels awful. It took hours to warm up again totally after that.

I knew that if I was fortunate enough to notice the first signs of hypothermia, that I would be running for the nearest town, although if I caught the hypothermia early enough, I might try to get a fire going in the woodland. On the exposed moors, however, there would be no chance of that. The first cry of the evening came just after the sun had set and the moon was the only light that could make it through the clouds. I tried to decipher if it was the Hound of the Baskervilles, an American Werewolf, or the WereRabbit. Then I realised that it was grouse. Dinner; if I could catch one of the things. I had my knife and matches, and there were trees a few miles away where I could get the fire going and cook the thing. Much as the torment of listening to these things went on, there was no way that I could see them on the ground, and by the time they made flight, they were already too far away for me to hit them with a stone. That does not mean that I did not try though, obviously. All I could hope for was a deaf one that just sat there and let me step on it. Grouse were not the only wildlife out that night. From time to time I also saw perfectly white rabbits running across the hills. There were probably rabbits of other colours as well, but I obviously failed to see those ones.

I was moving at a good pace for those first few hours. The average velocity would not have been much, because a lot of the time I was climbing over rocks, or scrambling up the side of a hill, but nevertheless I was moving fast. When I passed the waterfall and got back to the top of the Kinder Scout, ready to head off towards the reservoir and plantation, visibility was down to about 10 metres because of the low cloud. I knew that I would be walking across the flat moor, avoiding any change in height, until I was in sight of the reservoir several miles away. I also knew that I needed to be heading east-south-east, although without a compass or fix, I could only make a best judgement (some might use the term 'guess') as to where that was. Walking was tough, mainly because if I was not crossing a stream, then I was falling into a peat bog.

For every ten metres forward, I was walking twenty metres around something, with two or three metres of up and down. At last there was a break in the clouds, just enough to reveal the constellation of Cassiopeia, which was sufficient for me to get a good idea of where north was, and then to confirm that I was heading in the right direction. At the time, this also meant that the moon was lying just off east, so I could head towards that whenever the clouds did not cover it. I checked the time and decided that I would need to check my heading again in about an hour, sometime around 19:00. Without a constant fix on a point and with all the walking around in semicircles to avoid streams and bogs, it was difficult to have a lot of confidence in my sense of direction.

The ground was really annoying me. Particularly when it was not there. It was covered in ferns, shrubs and bracken, and I would try to plant my feet (sorry) on the centre of whatever it was. Sometimes that did not work and I would lose my leg into a hole, only to have to expend vast amounts of energy climbing out of the thing. The same difficulties occurred when crossing the peat bogs and streams; I would have to use one leg to perform the deepest single-leg squat possible, whilst hoping that the weight of my rucksack (just shy of 15 kg with all the food, water and clothing), would not tip me over backwards. Another 'embuggerance' was the fact that the prickliest bush in the Peak District seemed to be following me around, because every time I needed to put my hand out to catch myself, there the bugger was. At one point I managed to walk straight through the middle of the thing, and spent the next five minutes picking thorns out of my legs, which, when you cannot actually see the things, is really quite annoying. For flat ground I was doing far too much climbing.

Then came the relief of seeing a light over my left shoulder, some way off and beneath me in the distance. I checked again and was happy to conclude that it was moving. I was passing level with the part of a main road into Sheffield that should have been on a hill and lying perpendicular to me – which it was. Half an hour later the road had turned and was parallel to me. The headlights were going very slowly, presumably because the clouds were creating dense fog and the traffic was erring on the side of caution.

I could make out a climb to what I thought was the top of the hill I was heading to, and made the decision to head across to my right to avoid it, and thus bring into my view the reservoir and road plantation. As I lost sight of the road off into the distance behind me, I could make out the bright streetlights of Hope off to my front. After some slipping, some scrambling, and some falling, I then had to box around some farmland, and found myself walking next to the plantation. I was on a track that would take me into Hope, from where I would then head on to Bamford, and thereupon find the pub that I had been dreaming about for the last few hours. I had also been dreaming about a warm Radox and the possibility of spending the rest of the night in a B&B, safe in the knowledge that I would not make any last train into Sheffield, and even if I did that there would not be any trains heading from there to Cambridge tonight.

I eventually reached the A6187 at Hope and walked towards Bamford. Along the way I walked past a pub with a sign stating 'Travellers Rest', so I did, briefly underneath the sign to check the map, before continuing on to Bamford. There I passed by a pub called 'The Derwent Hotel', and walked up to the 'Anglers Rest'. I decided that going in there would be a liberty, so I headed back to the 'Derwent' at 22:40 for a pint of Abbot's, the chance to charge my mobile, and to re-evaluate the journey ahead. I decided to walk on to Sheffield. I knew that this would take my total actually walked to about 50 miles, including the meandering route I took across the hills, and the changes in elevation. At 23:30 I left the pub and headed back for the moors.

One of the good things about an active mind is that I was running through scenes and quotes from some great films. If it was not the *Hound of the Baskervilles* or *Dog Soldiers*, then it was *An American Werewolf in London* - 'Stay on the road; don't stray onto the moors'. I was also thinking about the risks of what I was doing, typically whenever the wind starting clawing at my face and I could feel the cold through my coat. Walking on the roads, when I could, kept my speed up, but at times walking downhill started telling on my joints and I would walk backwards for a bit. If I ever stopped for a couple of minutes to take on some water, to get some food out, or to check the map, then I would find it difficult to get the joints going again. The solution was quite straightforward (keep moving), but my average walking pace was still down to well below my usual 4 mph. I was also thinking about the people that could enjoy this experience with me, namely Stuart, who is an outdoors chap as well, although we will no doubt be heading out for walks together in the future. I also remembered the people that I have gone out walking with before. When I was 15, I went on an expedition to the Pyrenees, as I mentioned earlier. It was with the Air Training Corps. I was the baby of the group, with the other guys being 18; and there were a couple of instructors to make sure that we all did all right. It was Ross, and his quote from *Hamburger Hill*, which I kept replaying to myself whenever the climbing got tough; 'Let's take this fucking hill.' He had repeated it when we were up against it in the Pyrenees, and it became something of a mantra then and has been ever since.

When I rounded the top of one hill, I could see a vast orange glow out in front of me. It looked like sunrise, although at 02:30 the sun still had quite a bit to wait. As I walked on, another area of orange lit up over to my half-right. I could see Sheffield at last. The first train from Sheffield would be leaving at 05:07 to Doncaster, which I needed to get me back to Cambridge. I could not really pick up my pace any more, and after an hour and a half, having walked between another 4 and 6 miles; Sheffield was not getting any closer. At 04:45 I eventually found myself in Sheffield proper, but knew that it was unlikely that I would make it to the station for the first train. When I did get there, at 05:30, I could barely lift my legs to get me up the steps for the platform.

It was while waiting for my next train, at 06:18, that I actually felt cold for the first time. My knees were too sore for me to walk to the waiting room, so I just sat there on the platform waiting for the train's doors to open. I had not damaged anything, although my knees did feel quite tender, but it was just that my hamstrings had been doing so much work, not just because of walking with the rucksack, but because of all that climbing during the first few hours of the journey.

I made it home at 10:45 on Thursday morning. I closed the front door and undressed where I was, and then climbed into bed for a few hours. The rest of the day I took it easy, just relaxing and recovering in the flat. I felt quite good for what I had managed, although my body was still quite tender, but I was not injured and not even particularly tired.

SEVEN DAYS IN THE SAHARA

Friday, 16th December 2005

Today was a godsend. I could confirm to myself that I was not injured and had not damaged anything. I did not even have any blisters from my double marathon. I had to walk into town to get to an Internet café, and, although I was still a little bit tender, I managed a comfortable 10-mile round trip. The night walk was far more difficult than the same distance in the desert, because even though it will be incredibly hot rather than cold, I will not have the disruptions of navigating or boxing around so many obstacles, nor will I have to climb so much. The ground should also be easier to move over, unlike the spongy earth and the peat bogs of the Peak District. What I need to do next is to manage a 50-mile walk followed by a marathon the next day. I had about 24 hours between the night walk and the 10-mile follow-up this time, and what I needed to do was to ensure that my connective tissue and muscles were efficient enough to recover much faster.

This is the sort of thing that no doubt catches a lot of people out in the marathon, and the reason that I am putting more emphasis on total distances travelled rather than simply improving my running distances. I am still confident that I can do all that I need to before the event, cramming everything that I need to do into just one solid year of hard and purposeful training. There is just that operation that stands in my way, far away as it seems, on Tuesday the 10th of January 2006.

Thursday, 12th January 2006

Smarts a bit.

Friday, 20th January 2006

So, I had the operation on Tuesday of last week. The operation went surprisingly well, not that I should have been concerned, and my dear friend Russell picked me up from the hospital and drove me home. I had been told to get home and get to bed straightaway. I seem to remember something about anaesthetic. Ah yes, that was it; at about 20:00 hours the anaesthetic wore off so I was supposed to be in bed. I stayed up until about 22:30 and then made my move. A very slow, painful, and deliberate move to bed. In fact, sleeping was quite an experience for those first few days. It took ten minutes of acute agony, radiating across most of my body, just to get into a position that did not hurt anymore, and by then I was hot and needed to move. During the day I would try to stretch myself out, even performing the world's smallest squats and so on, just to feed that psychological need. I would still walk in a stooped posture, and I was aware that protecting the operation meant that I was putting stress on other areas, and would probably need to do some corrective exercise for my hips and knees once I was back on form.

I only took one dose of painkillers the morning after the operation, and none after that. I decided that pain was telling me something, and that clouding my brain to those inputs was not going to be of any physical benefit. It did mean that I said little more than 'smarts a bit' for that first week. I was also unable to laugh, cough or sneeze, without being in quite a lot of pain. Going to the toilet scared the crap out of me, although not enough to get the job done.

Last Friday I left my Cambridge home to come into London. Really, I should have been taking it easier for that first week, but I just had to get away from the flat and to a friend's place in London. Hence, with a rather heavy rucksack, I managed to walk the five miles that made up the total distance on either side of the train stations. Since then, I have been getting significantly better on a daily basis. I am getting out and walking around, and although I am barely totally upright, it is certainly getting blood to the area to help it heal.

Thursday, 23rd February 2006

Well, despite the odd niggling bit of soreness I barely have any sign of the operation. I have managed walks of about twenty miles, and even managed the occasional run over shorter distances. Last weekend I visited my parents in Hertfordshire and had a run across some fields on my way. Everything seems to be in good working order for getting back into my proper training at the beginning of March.

Saturday, March 11th 2006

Finally, after a few months of nothing much happening I found myself a new job. It was one of those instances when I had to choose between money and happiness, and happiness won the day. I have been employed as an operations manager, meaning that I am responsible for running a site with around 5500 members in the City of London. It is a big club with a lot of issues, which is just the sort of stress that I thrive on.

I was given a membership card and invited to 'mystery shop' the club over the Friday and weekend before I started work officially. I did not really use the opportunity to train with weights but just went straight for the treadmill. This was something that I had been thinking about for a while, anyway. Just recovering from the operation, I still need to take things easy. I can begin running again, but I am somewhat tentative about running a lot outside, where there is the opportunity to trip up on something and put an enormous amount of stress through my abdominal area. And the last thing that I want is to be running around London with my giblets hanging out.

So I took it easy, training two days out of the three that were available to me, and started out with just a mile of easy treadmill running. I could feel that there was what can only be described as 'insecurities' within the muscles that had until recently been fighting to get back together. By the time of my second run, I felt fine over the first mile, but that same feeling of weakness came back for the second.

Wednesday, March 15th 2006

Another good thing about my new job is that it takes about forty minutes to walk there. I am not a fan of the underground, and because of my position it is far better to use a reliable means of transport, such as my legs. I have incorporated some running outside now, in conjunction with all the walking and the treadmill running. There are definitely improvements, but I can still feel these nagging signs coming up from the region of the operation.

Friday, March 17th 2006

Treadmill Half Marathon

I decided that this afternoon would be the time to test myself and get an idea of where I am with my training. The plan is to complete a half marathon on a treadmill. I have been gradually increasing the mileage over the month to-date, but now I just want to get an idea of how tough a half marathon is. If I manage this, then it will be the farthest that I have ever run in my life.

As I am starting to discover, it is the first ten minutes of running that are the hardest and most demoralising. It is during that period that I start asking myself precisely what it is that I think I am trying to accomplish. What is actually happening is that I have created an oxygen deficit, because running causes my heart rate to increase over a very short space of time, so that it can deliver oxygen and nutrients to the exercising muscles. The problem is that the heart rate increases straightaway and breathing rate increases just afterwards, leaving this deficit that makes us feel out of breath and uncomfortable. Coinciding with this, the body's various energy systems are also getting a rude awakening, and they too take time before they are working efficiently. Basically, the body responds to running in the same way that the mind responds to the alarm clock on a Monday morning: There is a lot of confusion at first, followed by resistance, and then eventually comes the knowledge and acceptance that things are going to be a little bit harsh for a while (you learn these technical details on exercise science degree courses nowadays).

The run itself was tough, more so than I would have predicted. I kept on going; running on and on, mile after mile, but I did not really enjoy it that much. The lessons learnt were that half marathons are not easy with insufficient training, isotonic drinks are important, running pace needs to be developed over time and not guestimated from the outset, some underwear does chafe, and a whopper meal is about right for me as a pre-workout meal (about ten minutes before, in fact).

I am not an advocate of fast food, or junk food at all for that matter, but poor preparation meant that I did not bring enough food with me. Experience also told me that I get really hungry after about an hour of exercise, and red meat is about the slowest thing that I can eat that gives me energy for this sort of endeavour. It is relatively irrelevant for preparation for the actual event, because then I will be living off dehydrated processed rubbish, which I would never normally even poke at with a stick. Unfortunately, that is the nature of the beast, and indeed the nature of such a challenge as the *Marathon des Sables* is that I will be pushing myself to my limits, not just in terms of what my body can manage, but also in terms of what it can manage with a poor diet. If I could eat some fresh fruits, vegetables, salads, seafood and lean meats then I would be a very happy chap indeed, but, alas, none of that would last half an hour in the desert. But today I learnt that about 1500 kcals of processed red meat, chips and sugary drink allows me to run for almost an hour and a half without being hungry. I also know that I do not need to leave much time between eating and exercising, as my stomach seems to manage just fine.

The run actually took almost two hours, which was largely a reflection of my current training status, and was compounded by the inaccuracies inherent in the way that treadmills calculate distances. The treadmill was also set on an incline to give me some work to do. I obviously would not have wanted it to be *too* easy, after all. But still, I am in my first month of training since the operation and this was my first run over any respectable distance. I think that it was acceptable.

Friday, 24th March 2006

Another aspect of the rehabilitation, and my general exercise programme, is the resistance-training element. Depending on my shifts, and how the running is going, I am training with weights up to four days a week, which is about average for me. The resistance training is based on the functional, movement-based training that I wrote about in *Built to Last*. These exercises are adapted for what I have available in the gym, including cable pulls and presses, cable Russian twists, and medicine ball work. This is combined with some strength, power and hypertrophy training. This has less bearing on my running, and more on my general all-round health and fitness. These exercises include Military Presses, Deadlifts, Weighted Chin-Ups, and so on. Finally, the other element of my resistance training is specific to training squat patterns, as this will have the greatest bearing on injury prevention.

In *Built to Last* I wrote a preliminary exercise section, the idea of which was to improve joint alignment and function prior to starting more powerful movements. Those exercises are really the foundation for training movement patterns, and so are important for injury prevention, and rehabilitation. Once those exercises can be completed with proper technique, then it is possible to develop other running-specific strength and power elements in the training. The idea is that if the joints can produce power in a manner that is specific to running, then there should be a reduced likelihood of twisting an ankle or producing sprains and strains. In practical terms, if you were to lose your footing, then the ankle should be able to produce force through a greater range of motion than if you did not do the specific training. That means that the joint is less likely to be injured, and if it is, then the injuries will be less severe than if the training had not taken place.

Friday, 7th April 2006

I have to travel to Acton for a staff training today, which is not as much of a chore as it might be in other companies. I spent last night checking *streetmap.com* and *Google Earth*, and worked out a route back to the flat along the river. The route along the South Bank is close to a half marathon, and I have brought plenty of kit with me to carry, so this will be a tall order at this stage in my training. When the staff training comes to an end, I get changed and start walking towards the Thames. I make a stop at a petrol station along the way so that I can get some food in. As I have established, I can take food on quite late before I start training, and not suffer from ill effects, so taking some food in now should be fine. I would actually prefer to run with slight stomach discomfort than run hungry, just because at least if I have food in me then I am in a better state of mind for whatever is coming up. Anyway, it is not usually a problem, so I buy a couple of flapjacks and a bottle of Lucozade, and make a start on getting through it.

I finish the food and get to a park. I spotted the park on the maps, but had not decided to include it in the run, as I still have a little distance to go on the other side before reaching the river. Having got to the gate, I change my mind and head through. I sort out my rucksack and then get into a light jog. I can use the park as a warm-up, and then recover for the rest of the way to the Thames. I leave the park and drop back to a walk. That felt fine. I had no stomach discomfort and felt fit enough, so that was nice. Quarter of an hour later I reach the north bank of the Thames, and once again pause to sort out my kit, which mainly consists of getting the Platypus tube and mouthpiece into a convenient position, and tightening the shoulder and hip straps.

I head east towards Hammersmith Bridge, passing a pub where the benches are kindly set up to present an obstacle course, and I dodge past a few runners coming in the opposite direction. I run up the steps to the bridge and across to the other side, again making the effort to get past pedestrians and runners so as to keep to a running pace. I make a series of right turns at the other end of the bridge, ducking to save my head from the steel, and then I am on the Thames path proper. The ground has been made into a half-decent stony pathway, albeit a pot-holed and water-sodden one. It is a nice and cool day, and although it is only 17:30 there are not many other people around on the path, possibly because it is a little too cool.

After ten minutes, I leave the stony path as I reach the road and pavement that leads to Putney Bridge. I have to cross a junction, which is annoying, but it seems that when you are running you can pick your way across traffic far more efficiently than when walking. It might be related to heart rate, or it might just be down to frustration, but either way I am across and running around a church, a couple of restaurants and a pub. The path takes a detour onto a street, and then, I am at Wandsworth Park, and I make my way back to the riverside. There are some nice developments coming up here, but unfortunately signage for the Thames path is lacking, and I take what feels like a ten-minute run off course as I follow the river in front of some apartments only to reach a dead end and have to work my way back the way that I came.

I am back on a street again, around an industrial estate and then on to a retail park and hotel. I run past McDonald's and across a roundabout, and eventually find signs taking me back to the river. This is the worst bit about the Thames path – it is not really there! I had ideas that the Thames path was a continuous path along the river, but the reality is that it stops and starts, with retail, housing and industrial estates along the way, and signage that leads you twenty yards to the river but only goes by the river for ten yards before you have to work your way back again. This is very frustrating, Ken, and I really think you need to get on your bike along here to see what it is like.

I run along the side of the river in front of flats, and then in front of another church and some new apartments. I get to Battersea Bridge in just short of an hour, and then the path leads across Battersea Park to Chelsea Bridge, and once again I am working my way around new apartments and the old power station. Again there is no signage and I cannot get any further without either turning back the way that I came or doing a circle of the apartments. I do the circle just because I am loathed to run back the same way, and then I head off to a roundabout and then an incline by the Dogs' Home, before seeing the power station to my left. I reach the river after yet another detour, and see the headquarters of the Secret Intelligence Service (SIS - commonly and inaccurately referred to as MI6), just on the south bank on the far side of Vauxhall Bridge. I know that I am nearly back now. Which is nice, because I am hot and sweaty, and although I am not struggling to the point of wanting to quit, this is easily the longest continuous run that I have ever managed.

I skirt around SIS HQ and get back to the river and on towards Westminster and the Eye. I am going at a comfortable pace, and it is in this area that runners seem to be out all over the place. They are not as numerous as the tourists though, and I have to concentrate to get through them all at the Eye. I am sure that I ruined an otherwise perfectly good photograph or two of Westminster Palace by night. From here on I am just counting down the bridges; I have passed Westminster Bridge, so next up is Jubilee Bridge, then Waterloo, then Blackfriars (all two and half of them), then Southwark, and I come to a stop just outside the Anchor pub. I throw another top on and walk back to the flat. My clothes are saturated, but I am sure that this will be the case less and less, the fitter I become. All in all though, it was a very good run, if frustrating for the numerous detours away from the Thames path. It was definitely good to get a distance in with heavy kit, and now all that is left is to have a Radox and then get some food in. Not a bad day's work at all.

Friday, 14th April 2006

From the end of March through to this month I have had cause to travel down to Portsmouth and Gosport for a couple of weekends. It is good to get down to the coast, but running along the pebble beaches seems far harder than running on sand. Alternatively, it might just be that having barely moved on from treadmill running, that running on any relatively unstable surface feels like incredibly hard work. I give it a try for a bit, but spend most of the time running on the grass as I head westward by the sea. I am running at a good pace, stretching out and so on, without causing any issues around my core or viscera (which I can only judge by the fact that I am not getting the pulling or sore feeling of connective tissue straining around my midsection, which I had when I first took to the treadmill in March). I finish the run at about 20:00, and take my sweaty self out of the cold, night-time sea air, and into a nice, hot bath.

Saturday, 27th May 2006

I have very fond memories of the New Forest. In particular, I recall camping at Sandy Balls with my family, and us going out for walks around the countryside. I also have a particularly accurate memory of my father being chased by a bull. I suggest that it was my father being chased by the bull, essentially for no reason other than the fact that he was behind the rest of us, and therefore, the closest to the bull. It is, therefore, fair to suggest, again on the basis of this logic, that the bull was very much running after my mother, my sister and me, at precisely the same time as my father went charging past us. What followed is now somewhat vague, and I can only assume that either the bull became bored very quickly, or else the ground swallowed it up.

Now far too much time has passed since my last good walk. I need to head out somewhere in order to fit in a couple of days of walking before the close of spring. I check *Google Earth* and can see that the New Forest is quite easy to get to from London. I can take a train out of London Bridge and get to Southampton, which is close to the eastern side of the Forest.

I get off the train at Southampton and head into the town centre to pick up a couple of Ordnance Survey maps and some food. I pass the station as I head off in the other direction towards the forest. I am carrying pretty heavy kit, which is the result of deliberately not packing light, by including a thermos flask of tea, for example. I am also carrying my rucksack, a blanket and some bits that I can use to rig up a shelter if need be. I am not carrying my tent because that would be too easy. Besides, it would be nice if I can walk through the night and get some good miles into my boots.

Having reached the forest, I get off the beaten track and head west, enjoying the smell of the ferns and the sight of horses all over the place. During the course of the day, I see not only horses, but deer and one massive owl as well.

I had vaguely remembered that the New Forest was populated by such a huge number of horses. That bull incident seemed to cloud things a bit.

I cross streams and rivers about a hundred times before I manage to land in the middle of one. I was walking along a low branch and holding onto the branch above. When the branch I was walking on broke, I did not expect my hands to slip off the one above, but then I also did not expect a stream a metre and a half wide to be a metre deep. I walked the last bit to the bank and climbed out and carried on. Perhaps on a colder day I would have been upset about something like that, but happily the squelching subsided after less than a couple of hours, and I felt quite dry and comfy again. My lightweight trousers dry off quickly anyway, and fortunately the rest of my kit did not get wet.

After watching a mob of deer moving across the hills, I head up there myself to have a look around. It is dusk now and I am starting to get more than a little fed up with all of the bogs and puddles that I seem expert at finding. In the twilight the only thing that is clear is the fact that I will continue to find means of getting my feet wet just so long as I am in the forest. I head north until I am able to leave the forest, and then start heading west to box around until I can head south towards the coast. It means walking around almost the whole of the forest, but as I am on terra firma again, it does not matter that it is pitch black. Some stars are out and the sky is clear enough for my night vision to give me a good enough perspective on the road ahead and the moors around me: 'Don't stray onto the moors!'

As the evening draws in the night descends and I am soon making my way out of the forest and onto more predictable ground.

The minor metalled road eventually leads me onto a major road, and I head south-west until I reach Christchurch. At about 04:00 I come to a stop on a tall grassy bank by the sea, and unpack the sleeping bag and blanket by some bracken, which happens to be the only cover along the slope. I have some food and get some sleep. At about 06:15 I wake up, as the light is now good enough for me to check my feet. Having been soaked in the stream and bogs I could only imagine what state they might have gotten themselves into as I continued to walk for hours in wet socks. A couple of my nails had become best friends with the toes next to them, and although the nails could not have been much shorter, they had found a way of digging into my skin and drawing some blood. It had already dried up and was healing, so I just cleaned it to make it look pretty and then put my socks back on. After laying there for half an hour, looking across at the Isle of Wight, I decide that a nice stroll along the seafront is very much the order of the day.

My waking view as the sun rose above the horizon, allowing me to see for the first time where I had slept during the night. The Isle of Wight is to the right of the picture.

The view out to the west along the coast towards Christchurch.

I sort out my kit and have some food. I had finished my thermos of tea before going to sleep, although it had been warm until midnight, and still drinkable at 4. I headed east along the beach, scrambling here and there and then climbing up a shorter part of the cliff to get onto the coastal path. The plan is to head east along the coast, and then head north back towards Southampton. I spend the whole of the morning walking directly towards the sun as it rose up from the horizon. It was not outrageously hot, but it was a beautiful blue sky and I realised that I should have brought something with me to protect my face. But in true British fashion I decided to just enjoy it and work on my tan.

The view along the coastal path as I head east towards the sun.

The pathway was busy with people out getting their exercise in, and I enjoyed some brief banter with various people as I went; many of whom were intrigued by the size of the rucksack. The 'drawn through a hedge backwards' look, combined with the 'eau de lumberjack' smell, probably intrigued them even more as they drew closer though.

After walking around some marinas, I start working my way north through some small towns and villages, and then find myself heading back through the forest. The landscape is completely different today. The land is open with only a few trees dotted around, and everything is looking a striking green, on what has now become a particularly hot and sunny day indeed. I lay down for a couple of minutes to have a rest, but I cannot get out of the sun, try as I do amongst a hedgerow. I give in and head on. There is some woodland ahead, so I can take a chance there in about half an hour or so. By the time I reach it, I have already checked the map and worked out where I want to be heading, so I carry on past and straight into a town.

Then I carry on straight through the town and out the other side, straight into a pub. After a pretty good steak and ale pie, washed down with a pint of ale, I head off towards the ferry port. The plan was to take the ferry and then head up to the station, but when I get to the port no ferries appear to be running and I have already walked off course to get there. I jumped on a bus to take me up to the station, as there was no pleasure to be derived from walking that last familiar section. About twenty minutes later I am at the station and waiting for a train, stuffing my face and drinking coffee. I could not have wished for better weather and I loved every minute of the walk.

Wednesday, 21st June 2006

Following no ill effects after my walk around the New Forest, which did indeed end up being almost entirely 'around' the New Forest, everything has been going well this month. Debbie from Survival International approached me at the health club where I work, regarding the upcoming London Triathlon, and we were asked if we wanted to put a team together and raise them some money. I am not entirely sure whether it was the charity, the thought of the thrill of the competition, or the smile that did it, but for whatever reason I agreed. I am interested in it because I am genuinely a big fan of the charity's work (www.survival-international.org). Running a 10 K will also be a good chance to see how I fair against other runners, although I imagine the answer will be 'quite badly'. The rest of the team will include my manager, Jono, and fitness manager, Johann. They can both be great fun to be around and very competitive, so that is perfect. We are putting ourselves down to do the Olympic team event, meaning that Jono will lead with the 1500 m swim, Johann will follow on with a 40 km cycle, and I will run the 10 km to the finish. For me this is an awesome opportunity to get focussed for a race and have something short-term to work towards.

Monday, 26th June 2006

I leave work and get into a run straightaway. It is all downhill along Aldersgate past the Barbican, around the Museum of London and past Guildhall, continuing on until I reach Southwark Bridge, at which point it evens out. I stay on the north side and turn right, heading west towards Westminster. I pass Blackfriars, Waterloo and the Hungerford/Jubilee Bridges before reaching Westminster Bridge. I turn left and end up in the cycle lane going over the bridge to avoid all the tourists blocking the path. At the other side I turn left again, running back along the South Bank past the Eye, the bridges again, and then finishing just outside the Anchor pub. I walk the rest as a cool-down.

I was carrying a pack, by virtue of the fact that I had just finished work, and the plan from now until the triathlon is to carry minimal, if any, kit. Having been working with the goal of going for distance, I now need to get fit to run a shorter distance without a rucksack. It is a compromise already. I have been training myself to be relatively slow, and I am not going to change that a great deal in a little over a month, but at least it breaks up my training a bit.

Monday, 3rd July 2006

I start running as soon as I leave work again. I am not a fan of running along by the side of the road, but I have not got many other options, and the race will be along pavement and roads, anyway. I take the right at the bridge and start working my way towards Westminster. I am carrying a rucksack again, but it is as light as I could make it, and I am running much faster now already. It is interesting dodging past all the pedestrians. There are various. Some are considerate and make an effort to get out of the way. Some people pay no attention to their surroundings whatsoever, and just take their time at bottlenecks. They disturb me. Some people pay no attention until I am right in front of them, and they almost throw themselves into the river in a blind panic. It is the people walking in the same direction that amuse me the most. Few people walk in a straight line along the pavement and most just meander from one side to the other. Sort of like a drunk but with less energy and enthusiasm.

I turn right and run around Westminster this time, and then on through the gardens and along the north bank to Vauxhall Bridge. I run across and down the steps on the other side, in front of SIS HQ, onto the South Bank and head back towards the City. Westminster is the first landmark to draw level with, then under the bridge and past the Eye, under the Jubilee Bridge, then Waterloo, Blackfriars, past the pub, the Tate Modern, the Millennium Bridge and St. Paul's; then it is under Southwark Bridge and a sprint to the Anchor. That run is the 10 km distance that I will be running in the race, but I am too sluggish for my liking, and the long downhill makes it too easy for a reasonable comparison. But, that is the course that I have available to run, so it will have to do for now.

Thursday, 6th July 2006

I had flown out to Antalya in Turkey for the engagement celebrations of my sister-in-law. Although the wife and I are separated, we are still getting on amicably. She will update her parents about all of this one day. Probably.

Friday, 7th July 2006

I need to get a run or two in whilst I am here. The climate is great for desert training, and in the past I have felt the combination of heat and humidity here to be more uncomfortable than anywhere else. Having spent the day with the family and around Antalya, I was able to head out in the late evening after dinner. The family had not been very keen on the idea, and I would have preferred to get going in daylight and midday temperatures, but this should make for a good first run.

I loaded up my rucksack until it weighed around 10 kgs, and then headed off. I got onto the main road out of Antalya, which heads west towards the mountains and parallel to the sea, although I was too low and too far inland to see it. There are not any smaller roads or paths that I could use, because there is too much development all around this area, so I just stick to the side of the road and start running. I pass a couple of junctions, and then the traffic subsides and there are big enough breaks between cars for me to lose sight of the road beneath my feet. As I pass a cemetery, the roadside is broken and full of potholes, meaning that I have to go slow a little to reduce the likelihood of a trip or fall. The road goes downhill for a few minutes, across a bridge, and then goes up and around the first of the hills. I am very much out on my own now, with just the odd building every couple of kilometres.

As I run on, I pass through the occasional village, before leaving it behind and finding myself back in the darkness. Once I have left the village, there are no streetlights, few cars, and with woodland surrounding most of the roads, and a lack of moonlight, my night vision is sluggish to return. However, one thing far more annoying and concerning than my night vision is the abundance of dogs. They would usually just bark, but because I am running they instinctively want to run after me, and I almost trip over one that is lying by the side of the road. I am constantly crossing from one side of the road to the other, trying to create some distance between us, but they still come out into the road barking and running. One followed me for about five minutes. Getting bitten would not be a good thing, and I imagine that a few have probably got rabies. I come to a river before the next village or town, and decide to turn around and head back. It would have been a pleasant run but for the dogs.

At least on the way back I know where they are, so I can cross the road earlier, pick up my pace when I want to, or slow to a walk to get past some of the others. (If I walk then they do not chase after me, although if they chase after me then I run faster until I get bored and turn to run after them. At least it all keeps me thinking.) It was a good run and a good introduction to running somewhere unfamiliar. I am going to be busy with the celebrations for most of the rest of the week, but I will see when I can fit in some more. I will probably try to avoid running the same course though after dark. I spent most of the run surrounded by beautiful green trees and high mountains, but could not see any of them.

Monday, 10th July 2006

One of the nice things about being out here is that I am getting to go swimming in the sea in the mornings. The father-in-law and uncles get up at silly o'clock, and we head off to the beach for a swim and to enjoy some 'man time' before we go back for breakfast. The way of life in Turkey does seem to be that the men work and the women look after the household. It is very sociable though, with the women preparing the food *en masse*, with half a dozen or so friends and relatives all crammed into the kitchen, whilst the men, usually in similar numbers, take pleasure in sitting around and enjoying a good drink, or glass of tea.

The seafront in Antalya, where I would be swimming in the mornings, and the mountains in the background, that I ran out towards the previous night.

For me, it is nice to be out in the heat of a Turkish summer on the Med., and I am getting plenty of walking in as well. The beach is over four miles from the apartment, and there are plenty of shops, restaurants and cafés around, so I have been heading over there in the afternoons as well. Today though, one of my uncles is taking me out to see some places outside of Antalya, such as the Roman Amphitheatre at Aspendos, and then on to Side.

We spend an hour or so in the car on the way out there. I have been to the amphitheatre before, on a previous visit, but it is a wonderful place to go and take in some beautiful country.

Having finished doing the tourist thing, I head off to the hillside that the amphitheatre is set into. There are some ruins at the top and I decide to use the opportunity to have a run around, so as to get into the feeling of running in some heat and up hills. The ground is uneven as well, ranging from the stones of the aqueduct to thin, winding paths to loose stones and grassland.

I run and climb around, taking photos of everything, and then decide to head back. I choose a direct route down a winding, but open, stony path. On the way I see a sign pointing off to a stadium in the distance, and make the mistake of letting my gaze wander off in that direction, whilst the rest of me continues down the path. My right foot connects with some loose stones, and as I turn back to look where I am going, I have already slipped and gone over the now twisted ankle. I did not fall, but my right ankle had to work in some stretched positions, and as a consequence, I know that I have screwed it up.

The amphitheatre at Aspendos (top) and the ruins in the hills above and behind it (above).

I stop at once and shift the foot through a few positions. There is no pain, but it is tender, and I walk the couple of hundred metres the rest of the way to the car park. I am not hobbling along, but just taking it easy. I get into the car and have a check, only to find a minimal amount of swelling. I am thanking myself for the stability work that I have done, knowing that the trip could have easily caused a lot more damage without it.

An annoying little injury is no reason not to enjoy the sights of Side.

The tour of the area continues on to Side, where we have a pleasant stroll around, and then we head back to the apartment in Antalya. When we arrive, I get some strapping onto the ankle, so as to restrict movement through the plane that has been damaged, and I use any opportunity to put my feet up.

Tuesday, 11th July 2006

I woke up early again for another swim, and checked the strapping on my ankle. The damage was not too great, and the strapping had done the trick, so there was hardly any inflammation whatsoever.

I had a few issues when I was swimming, and it was a lot easier to control my foot in breaststroke than in front crawl. But, other than that minor inconvenience, I had another good morning swim. In the afternoon, as it was my last full day in Turkey, we headed out into the mountains for a picnic (a proper picnic, mind you, with barbecued meat, vegetables and salad). Whilst the food was getting prepared, I went out for another run. The ankle was feeling manageable, and I had replaced the strapping.

The first twenty or so minutes was along a minor road, but I then took a detour to get to the top of the mountain, and the steep incline was strewn with rocks, roots and fallen branches. I made it to the top and started working my way back to the others. The toughest parts of the run were very much the climbs, rather than the amount of time spent running or even the heat. Falling over roots was just annoying.

The mountains, some rocky and some tree-covered,
that lie out to the west of Antalya.

Tuesday, 18th July 2006

One annoying thing about shift work is the difficulty in fitting in one's social life. We are now well into Proms season and I have hardly managed to attend any concerts at the Royal Albert Hall. This evening is an exception though. Having finished work I run along to Westminster and then across St. James's Park, Green Park and Hyde Park until I reach the hall. It was not the most direct route, but it was the most pleasant to run, although I did not arrive in a state appropriate for standing around in the arena amongst other, less sweaty bodies. I use the opportunity to run back afterwards as well.

Wednesday, 26th July 2006

I leave the Royal Albert Hall after another concert and run down to Westminster. The going is fast, as once again, so much of it is downhill, and I turn right and head over to Vauxhall Bridge, then crossing to the South Bank and heading back to the flat. I am fit enough to be running the distance without too much trouble, but as I am training for daily marathons that should certainly be the case, anyway. I am also getting faster, but nowhere near the sort of pace of the diehard 10 K runners and triathletes. I just have to keep plugging away and hope to develop my speed some more before the big day.

Saturday, 5th August 2006

The London Triathlon

Probably the best way of getting to a 10 km footrace is not to cycle the 20 km from the flat. But, alas, this was the only way that we could think of to get the bike to Excel. It was not as if we could ask Johann, our cyclist, to ride it there.

Having taken a slightly scenic route to the Excel centre, by taking the direct route to the last roundabout and then taking the wrong exit and having to come back on myself, I was privileged with a good view out over the Royal Victoria Docks where the swim stage would take place. I rode into the car park, and made my way to the registration desk in the main centre, and then racked the bike. I was there early enough, so I chose a position along the stand that would have Johann closest to his exit point onto the cycle course. This also meant that when he dismounted on re-entering the building at the end of his section, he could run the bike directly onto the stand without having to negotiate his way down the length of the rack, between all of the other competitors. It made much more sense that we did things that way, and then I would run that length instead, which would be much more convenient for me than for him with a bike.

I checked my kit and went off to wait for Jono and Johann in the main centre. They were not due for a while yet, so I found somewhere to sit down and made a start on my pre-race food. This was essentially a tub of rice, tuna, salad and peppers. I knew it was good, because people walking past were looking at me either in astonishment or amusement. The more experienced amongst them had a clear look of approval about them.

It reminded me of going to bodybuilding competitions to see friends compete, and the rituals of dieting and contest-day eating habits. Everything had to be just right. Besides, on this occasion, I had just cycled about 20 km and I needed to get some glycogen back into my legs for the big race. I put my food away and went off to nab some isotonic drinks that were being given out to competitors. Naturally I made a point of picking up some for my friends. And then I went to the next person and did the same routine with them. Well, you cannot mess about when it comes to pre-race nutrition. It is better to have it and not need it than be at the start and realise that your energy stores are depleted.

.....

Johann and I picked up a water bottle and carrier for the bike, and secured it in place. We racked the bike and wandered off to watch the start of the swim section. The gun went off and the race started. We watched the lead group move forward in the water, knowing that Jono was amongst them somewhere, carving up the water and hacking to get through the bodies around him. We headed back to the bike and checked that we knew our routine for the changeover. We talked it through, explaining exactly who did what, as we needed to make it as efficient as possible. The timing chip on the ankle and the race number on Johann's back needed to be swapped over, once the bike had been racked, and screwing up meant losing time and possibly even being disqualified. We rehearsed it, partly through descriptions and partly through acting it out. Check, re-check and then check again. Just making sure that we knew what we were doing. Then I headed off to wait for Jono to run into the centre so that I could get a picture.

.....

The atmosphere in the Excel centre had reached fever pitch as the swimmers were all in and the cyclists were all out on the course. Hundreds of people all standing together, waiting to run, as the time ticked by before the first of the cyclists came in. And then they did. The first dozen flew into the building, with those of us waiting to do the run section having to move out of the way to save ourselves from getting hacked up by cycle peddles. The bikes were racked and the runners took off. Shouts went out for people to make the space for them to get through and onto the running track that led outside.

More cyclists came in, and more runners left. No Johann. Johann was good. He was fit and he had been training. The training was not great and the bike was old, but he was in good shape. And he was not here. I waited. Those of us left were losing patience fast. Another cyclist would come in. Was it ours? Another runner would leave. Half the runners had left. Then three-quarters. The racks that were empty were now almost full again of bikes, and people were just standing around talking. Then he came in. He ran the bike right into the rack and as he turned, I was on one knee to remove the timing chip from his ankle and place it on mine. As I was putting the chip strap around my ankle, Johann's arms went around my chest from above as he secured his race number on me. We both finished at the same time, less than two seconds, and I stood up. The final, perfect touch, was Johann taking his sunglasses off and passing them to me, the perfect cool baton, and I was off.

The racks ran the width of the hall and the area between was filled with bodies. 'M-O-O-O-O-V-E!' No sooner had I started the shout than shouts went up all around me and to the front - 'CLEAR THE PATH!' 'BACKS!'

I was at the end of the racks and onto the running track to go out of the building. I turned left out of the changeover area. Two runners in front of me. They were hardly moving. I could not work it out. Were we supposed to go this slow? Were we supposed to pace ourselves like this? I heard a shout from behind and I turned to see two friends, Coral and Janice, who had come to see us race, shouting support. I raised an arm in acknowledgement as I was already turning back to the other two. No. This was not what we were supposed to do. This was not my pace. I accelerated and moved past him in two seconds, her in less than another five. I accelerated up to running pace as I reached the start of the main circuit; runners that were finishing a lap were coming around at the same time; the few metres to the finish line was just off to the other side. A sharp right arch lead me out of the building and into the sun. Some supporters of my charity, Survival International, shouted after me, 'COME ON SURVIVAL, SAA…SAA…SAA!!!'

The course went down a ramp, then arched around to the left, went uphill slightly and over to the right. People were giving out water. I took some. Some even managed to make it into my mouth before I threw the cup off to the side of the track. Huge speakers blared out Queen's 'Don't stop me now', and by this point I was well into my pace. The course evened out and was flat for the two kilometres of the circuit that took me back to the point opposite the guys with the water. The course was packed full of runners, some doing the same event as me, some doing the shorter distances of the super-sprint and sprint triathlons. There were hundreds of them. And I was faster.

The sun was bright, and as I passed the cool water showers, it was a chance to get hit by some refreshing water as I lined myself up to overtake some fellow competitors. I could not help but feel aggressive to some of these guys. It seemed that they had spent longer choosing their top of the range kit than they had training. I tore past the guys in their Nike 'I will run a year' tops.

Hundreds of them. I would slow down when I had to, purely because of the number of people creating congestion along the course, and then I would use it to accelerate past them. I was not the fastest on the course, and I knew that the best runners had already finished, but this was me running now.

This was my race. And all that I had to do was run my pace and complete four laps. I passed the pub on my left, with another cry from some other Survival International supporters; downhill slightly, round to the right, along, then up the ramp. I had been advised not to go crazy at this point; that lots of people were draining themselves of energy and making a big mistake for the rest of the race. So I waited, I denied my desire to dig in and accelerate up, and I kept to my pace. I looped around the top of the circuit and went back for lap number two. Johann and Jono were nowhere to be seen. Bastards. I thought that the least they could do was to come and give me some support.

The runners lined up along the course in front of me. I really was not the fastest. People ran past me. But the difference was simple. I was overtaking tens of people for every minute that I was on the track. During the whole four circuits, I was overtaken by about eight people, and I took at least three of those back on my next circuit; I had remembered them. Top of the second circuit, starting the third, I looped around and saw Johann and Jono there, taking a picture of me and giving me a shout. Where had they been? Bastards. Anyway, I had two more laps left and I was feeling good. Down the slope, around, then up. Was it going to be Queen this time or the theme from *Rocky*? Was any of the water going to get into my stomach this time or just all over my face like every other time? It was not deliberate. I was not trying to cool my face down; I just could not for the life of me slow down and take my time trying to get it right, and as a consequence I ended up throwing it all over myself.

Just coming out of the arena for circuit number two.

I had realised that the best tactic was not to take water every time, but rather to ration it out and allow myself the chance to try to take it on board properly, instead of depositing it on me and the runner behind. This was good, I was in my pace and it was not letting me down. I was enjoying being a runner; the supporters were lined up along the barriers and outside the pubs. This was a good day. The Survival guys had left their position outside the pub, no doubt to go inside and get some drinks. Bastards! Anyway, it was just down to me now, running for the team and myself.

I reached the top of the circuit, looped around to the right, and heard the shout go up from Jono and Joey. I gave them a smile and a wave and carried on towards the ramp, this circuit being very much like the one that I had done before. As I came around the top of the circuit for the third time, I held up my index finger and shouted out, 'Last lap – see you at the finish line.'

Johann had looked a bit surprised, but he had definitely heard me. I gave myself a mental slap to check that I could indeed count to four. Yes. Definitely. This was it; lap number four. The last one. My watch told me that I was running ten-minute laps. Nice and comfortable. I could have run faster, most definitely, but I still had this lap to go, and I did not want to be working myself into the ground just yet. Besides, as long as I was still the one doing the overtaking, what was the point in running faster? I might need it later. I was well into the rhythm of the circuit, and there were fewer runners on my final lap than there had been on the previous three. But I was not running against them, only me.

Past the pub, downhill, round to the right. There it was; the ramp, at the top of which was the arch around to the left into the Excel centre. This time, instead of looping around to the right, I would continue left to the finish line. Just that ramp ahead of me, and there is a group of runners just getting to the top. When would I do it? When would it begin? I reached the bottom of the ramp, and I leaned in and started to stride up towards the top. Ten metres to the top; the other runners have just gone out of sight to my left. It started. My legs punch down into the ramp and I accelerate. Heart rate increases; breathing rate increases; focus increases. I move in behind them, right behind them, and have to take the left arch wide to overtake them and get around it. I move in to the left again, runners spilling into the final few tens of metres to the finish line. They are everywhere – to the front, the left and the right. Right in my way. Bastards. Last few metres and I do not care if they haven't got anything for a sprint finish. I have. And in my head it goes up: 'M-O-O-O-V-E!' And with everything I have got I get past them and cross the line.

I hit the barrier, resting on it with my forearms before bending down to take off the timing chip and throw it in the bucket. I am given a bottle of water as I lean back to take in some deep breaths. I feel a little dizzy; it was not as if

I had a cool-down. Off I go to find my teammates. I find them straightaway, a few metres away from the finish, and we give each other some congratulatory hugs. I swig some more water as I put my medal around my neck, Coral and Janice take our picture, and then the feedback came in:

From Johann 'You flew; you were awesome.'

From Coral: 'I'm very impressed!'

She looked impressed too. I was impressed. It was my first race, and I felt great. Then came the slagging, care of Johann: 'What's the matter with you? It doesn't look like you've done anything!'

He was right, I was back in the world of the living again now. My breathing felt back to normal, colour had returned to my face, and I was one happy bunny. Had I the pleasure of starting with the other lead runners then it would have been a whole new kettle of fish and I would have had to work for it, but I was happy with what I had managed. And Johann? The chain had come off his bike just a short distance from the end of his stage, and he had put it back on as all the cyclists he had worked so hard to get past, passed him. Some might say that it had something to do with the comment that immediately preceded the knackered chain incident '…Old Faithful'. That would be sure to bugger up any winning situation and shower it with bad luck.

Jono had put in an awesome swim, Johann had managed a superb race up until and after the chain came off, and even then he had the presence of mind to fix the situation and get back on the saddle (as it were). As for me, I had an awesome birthday, and when I turned up at the flat with the bike, Coral and Janice were already waiting for me. I made up some food and then the three of us headed off to the pub for last orders. There had been talk of meeting up with the others and doing a pub crawl, but we were pretty tired and just happy to do our own thing, and I had a birthday that I will remember for a long time to come.

Not a bad birthday at all.
Jono (left), yours truly (centre) and Johann (right).

Competing again next year? Not me. Once the *Marathon des Sables* is over, I can hang up my competition trainers and concentrate on the next endurance project, but the Michelob Ultra-Triathlon will always be my first race since I was a schoolboy, and it was an incredible introduction. More important than just my inherent desire to run past everyone, was the spirit of the day. We were all there to race and none of us wanted to look at this as just a fun run. But the spirit of camaraderie created an electric atmosphere of excitement and anticipation of the race ahead. We were all in this together, hundreds of us on the Olympic Team event, and thousands of us competing in some event of the London Triathlon over that weekend. Yes, we all had our motivation to give as good as we could, but it was an excitement that meant we had something in common with everybody else, and a reason to help each other out and be friendly.

That was something that I had not expected, and really appreciated on the day. I also did not expect to be running faster than so many other competitors, and upon reflection really wished that I could have been setting out with some top runners. Not because I would have wanted to see them racing off ahead of me, or even for the chance of raising my game and getting past some of them, but purely from a pacing point of view to really challenge myself. Because really, there were thousands of people out there, but only one person that I was racing against, and I absolutely loved it.

Saturday, 9th September 2006

The Last Night of the Proms

Following a fair close to the Proms season, I headed back to the flat to collect my kit and then set off to Heathrow for an overnight flight out to Cairo. Although I had not managed any running today, I had clocked up about fifteen miles of walking, including a few miles with the heavy kit needed for my week in Egypt.

Sunday, 10th September 2006

I arrived at Cairo airport in the morning, and was taken by Mahmoud's driver to his apartment in Maadi. I was in Egypt for the wedding of a dear friend of mine, Mahmoud's daughter, Dalia, and I was expecting to use the rest of my time here for training.

Monday, 11th September 2006

Today I mainly slept and took it easy. I returned to the apartment from the wedding in the early hours, and spent most of the day being lazy and just wandering around the local area by the Nile.

The evening view from the apartment in Maadi, with the sun setting behind the Feluccas on the Nile.

Tuesday, 12th September 2006

Mahmoud drove me into Cairo for a meeting, after which I decided to go for a stroll. I enjoy walking around Cairo. Unlike the time I spent in Russia, where I could fit in and look like a local, there is no way that an Egyptian would confuse me for one of them. I do not tend to enjoy sticking out from a crowd as a foreigner, but the good thing about Cairo is that a lot of Brits and Americans study or work over here, so the locals do not know if I am really a visitor or if I have lived here for ten years.

It is a beautiful blue sunny day, and the temperatures are in the high twenties or low thirties. I find it difficult to tell how hot it is here, because it never seems that uncomfortable, as it is so dry. Similarly in Russia, where I could not tell the difference between minus fifteen and minus thirty; I just recognised it as 'a bit parky'. I head across the Nile and Zamalek, past the Egyptian Museum and then on downtown, via some marketplaces. I work my way across town until I reach the City of the Dead. The name is a title given to it by the Brits. When Cairo's population began to expand, people started making homes for themselves around the tombs in the northern and southern cemeteries. I looked in from outside and then took a walk through it. The tombs are incredibly well looked after, and children were playing in the streets. I was certainly the only white-eye wandering around, but then there were not many people here, anyway. I took a right turn and met up with a main road that took me to the Citadel. I had a walk around the Citadel complex, including the military museum, and then got back onto the road and headed into the next part of the cemetery.

I worked my way along backstreets and then eventually arrived back at the Nile, albeit a few miles further along from where I had started. I was not wearing proper walking kit, and I had not had that much to eat during the day, but the last couple of hours to the apartment in Maadi did make me feel that I was doing something to train myself. The desert is hotter, but being in the dry heat of Cairo is a good way to get accustomed to the heat before I make my way out to Mahmoud's stud farm later in the week. I get back to Maadi and head down into a restaurant by the river. I have walked about twenty miles today, at a very easy pace, so I did make the distance and it was a good reintroduction to Cairo and the local climate.

Wednesday, 13th September 2006

One of Mahmoud's staff took me out to Khan al Khalili today. The area is often regarded as 'Old Cairo', and the bazaar itself is a massive tourist trap. Unlike the markets that I walked through yesterday, which were along backstreets and populated only by locals, Khan al Khalili is much more difficult to move around. Shop owners work hard to encourage you into their shops, there always seems to be someone at your side trying to sell you something, and turnover of stock is such that the muddy ground is littered with discarded boxes and plastic. It gets cleaned, but not enough to actually look clean. The markets yesterday were clean, the ground was not littered, and nobody approached me at all. I could even browse the stalls without the shop owners harassing me. But I think that Khan al Khalili is charming in its own way. It is just another aspect of Cairo, and I still enjoy coming here on most of my visits to the city.

Thursday, 14th September 2006

Following about four miles of walking yesterday, today I move out to the pool house at Mahmoud's farm by the desert in Giza. I make myself at home, put some food into the fridge, and then head out for a run in the desert. The first part of running in the desert is actually getting to a good starting point. Leaving the farm's main gates, I walk along by some irrigation channels and around other farms, until after less than half an hour I am by the desert. I head left, with farms and farmland to my left, and tombs and the desert proper to my right. There is a mound that some dogs seem to like living on, and they start barking for Egypt whenever something organic comes along. A few well-aimed stones seem to do the trick, although a big stick also works quite well. After walking through some small trees, I cross over a road used almost entirely by lorries that head to and from an industrial area further out, and then I am at my starting position. I get to the top of a mound by the roadside and look back at where I have come from, whilst I sort out my kit. I can see the pyramids at Giza from here, which are always a welcome sight when I am heading back from the desert.

The older pyramids appear above the horizon to my half-left as I head out towards Saqqara.

I turn around and start running. I have the choice of a steep climb or no climb but soft sand, and I choose the climb. I dig deep and get to the top. The ground is quite hard; hence I prefer it to the soft sand around the base, although between plateaus I am bound to be running up and down as I move from one to the next. But it is fun, so it is okay. The sky is yet again a perfect deep blue, and the sun feels like it is concentrating on me directly, with the air temperature noticeably hotter than in the city. I run around the hills, then down onto the flat towards Saqqara, but turn around and start heading back before I get there.

Passing closer to some step pyramids as I reach a flat a few
miles north of Saqqara.

I get back to the start point and then walk the rest of the way to the farm. I probably only managed about 6 miles, and it took two hours, but that is the desert for you. You are either slowed by the sand or by the hills, but at least for me the heat was quite tolerable. It was hot, but I was sweating and taking on water, so I did not overheat or feel any worse for the environment.

When I reached the farm I dumped my kit down and jumped into the pool briefly before making a start on some of my food. I then took out an aerial map of the area, which I had bought back in England, and started planning a route out across the desert. The plan is to spend one or two days heading south-west towards the lake at Al Fayoum, carrying all of the kit and water that I will need with me. The route is not difficult to plot, but I will be navigating using the sun, and a friend that would have liked to have been my support crew is out of town. Mahmoud's wife, Nihal, comes over to the farm to check that everything is in order, and I go through my plan. The idea is to reach the lake and then head back, but I appreciate that I may need to make some contingencies. My mobile will work for some of the journey, so I can be in contact with Nihal.

My Emergency Action Plan (EAP) for anything that goes wrong is to head east until I reach a main road that parallels the Nile, and to call for help from there. Nihal seems quite happy with everything, although everybody else has already told me in no uncertain terms that I *will* die. As Mohammed, the farmhand, puts it, 'the car gets exhausted and cannot make it that far'. Mahmoud's brother, also called Mohammed, is confident that I will be killed by snakes or scorpions, and Nihal is primarily concerned that she cannot tell me where there is quicksand or landmines. Landmines? I remember hearing about this before. Landmines litter the desert here and have been moved around with the dunes. Consequently, 'There is no such thing as "safe" desert'.

It seems that everybody knows of someone, usually a friend, who was maimed or killed by landmines. Although I try not to show it, that changes everything, because now I need a contingency for not getting myself blown up. I can obviously keep a lookout for metal surfaces above the sand, and any abnormal shapes just under the surface, but anything resting under the sand is going to be impossible to identify before it is too late. I am not too sure about how to identify quicksand either, but again will need to be very attentive regarding my observations of the ground that I am travelling across. My first thought, to reduce my risk of coming into contact with either landmines or quicksand, is to stick to the 4 x 4 tracks. People love taking their jeeps out into the desert, and it is possible to travel almost anywhere within continuous tracks left by those cars.

Friday, 15th September 2006

I leave the farm at 06:45 and head off to my start position. Once there I check that everything is in order and I start running. I am carrying a rucksack full of food and twelve litres of water. All in it weighs just over 17 kg (38 lbs). I am dressed in my usual desert combats and Magnums, with a Mountain Warehouse lightweight T-shirt and a jungle shirt over the top. I am also wearing sunglasses and a shamagh. With all the weight, I am not going to be able to run continuously for very long. My kit is much better suited to walking than running, but it is tried and tested and will be fine for today. Trail running shoes would be better than boots, but as I do not have any gaiters, they would fill up with sand, and despite being a bit cumbersome, the desert Magnums are actually fine to run in over short distances. I have worn them so much that they feel like slippers now.

I run past the step pyramids and then on to Saqqara. This is farthest that I have ever travelled by foot in the desert (or on horseback, for that matter), so I am now entering unknown territory. I check my bearing with the rising sun, and am forced to box around a military installation and some land that is fenced off. The skull and crossbones on the markers suggest that taking a short cut is not recommended. I follow a track between installations and then get back to my cross-country. There is a road up ahead, leading away from Saqqara, and I cross over that and carry on heading south-west. Something resembling a giant crow lands on a mound over to my right, and I consider that he must be taking first dibs on my eyeballs.

Leaving the Nile Valley behind me as I head southwest towards Saqqara.

At 10:00 I take the rucksack off and sit down, whilst I take in some food and some water. I am still close to the military installations, and I am in sight of Saqqara. I am looking forward to getting away from it all, just being alone and making my way across the barren desert. I get my rucksack on and I start moving off from the resting point, which was no more than a small mound by the side of the track, and I have a go at another run. I can run along the tracks, but tend to walk when I am over softer and less predictable ground. The Saqqara pyramids had been in sight for hours, and as they become more distant, I find myself checking the bearing every half an hour. As it approaches midday, I find that I am truly on my own, with no hope of finding shade, and the sun is beating down hard from a cloudless blue sky. I am fit for the task and I am carrying plenty of food and water to survive, but if I succumb to heatstroke, then I am in real trouble. I have no means of finding shelter in such

The headgear will usually be kept loose, but it is good to check that it will do the job, along with the sunglasses, should the sun become unbearably strong or if a dust devil (check Google Images) starts throwing sand at me.

an open landscape. Even though there are hills, with the sun directly overhead, there is no shade created, so I must just grin and bear it.

At 12:30 I decide to take another break. I sit down at the top of a plateau, with my legs hanging down over the steep face to the valley bottom below. The sun is still hot, and a warm breeze wicks away any sweat that has formed to cool me down. The nicest feeling is taking off the rucksack and letting the breeze push my soaking wet shirt and T-shirt into my back, which

The squashed appearance of the Saqqara pyramids, which remain over my shoulder for more than an hour as I make my way out into the desert.

feels wonderfully cooling, albeit just for a few moments before it dries. I rest for about twenty minutes before I continue heading towards Al Fayoum.

I am walking/running a good distance, but I am sticking to 4 x 4 tracks whenever I can. The plateaus are quite solid, so I am confident that there is not likely to be any quicksand up here, nor any landmines that could move under this surface. On the lower ground though, and on the climbs, the ground is far less stable and I am, therefore, on the lookout for anomalies in the sand and the presence of metallic surfaces. It seems that every idiot with a jeep drives around in semicircles. I gather that this is because they think that there will be less chance of driving over a landmine by doing so, but if they were to drive in a straight line then they would cover far less ground and be significantly less likely to hit a mine. As a consequence of their bizarre logic, however, I have to cross the desert in semi-circles, and it means that I am taking a lot longer than I would like to cover the distance between two landmarks (usually hills).

The slight and rolling landscape that presents the first, and still familiar desert landscape that I am accustomed to.

One thought keeps coming back to me though. It has been hours now since my last sighting of animal life. That was five hours from when I started, and it was a rabid dog, which was dead. The last sighting of anything *alive*, other than the sparse desert brush, was that crow, and he is still probably around somewhere, waiting for a chance to take a peck at the nice juicy fluid in my eyeballs.

Every now and again, an area of breathtaking beauty opens up in front of me, and I take a five-minute break as I check navigation and work out my route.

At 15:00 I take another twenty minutes. This time a mound has created some shade over to my right. The mound is dotted with holes, which I would guess belong to either scorpions or beetles. There is no sign of snakes or anything else, so scorpions are the biggest risk. Fortunately, because it is so hot, everything sensible is staying in its hole at the moment. When I take the rucksack off, I make a point of falling back against the mound as heavily as I can, just to confirm to anything at home that something outside weighs far too much to get out of bed to have a set-to with. I look out across the valley to the plateau on the far side. The lake is miles away on the other side of that, and I need to keep heading towards it until night falls. My original plan had been to give myself a cut-off time of 2 am. If I had not reached the lake by then, I would turn around and start heading back, anyway. The problem will be that when it gets dark I will not be able to see the tracks anymore, and I will be much harder to find if anything goes wrong.

I head off towards the other side of the valley, a few miles ahead in the distance. In fairness I am also not feeling that healthy at the moment. I have been taking on plenty of water, but not enough food. When it is hot, and especially when exercising, it is not easy to take in a lot of calories. I have been eating, but it has just been some snack foods, and nowhere near enough to balance out the calories that I am expending. That should not be an issue, but because I am drinking water instead of an isotonic drink with electrolytes, I am diluting my cell chemistry. I am sweating continuously, and therefore, losing a lot of minerals. Salt is one of them, and I am replacing that by dipping into a bag of salt that I have brought with me (the nomads suck on stones to get a similar, and probably, better result). The problem is that I am losing more than salt.

I am losing potassium as well, and magnesium, calcium, and everything else that can come out in the sweat. At 16:30 I lie down on the floor by a small area of uplifted ground, and take relief at the feeling that the sun is lower in the sky and it is much cooler and more bearable now. I take on another snack bar and feel instantly better. I have no appetite whatsoever, but force it down me with a minimum of water, and just feel a little bit more normal. I am thirsty, but I do not want the taste of water, and that is why I believe that I am short on electrolytes, rather than just dehydrated. I am carrying enough water to kill me, if I take it in without all the minerals that I need to maintain cell homeostasis, but it is also a ration of six litres per day, reckoning on two full days of travel. The problem is that I have now had eight litres, and it is only approaching 17:00.

The decision to just drink *ad libitum* is because I must stay hydrated as my first priority. If I am thirsty then I must drink, because I am already slightly dehydrated by the time the thirst mechanism kicks in. Essentially, my priority is to live, with going the distance taking second place. The lake is not far away from where I am now, close to the end of the valley, and I can even see birds flying a little way overhead, just about where I reckon the lake should begin. Knowing it is so close is why it is so annoying that I have to break off and head east. I spent the last half an hour going south, so as to cut down on the distance between the edge of the lake and the road by the Nile, but I know that there is no way that I can travel even the 20 km from the lake to the road at night. The risks are just too high. As I pass a track, I can see a watchtower off to my right and a car is outside. I have been informed that actually getting to the lake would be incredibly difficult because of the military installations, and anyway, access is forbidden due to the archaeological sites around it. That had not really bothered me, as one guy that does not want to be seen can probably make it through. The lake is vast and cannot be policed that effectively.

The sun is setting directly behind me, and the birds flying around above me are there purely to tease me. I am really moving now. I need to get as close to civilisation as possible before the sun disappears and I can no longer see the tracks. It is getting significantly cooler now, and the breeze carries a cool rather than a warm air. It takes about an hour for the sun to set completely, and there was the illusion that the sun just rested on the horizon for about forty-five minutes, before getting its head down for the night. The sky is clear, and I can navigate using the stars now, which is far easier for me than using the sun. Both methods are straightforward, but I have been working out bearings from the stars since I was a child, and in the past I always used a compass when navigating in the day. To think that my Egyptian friends thought that I was mad for not carrying GPS! In any case, GPS can go wrong, and should only be used as a backup, rather than as the primary tool for navigation. At least the sun does not play silly buggers.

I switch on my torch so that I can see the tracks. Even so, there is barely enough light to be able to pick up a new set of tracks when the current one goes off on the rest of its semicircle. There is the glow of lights in the distance, but it is still many miles away, and there is a lot of unknown ground between us. I eventually find some farmland, given away by the presence of a wall, rather than crops or animals, and I work my way around and then back on a course to the lights. I see a farmhouse up ahead and turn off the torch. It is a thin road and if they are looking out then they will see me, but I really want to avoid that. Too late! A boy came running out of the house with his brothers and they start shouting at me as I pass. I carry on and try to signal that everything is okay and I will just carry on, but they are not having any of it, and look ready to jump into their van to come after me.

I go back to talk to them, greeting them with a 'Salaam alaykum!' and they shake my hand and ask me where I am going. They are in the process of moving into the house, and the boy insists on showing me around and introducing me to the family. Having been out in the desert on my own for the last thirteen hours, with all the sudden fuss and attention, I was beginning to wish that I had taken my chances with the landmines. I take a seat and call it an end to the day's adventure. They have informed me that the town is too far away to walk, as it is an incredible seven kilometres away, and so they insist on driving me there in a couple of minutes. They offer me drinks, but I am happy to just sit down and take the weight off my feet.

They drive me off, and as the bumpy, pot-holed road winds around all the farms I realise that I would have had a nightmare to work my way around all the private land. At least in the desert there are not any boundaries, but in this area I would probably be walking along all the roads to every dead end before I eventually worked my way to the town. I was a little concerned that they might just be driving me out to a friend's place and the nightmare would continue, but after about fifteen minutes, we pull up in the town. When they had asked me where I was heading, I had just told them the Nile; heaven forbid that they might have driven me to Cairo. They refuse to take any money from me for the petrol and then they drive off to somewhere else in the town. As I walk along the side of the tributary towards the Nile proper, and hopefully that main road to Cairo, I attract the attention of the locals.

A white-eye with a rucksack is probably a rare occurrence in this place, and I have no idea where 'this place' actually is. I return the kind greetings from the locals, and avoid the looks from any young women, and just try to look casual as I consider that some small Egyptian village has just found itself a new idiot. A group of teenage boys on bikes ride along at the side of me, some wanting to shake my hand, and others wanting me to present them with money. This really annoys me. I work out my contingency for throwing them all in the river if they get aggressive, but it is just the cheek of asking for money that grates. They are doing it because they associate me with money, rather than in connection with their providing me with merchandise or a service as most would. It is not right to think that this is a negative reflection of the Egyptians, as their parents would take no pride in what they are doing, and would no doubt reprimand them accordingly.

The boys eventually get bored and give up a little while before I reach the next town, this one being on the main road. So, thirteen hours in the desert? Not bad for a day's stroll. I wander around looking for a taxi, and instead, manage to cram myself and my kit into what already looks like an overcrowded minibus. Some people are smoking, and the Arabic music is wailing out of the radio, and nobody is particularly fussed about me being in there. I sit back and get comfy, then start looking at the photos and thinking about what I have been through. It was sort of my own personal debrief.

Saturday, 16th September 2006

Having reached the farm in the wee small hours, I put my head down and got some sleep. In the morning I checked the sores from the previous day, attended to them accordingly, and then went out into the desert for a run for a few hours. This was great fun. After the full day of working towards a distance, this was just a nice little fun run for about three and a half hours.

Today's run was mainly spent doing hill running and working at higher intensities and shorter durations than yesterday, so as to promote recovery whilst still keeping active.

I headed back out towards Saqqara, although I refrained from going the whole distance, and instead just did some hill work in that general area, charging up and down the dunes, before returning to the farm, and then travelling back to Maadi.

Thursday, 12th October 2006

I went down to the gym to have a chat with the guys and check that everything was in good order. It was at this time that Sam, one of the fitness consultants and personal trainers, asked me if I had heard about the Hellrunner race in November. Well, the answer was 'No', but I did like the idea, based on the name rather than anything else. Sam went on to tell me that it was just shy of a half marathon, on land where they test the Challenger II tanks. There are wetlands, bogs and all that sort of shenanigans. It sounds good. It has a certain appeal. Considering how much I dislike running around town, the opportunity of doing some proper cross-country running sounds very appealing indeed. So we signed up.

Saturday, 11th November 2006

The plan was to complete a half marathon or 10 K in the week before the event. The way my schedule was looking, it would have to be on the Wednesday, which would be about right. It should definitely have happened by the Saturday. At least a brief 2-mile run along the South Bank would remind my body that running does occasionally happen. But unfortunately none of that occurred. Instead, I had thrown myself, with gusto, into planning logistics for a couple of days in some countryside.

I had booked a return journey to Snowdon (or Porthmadog, which is the closest train station that I could find), and come eleven at night I was going through a kit check. By half past midnight I was just finishing off a curry. My last run was the half marathon a couple of weeks before. The last run before that was in the desert. Training for the Hellrunner was very much a non-starter. Instead, I decided to view the Hellrunner as a practice run for my adventures in Snowdon.

Sunday, 12th November 2006

Getting to Longmoor camp was quite straightforward. I took the tube to Victoria, the over-ground to Bromley South, and met a friend who drove us both down the M25 and A3 to the site. At the first petrol station, I picked up a couple of flapjacks, a bottle of Lucozade and some Evian. The flapjacks went down easily, and I was hoping to find somewhere that I could buy something altogether more meaty and calorific. Unfortunately that was not to be. We made a final pit stop at what advertised itself as services, but with only one toilet for all customers and with a dozen people in the queue, I was not going to stay to say my farewells to last night's curry just yet. I did manage to catch up with a Kiwi who was also to be competing in her first Hellrunner event, and it had not taken long to realise that Shell was becoming crowded with a hardcore breed of adventure runners. There was a key difference between these guys and the guys at the London Triathlon. At the London Triathlon, everybody was wearing nice and shiny logos and professional-looking kit, and most of them were really finding the flat road running tough. This time the guys were dressed much more modestly, and there were far fewer fashion-based telltales that they were athletes. They just looked outrageously fit.

The toilets at the barracks were less than inspirational. They were divided into male and female, although there was only one cubicle in each. The curry was well on its way through the system so there was no way that I could take it with me. I was just waiting to have to apologise to the guy in the queue behind me. As it turned out an apology regarding any lingering smell was not required. Not considering that the plumbing had given up the ghost about four people or so before me, not that my bowels were in any frame of mind to care or object.

The race was preceded by a minute's silence, and considering the fact that we were at an army training ground, it would not have been right to go without it. The race started amidst clouds of red smoke, which we passed through on our way to the first corner and uphill. It was a reasonable uphill, and there was not really much to worry about for the first few miles after that. In fact, it was just nice to get into a comfortable running pace and enjoy the scenery.

The route continued up and around a slight hill, during which the field spread out from this horde that just left the start line.

It is normal practice in running to keep the head positioned forward, which alleviates strain on the neck and improves running posture. However, when now wearing grip-free, knackered trainers, and running at pace over sand, mud, loose rocks and deep tracks, it is much more important to look at where the feet are landing and going to land.

The first length of water came in after about four miles, and came up to about my knees. This had the effect of soaking my socks, but not much more. Over the following miles the terrain gradually seemed to get more varied, with greater variances in steepness of the inclines, and the nature of the ground. It was just about trying to keep a consistent pace during the flats, then digging in on the uphills, and controlling my pace enough not to fall arse over tit on the downhills. The route took us through woodland and out into the open moorland. I took the opportunity to look around at the countryside whenever I could, just continually reminding myself that it was so beautiful and exactly whereI wanted to be, especially as I am usually confined to the flatness of London, with nothing underfoot but paving slabs and chewing gum.

I managed quite happily for the first fifty minutes, after which the two pathetic flapjacks had given up all their available energy and I was in need of more carbs. I knew that I was not going to get them and I knew that I would have to just do the best that I could without them, but it did mean that I could not stop my pace from gradually slowing over the remainder of the race. The slight dizziness did not do much to help either, especially as I had to concentrate so hard on the loose rocks and mud and generally all the places that I did not want my feet to be. The dizziness was a result of being dehydrated and lacking carbohydrates. The brain requires about six grams of glucose every hour, and more if you are asking it to actually do stuff, such as not let you fall on your arse. Consequently, when the body cannot liberate enough or the stores have run dry, then it is quite understandable that the brain starts to slow down a bit. My body followed.

I did not struggle to keep my legs moving, as my fat stores could keep those going around, but the concentration issue and hunger just made for slower progress. Hydration is important because the average athlete needs about 250 ml of fluid every fifteen minutes. I had run for fifty minutes and taken on about 100 ml of fluid. The body only needs to be dehydrated by one per cent for there to be adverse effects on co-ordination. Because it was cold I did not feel particularly thirsty, but it was definitely having an effect. At least in the desert I would be continually taking on isotonic drinks, which would deliver both the water and glucose that I needed.

There was one water station on route, which was about halfway around the course, at close to 6 miles. It was only a couple of miles after that, whilst the track took us left through the woods, that we saw a sign informing us that we were at the 'Bog of Doom'. The runner at my side at the time questioned me as to whether or not that was something from *Trainspotting*, which indeed it was. What happened next was a right turn and a bit of a downhill for a few metres. Then we both jumped into the bog in front of us – deep, red, sodden clay, up to the tops of our legs. The ground underneath was muddy and saturated, so there was nothing firm and we were sliding as we tried to wade through. The guy's next comment was to inform me that the last time he went home this dirty he received a spanking. As we came out of the bog and got back into our stride, I allowed my mind to wander as I thought of all the people that I would not mind having waiting to give me a spanking when I got home. It certainly passed a couple of minutes.

Not long after the bog, came some deep-water hazards. This had the effect of cleaning me, which was both helpful and welcomed. The main water hazard was twenty or so metres long, and the water was up past my waist. The ground underneath was a nightmare, as my feet were going everywhere, and thick roots were doing their bit to become a major embuggerance. There was no way of passing anyone, so all I could do was wade along in something of a queue as people filtered out up ahead. After that, there were a few nasty uphills, and the rather tame 'Hills of Hell' just a mile before the finish. The last hills were tame because they were steep but short, which meant that I would not get overly tired on them, although when I got there I was in a queue of people walking again.

By this stage I was very close to my limit; I was feeling exhausted, mainly due to poor hydration and energy availability, which made my body feel tired and heavy. My legs were still turning, but I was enjoying the race just a little bit less. As the finish line approached, I barely increased my pace. I got over the line after an hour and thirty-three minutes, which was nothing to jump up and down about, but certainly the furthest that I have run in competition (much as I viewed the whole thing as a bit of a fun run and a pleasant jaunt in the countryside).

There was no need for me to grab my ankles and try to catch my breath, because I had not lost any of it. I actually finished the race feeling quite reasonable, although very much aware that my legs' carbohydrate stores had been almost entirely depleted, and a few muscles were seriously peeved at me playing silly buggers with them without adequate consultation or training. I turned in my race chip, picked up my free goody bag, and sank a few cups of isotonic sports drink. Getting set for the homeward journey was quite straightforward. I took out a bin liner from the car, and started throwing my trainers and clothing in; I also took out a towel, which I used to remove as much dirt from my skin as possible. When I took off my shorts, the white liner was covered in mud, and the same was very much true of my boxer shorts.

The open, spacious, well-ventilated changing facilities were within easy reach of the car.

I did a complete change of clothes and footwear in the car park, walked and jogged for a bit to stay loose, and then got in the car to be driven off. My post-exercise meals consisted of the small cups of isotonic drink, the bottle of Lucozade, and then, when we got to London, it was a trip to my local carvery at the Anchor and a pint of Bombardier.

I part-jogged, mostly walked, the short distance back to the flat, whereupon I ate some minced beef, loosely in the guise of a Bolognese, as well as smoothies, fruit, chocolate, and anything else I could get my hands on.   A pleasant text from my old chum Stuart went as follows:

> 'Ha, Mr Hines you hellrunner you! Erm, I hope that went well today with no training and the curry last night and you weren't sort of blowing out your arse…' (Stu).

I had forgotten about that curry. It was on account of that curry that I had felt a major calling to evacuate my bowels about half an hour prior to kick-off.

I put on some music and jumped in the bath, and for the following forty minutes, I scrubbed away the more ingrained dirt that I had not been able to remove with the towel after the race. One thing that came as a surprise was the amount of mud in my nether regions. In fact, I cannot imagine being perfectly free from all the mud, dirt and debris associated with the race until after my next bowel movement.

It is currently thirty-three minutes past midnight on the morning of Monday the 13th of November. Various muscles and connective tissues are currently alerting me to the fact that I have been a bastard to them, and that they will need more than just a Radox bath to make them consider forgiving me. Unfortunately I cannot wait too long for them to repair themselves. Just one more day and then it is time to become acquainted with Snowdonia, and I can barely wait…

Tuesday, 15th November 2006

Thanks to London Underground's Northern Line making a meal out of what should have been a quarter of an hour's journey time, I arrived at London Euston station with minutes to spare. I made a move for the Virgin Trains fast ticket machines, which could not print out my pre-booked tickets, so I had to wait in a single queue for quarter of an hour to have them printed out at the service window. I would have been sorted quicker if the delays had not meant that I missed my first train and would need to have the train times moved on a bit and the tickets organised accordingly.

After a total of nine hours since I left the flat, the Welsh Highlands train pulled into a cold and dark Porthmadog station, at about quarter to seven in the evening. I checked the compass and headed off towards Snowdonia. After about ten minutes, I took the 20 kg rucksack off and pulled out my gloves and balaclava. The latter I rolled up to make a more presentable woollen hat. At my first option, I took the sign for Caernarfon, and continued walking along the road for a further three hours. It was a full seven miles before I came onto the bottom of the Ordnance Survey map. It was at this time that I realised that the road I had chosen was not the one that I had originally intended to take. I made a mental note to myself: NEXT TIME PRINT OUT ANY MISSING SECTIONS OF MAP, YOU ARSE. The only preference for the road that I had wanted to take was that it would bring me right up next to Snowdon itself. I could then head off between a couple of peaks in the opposite direction and make a camp on a third, so as to wake the next morning with a view of the highest peak in England and Wales.

As it was, that plan was completely buggered by my current location. I could not turn back and hope to find my way to the other road, because I did not have the map, and there were no roads that would take me east over to that road for another five or so miles (and then it would mean walking the same distance east, and the same again south) and there was no justifiable reason to do so. I scanned the map and saw another site that I had looked at before leaving, and decided that this would do the trick. It was on some flat land just next to a big lake at the base of a stream. That basically met all of my requirements for a good campsite; flat, water for making up my dehydrated food, and a nice view. Perfik.

I took a right turn onto a minor road and followed it around, parallel to the first road for the next hour and a half. The basic function of this road was to link the few farmhouses and homes in this area with the main road that I had just come from. One thing that I was not prepared for was the emergence from the darkness of what must have been the most dramatic and eerie cemetery that I have ever seen. The gravestones were big and seemed to loom over me from their position high up on the right side of the road. I had seen the cemetery marked on the map, but checked again to confirm my position. I was walking along towards a huge metal tower, with red lights that could be seen from miles away. As I walked closer, I wondered if it was a trick of the hills that I could see only two levels of lights, when half an hour before I could see six - which reminded me of a similar issue in the desert. When I was running towards the Saqqara pyramids, the subtle changes in elevation influenced how much of the first pyramid was visible, and there were times when I was actually very close, but the top of the pyramid had been completely taken over by the horizon.

This was not the same. The red lights that I could no longer see were on the upper parts of the mast. The clouds had consumed them. The road took a steep downhill, and then a track to my right took me out into a field by the lake, and then the track ended. I walked on to the back of the lake, the ground sodden and saturated, and I began climbing the hill. My idea of a nice campsite next to the lake disappeared into the boggy mud beneath my feet. I would instead have to cross the fast-flowing and wide stream, and then climb up the opposite bank, and find a flat area near the summit where the ground was less waterlogged and I could pitch the tent.

Easier said than done. There was no route around the lower areas of the lake and so I would have to climb the hill instead, and then once I had worked my way around the hill, drop down and cross the stream. This area of hillside predominantly consisted of outcrops of rock, which meant scrambling along. I am not a great climber, and I tend to consider myself as half-good at a number of things, climbing included. Consequently, drenched with sweat from the climb and scrambling, and carrying over 20 kg of kit that pulled my centre of gravity backwards, I was not particularly filled with confidence as I made my way around the loose and wet rocks. I would often pause to survey my options up, across and down. Sometimes I did this to confirm that I had no better options than the one that I was presently pursuing, even though that did have me clinging to the rock face vertically, pressing in with my fingernails, knees and feet.

My body was pressed tightly against the rocks and if it came to it I would be using my teeth if that gave me a better grip. I then thought about how easily a rescue team would find me when my friend Stuart raised the alarm on Thursday night, if I failed to phone him with the 'all clear'. I also considered that Stuart would be under the impression that I was about five miles east of my current location; mincing about in the country between the coordinates I had given him for my projected campsite and Snowdon itself. I impressed myself that I had the presence of mind to stop and fill one of my two litre water bottles, when I saw a thin stream of fast-moving water cascading down from above the outcrop. All of my food was dehydrated, and even if I was going to get by without food, I was still going to be desperate for a brew at some point. I was thirsty too and took a few sips directly from the running water. I did it more to wet my mouth than anything else. I dropped a couple of puritabs into the water bottle, accepting that I now would not have any more water unless it had been treated first. I thought that I could see close to the source of the stream, but there was no way of knowing if a dead sheep was out there somewhere, leaking all sorts of nastiness into the surrounding soil and water.

Considering that it had taken me about three hours to get to the front of the lake from the station, it took a further hour and a half just to get halfway around it. I dropped down to the base of the hill and found a way across the stream to the thin bank on the other side. I began working my way upstream, despite boggy ground that was taking every opportunity to pull my boots down into it, and after about twenty minutes I had to climb over the side of a stone wall so that I could start working my way up the side of the next hill. The climb was steep, again, and the ground was saturated. The ground varied equally between rocks and heather and bracken. There was no grass. I would walk along and slightly upwards, then turn into the face of the hill and climb directly upwards, sometimes on the fallen rocks that had slid their way to their present position, and sometimes pulling myself up using the branches and roots of whatever fauna happened to be within grasping distance. There were plenty of times when I slipped a little and there were a couple of times when I slipped a lot. There was one occasion when my footing on a rock slipped forwards and my whole body twisted around; my one handgrip and the trapped foot acting as a hinge for my body to swing around until my arse hit the rocks. That was annoying.

I was constantly out of breath from the effort, and the low clouds meant that I was drenched now not only from sweat, but also from the water vapour carried by the clouds. There was enough water vapour to ensure that everything was soaked. As if that was not enough, there would be sporadic rainfall as well, and the winds would sometimes be strong enough to almost knock me backwards, trying to push me and drag me off the rocks and hillside. My socks and boots were wet anyway, and my clothes were wet from sweat, and because all of my layers were in such a state, including my hat, I started to take this personally. I would stop to catch my breath and look up; 'Just another twenty yards and you'll be on the height of the tallest rocks,' then 'Just give me another five yards and you can take another breather'. At 01:30, I found an area near the summit that was relatively flat and relatively dry (or relatively less saturated) and I decided to pitch the tent.

Relatively flat is important descriptive terminology. The ground was flat by comparison to the varying degrees of climb that the hill had presented me with to this point. But when I climbed into the tent at 02:00, it was still necessary for me to sleep at an angle, with a rock under the ground pressing against my ribcage. The rock did two things. It told me that I had not slipped down. It also told me that the tent had not slipped down instead. My greatest concerns that night were that a rockfall would crush me to death, or that the tent would be hit by lightning (should a thunderstorm come along to compound the existing issue of the battering wind and torrential rain).

Another perfect campsite.
By the morning the ground was inches deep in water and the tent was still being bombarded by ferocious winds in the thick cloud.

Wednesday, 15th November 2006

I made the decision to get out of the tent and get moving at 09:45. I had not slept much, mostly lying awake as howling winds pounded the tent almost flat. The groundsheet was wet through, and all of my kit had continued to take on water from the damp. I would have liked to get breakfast going inside the tent, but a quick check outside the inner tent told me that the reasonably dry area where I had pitched my tent had since been beaten away and replaced by more saturated earth. I put on a reasonably dry change of trousers and woolly pully. Putting on the wet socks was not pleasant, nor was putting them into my wet boots, but it only took a couple of minutes before they were feeling warm, and not obviously uncomfortable. I packed away all the kit and began to make a move along the side of the hill at 10:25. It was only another half and hour and I found another stone wall, which was offering a perfect windbreak to the prevailing cloud and wind, and I set up the Trangia for a brew and some breakfast. The hot chocolate was nectar, and a Vesta beef curry had never tasted so good.

I packed away and checked the map and compass. I then headed off down the side of the hill until I came across a stream, and make a right. Within three quarters of an hour, I was looking at the lake that I had passed last night. It looked beautiful, as did the streams and waterfalls and all the surrounding countryside. I had just ducked out of the clouds and it had all opened up before me. I carried on for a while so that I could get a clear view of the mast again

195

and get a perfect bearing off the map. I checked the compass, and the three of us were in agreement.

I could continue off the map, take a right when I came to the road, work my way onto the main road, do a couple of right turns, and just over a dozen miles later I would be at the base of Snowdon. But I did not come all the way to Snowdonia to walk along roads.

Nothing beats a nice hot meal and a hot chocolate after a night like that and a morning like this.

I checked the map and where I wanted to end up. I checked it again, and then I turned 180 degrees and headed off again upstream. I passed the point where I had come down from my breakfast spot over to my left and on the other side of the stream, and I continued up. In no time at all I was back up in the clouds and facing a fearsome oncoming wind. There were times when it had nails in it.

After reaching the tops of a few fake summits, I eventually found myself heading downhill again. Even at the top these things were sodden bogs. I saw another stream off to my left heading in the same direction as me, but I avoided wandering too close, as the fauna around it gave a good indication that the surrounding ground was even wetter than what I had just been walking over. It was a good hour or so before I rejoined the side of the stream and followed it along downhill. I had to move away again, as the ground became too wet, and after a while a disused mine came into view between the river and my current position. The buildings no longer had roofs and I went on for another twenty minutes, to the point when the stream took a sharp right turn, and I found myself at the top of some rocky outcrops. It presented me with the view of the road that was the halfway point between the main road that I had left yesterday evening and the other main road running alongside Snowdon.

I stopped on the outcrop and set up the Trangia for lunch. At about 14:25 it seemed like the most reasonable thing to do. I sat there, my arse on a big rock, and looked across the valley to the road and the few faraway buildings, and over at the peaks opposite as their summits became lost from sight due to the clouds rolling in. Then they rolled above me as well, bringing the wind across at first, and then down came the rain. I picked up the rucksack and moved it around to a more secluded area of the rock, where I could manage some protection from the wind and rain, and made a couple more return trips to pick up the burning Trangia and the food that was still cooking on it.

The walk down from the hilltop took me into the valley that leads off to the lake. I, however, use this as an opportunity to check navigation, and then do an about-turn and head back up into the clouds.

The rain seemed to follow me, and the rocks were not high enough to protect my head and upper body from the downpour. I used the rucksack cover as a makeshift waterproof hat, and carried on about the chore of preparing my lunch. I started with a soup, which was quite disappointing, but carried on with a tinned strawberry jam pudding. Now my mum could make a better pudding than that with her eyes closed, without weighing scales, and without much care and attention whatsoever. But at that point, with wet clothes and soaking wet legs, with the rain biting in to the side of my face and wind rushing all around me, that pudding was the stuff of the gods.

I did not need to carry on along the compass bearing to the road, as I knew that if I just headed across the next peak, I would drop down the other side and meet the road further along and closer to where I wanted to be. Crossing the stream was the main issue, and walking through the bracken and high ferns made a good job of ensuring that any areas that had tried to dry up, were well and truly soaked again. Because the rucksack was so cumbersome, it was difficult to find an area where I could take it off and throw it the distance across the stream, with the intention of throwing myself across immediately afterwards. I did find a good crossing area, which I negotiated without landing in the water, and I then made my way up and around the next short peak. My intention of dropping down onto the road was waylaid by the sheer drop, the fence, and the number of sheep. This was all indicative of the fact that it was private farmland, and there was the suggestion that the fence at the other end might be harder to negotiate, and anyone working in sight might kick up a fuss. I chose to take the slightly longer route around using some tracks, and made my way through a succession of gates, making a point of checking that they were all properly closed behind me.

I reached the road and took a left turn on a heading north, and with the expectation of finding a path at the point that the road ended. What I found, at about five in the afternoon, was utter darkness. The road did end and a path began, but it was virtually impossible to see it with my night vision. I had to resort to my three-celled Maglite instead, which only concerned me because it used up a hand that I could not use to reach out for climbing or to steady myself, and presented me with the problem that if the batteries ran flat then I would not be able to use the torch at a later and possibly more needy point. Despite the light from the torch, the pathway seemed to disappear, although I managed to find it again every now and again. It was actually quite tough to work out sometimes if I was following a footpath or a stream, as on many occasions they seemed to be one and the same thing.

I knew that the path was supposed to take me to a forest, which I had thought would give me perfect cover to pitch the tent on that first night, from where I could have a crack at an ascent of Snowdon. What concerned me was that the last moments of dusk have presented three peaks in the area to my right that I needed to be on the other side of. The torch was not powerful enough to illuminate them, and whilst I could see their silhouette with my naked eye, there was no way of seeing what the terrain was like on the way. I could not use my map because it was now so soggy that it could not be opened. I made another mental note: 'BUY A MAP COVER, YOU ARSE.' That mental note went along with another one that I had logged when I realised that my puritabs were several years old, and that they might be even more toxic than the water that I was treating with them.

As with the rest of the journey to this point, the climb, when I decided to commence, was over wet ground, with wet fauna brushing against my body to ensure that I was reassuringly saturated. A small settlement at the top had a

The vivid colours were wonderful when I could see them, but this was one of the few times that I came out of the clouds, shortly after which I sat down and set up the stove for lunch.

footpath that led around the side of the next peak, where I then found myself once again clambering over rocks to find my way through between that peak and the next. Passing one lonely pine tree, I headed down and across the side of the slope. I could hear a wailing sound, like the wind rushing heavily around the summit of one of these hilltops, and I was bracing myself for the impact when I got there. Over to my half-right I could see some trees, on the other side of a fence. I took a second look because my mind was kicking me in the back of my head and the penny had not yet dropped. Trees… That would be the National Trust forest that I was expecting the path to lead me to. I could hardly believe that I was here. I just needed to cut through the woods for half a mile or so and I would be at the base of Snowdon.

I know now that I will not be able to climb Snowdon tonight. It might only take a few hours if managed at speed, but it was just too wet and too cold, and if I attempted it then I would be nothing more than a giant icicle at the top. I would have to come back on a nice day and do it then, hopefully with a friend like Stuart with whom I could enjoy the moment. If I climbed it tonight, I ran the risk of putting myself off Wales for life.

I climbed over the top of the fence and dropped myself down into the forest. The forest was made up of pine trees, and they were growing incredibly close together. My sleeping bag and roll-mat were getting caught as I tried to fight a way past the branches and across the fallen trunks. I came out onto a small track, and ended up following it for a mile or so, before I passed the closed gate of the forest. The forest was closed for the winter, hence there were so many fallen trees strewn all over the place. It seemed like a very long walk along the meandering minor road before I emerged onto the A487. Mount Snowdon was directly in front of me, but I could hardly see more than a dozen yards up its side. There was cloud everywhere, and at this height, being this cold and this wet, I confirmed to myself that there was no way that I was

The view from where I took my lunch as the heavens opened up on me. It would be nightfall by the time I reached the base of that climb ahead of me.

going to put myself in that position. However much I might have wanted to test my determination to get to the top, my overriding logic gave me all the right reasons as to why it would be the wrong thing to do. I had accomplished enough to this point and there was no need to be foolhardy now.

I did not stop to gaze at Snowdon. I just took the right turn onto the road and began the sub-ten-mile walk along it towards Porthmadog. I glanced across every few minutes, but there was no more of it visible, and there was still nothing to make me want to climb up it. I paused for a rest a few times along the journey, as both the miles and I dragged our heels as we slowly but steadily passed, and I staggered into Porthmadog at about eleven at night. I had remembered a kids' playing area, at the side of a much larger field, complete with stone circle and a few sheep. I had decided that this would be the place to get the tent up for a few hours, and was anything but surprised when my boots met the soaking wet mud and grass, which told me that it was unsuitable for pitching up for the night. After only a couple of minutes, I found an area further along where the mud was more solid, and pitched the tent. I stripped off and climbed into my partially wet sleeping bag at 23:30. I wished that the rucksack cover could have guarded against all of my kit being so wet, but, unfortunately, it had not.

Thursday, 16 November 2006

Once again the night saw winds vicious enough to almost flatten the tent down, but at least there was no risk of rocks rolling over the top of me, and less chance than previously of being hit by a bolt of lightning. At 05:30 I woke up and started climbing into my wet clothes. My underwear was so wet that I decided to go commando, and I only put on one of my two pairs of socks (the sports socks were in a dreadful state, so I went with the thicker, woolly, outer skiing socks instead). I packed away the kit for the last time and headed over to the station. The train arrived at 06:32 to take me back to London.

I could manage to sum up the journey into the Welsh Highlands quite easily with words such as wet, saturated, cold, hungry and tired. I also found that being in this position, where I was working so hard and in such adverse conditions, that it was almost sufficient to make me dislike the whole thing and never want to repeat it ever again. For example, I could have done the thing on a beautiful day in the middle of summer, when I could have seen everything around me instead of being in cloud cover and darkness for most of the time. I could have climbed Snowdon under a pleasantly dry and mild, starry night. I could have arranged for a later train, stayed an extra night, and climbed Snowdon on a beautiful and sunny day. But the sense of satisfaction would never compare. I love to think of what I accomplished.

The weather was rotten, the visibility was terrible and the ground was a nightmare. I was also against the clock to make my train back. But in light of all of that, I did some incredible walking, often at an impressive pace, along with climbing and scrambling that I would not have been confident attempting even in good conditions and without kit. So the satisfaction of doing this makes me feel wonderful. I had suggested to people prior to my departure that I would be half-killing myself. On many occasions it seemed to be the case that I had put myself in the very real risk of exposure, and whatever I did subsequently was to take me away from that risk and towards being safe. I put my body through a lot, specifically my shoulders for carrying the rucksack and my feet for carrying everything.

The main thing that I can carry over from this to my training for the sand marathon is the mental training. I have been told that people do not have to be incredibly fit to run the *Marathon des Sables*, because, however fit you are, whether or not you complete the race is all down to attitude. It never pays to be stubborn to the point that good judgements are clouded, but when it comes down to just cracking on and refusing to give up, I know that I can do it. I have no questions of myself regarding the mentality to complete the *Marathon des Sables*. What I need to sort out is the physical side. With five months left until the race, the weather is awful and I really do not take any pleasure at all in running in London, but I really must start to get my running in order.

Saturday, 2nd December 2006

The plan for today is a good one. It is time to get another distance under my belt, and see some country further out of London, if only just. I rarely get to see my parents nowadays, primarily on account of the fact that I work ridiculous hours, not just in my full-time employment but with my own projects as well. So, this weekend I am travelling up to Hertfordshire to see the family.

Ordinarily this journey would involve walking to Liverpool Street station, jumping on a train, and heading out of town for about an hour. Today though I am going to try something different. I walked to Bank and jumped on the Central Line. I got off at Woodford, bought some food from Budgens, sorted my rucksack out, and started running east. The route would be out of Woodford, past Epping Forest and through Epping, then on northwards through Harlow, Harlow Mill and then into Sawbridgeworth, my hometown.

The run was quite pleasant. There were just some gentle inclines along the way, and plenty of good scenery. I made a point of keeping to the pavements and roadsides through most of it, as I am more interested in making the distance rather than getting into the soft mud through the forest. I started feeling hot pretty soon after starting. Then I got over it and just got into my pace and my rhythm, switching off everything else in my mind and taking in the views across the countryside and the forest. I made a point of running through a section of woodland, but had to think twice, as the mud was ridiculous, and I was battling to keep my soaking wet feet away from more puddles and the like. I got myself back onto the pavement and found my pace again. Happy days. One nice long uphill stretch gave me the privilege of passing a very attractive blond running in the opposite direction. Her long hair was bouncing in time with her running, the wind flowing around her red tracksuit, her running appearing so comfortable, effortless and elegant. And then there was me, running uphill, a heavy pack on my back and breathing out of my arse, probably with spit all over my face. Somehow I think that I benefited the most from the view across the road. We gave each other a smile and a wave, and I carried on up the hill, wondering if the run was going to get any better.

As I ran into Epping, the high street came into view and my mind began to wander back to days gone by when I came here to see my orthodontist. I fought my way through the mass of people lollygagging around the market stalls, as I wondered where the pub was where I had a quiet pint of ale once whilst waiting for a bus, and then I was out of the melee and heading uphill and out of town. As I ran past the fork that goes off to the hospital, I had a thought of my grandfather after an operation there, a hip operation, if I remember correctly. I remember not being at all happy with the look of the place, but very happy to see my grandfather safe and well and in good spirits.

The rest of the run away from Epping and towards Harlow seemed rather longer than I had thought it would be. I accepted that this was because I usually drove through Harlow and into Epping, and have never done the route by foot before. After an hour and forty minutes of running, I was famished. At the top of a hill I thought that I would have to go through the bag and see what food I could find and stick down my neck. But then something terrible happened. Anybody that knows that final rise before the M11 roundabout by Harlow will know precisely what I saw. It is somewhere that I generally avoid like posh bars that do not sell ale. But at this moment, being this hungry and in need of calories, McDonald's was singing to me like the Sirens sang for Odysseus, and with no option to tie myself to a lorry to get past it, into McDonald's I went. Obviously, at any point in an 18-mile run, one would not normally consider throwing a quarter-pounder-with-cheese meal down one's neck. So I added a couple of apple pies as well, just to get the calorie count that bit closer to 1500 (although I *did* go for the orange juice instead of the nasty cola, so I was safe there).

Feeling much better, and with questionable feelings of guilt, I gave my body and digestive system the benefit of a full ten-minute rest before I continued my run up to Harlow, and then onwards toward Harlow Mill. By the time that I reached the road past the Gates garage, I had slowed to a walk, so as to give myself the benefit of a good recovery period of the final half an hour. I was not feeling as comfortable as I would have liked, and just generally felt that I would not particularly enjoy much of the last leg of the run, so I walked it instead. It gave me a chance to make some calls, and check that my dad had the kettle on so that a nice hot cup of tea would be waiting for me when I got home. I was quite happy with the run, overall, although it would have been better with lighter kit at this stage, and better still if I had eaten better and not gone crazy at that less than perfect ham and potato restaurant further back.

Saturday, 9th December 2006

The plan for today was to get up to Epping for a nice jaunt around the woods for a couple of hours. This time the intention was to derive some benefits from some nice soft ground and to make use of the little uphills where I could find them. Sadly, the plan, and a good plan I might add, was not to become a reality. The Central Line was all over the show and there was no chance of getting to Epping. Instead, I jumped onto the Docklands Light Railway (DLR), to see where that could take me. Woolwich was the answer. In all fairness, the run from Woolwich back to Borough was interesting, and I am glad that I did it, but as has been the case with my experiences of the Thames path, there are a lot of housing and industrial estates to negotiate, a few building sites, and even the pleasure of running through Deptford.

Highlights, and areas of local interest were the Barrier, the Millennium Dome, the magnificent Greenwich Maritime Museum and Naval Academy, and the Greenwich Observatory. It was also quite pleasant to see all the little boats along the side of the Thames between the Barrier and the Dome.

Canary Wharf is annoying along that route. I was looking at it, remembering my weekly running club run of up to four miles that I was doing last year. I was looking at it for a long time. The annoying thing is that it seems to take forever to get around the place. The only reason that I was not going completely mad was that I saw that I was facing different sides of the buildings there, which told me that I was still moving forwards, but it definitely seems that there is half an hour in which Canary Wharf gets no bigger or smaller. It is just sitting there, the bastard. You can imagine my glee when I eventually found myself at Surrey Quays and with Canary Wharf most definitely behind me for the first time. From there, it is just a quick run past Canada Water and Rotherhithe, and on towards Tower Bridge. This time it is the NatWest tower and Gherkin that seem to be taking forever to reach, all thanks to those wonderful, sweeping bends in the river. Then, out of the blue, I can see Tower Bridge bigger and brighter than ever, and in only a few minutes I am running underneath the southern end and over to Tooley Street and into Borough. I slowed to an easy jog at Tooley Street, and enjoyed a pleasant cool-down walk the rest of the way to the flat. All in all, it was a fair run, even if not the one that I had intended to complete, but at least it confirmed some possibilities about the Thames path east of Tower Bridge. It is rubbish that way as well.

If anybody else tries that run, see if you can do what I managed, which was to get to the other side of the Hilton to find that you cannot get any further and really should have paid more attention to the 'No Access' signs. My course of action was to pretend that I looked presentable and walk through the hotel lobby, out the front, and then I started running again from there. The receptionists barely batted an eyelid, but probably because they wanted to pretend that if they did not look at me, then maybe I did not really exist, and then none of the guests about to check-in would make any comments either.

Saturday, 16th December 2006

Today should have been a repeat of my previous weekend's exploits from Woodford to Sawbridgeworth. My family are heading off to British Columbia in Canada for Christmas, and so we are celebrating together a week early. It is because of this, that my kit is simply too heavy, and too fragile, to allow me to run that distance. Instead, and keeping to the spirit of staying unbroken, I decide to walk home from Epping instead.

Sunday, 17th December 2006

Today I chose to get in a nice 8-mile run, with kit, along the River Stort from Pishiobury Park to Pig Lane near Bishop's Stortford, and then back along roads and up Thorley Hill into Thorley. What I had intended to do was to run all the way into Bishop's Stortford and then back again. That would have been a good run. What actually happened, however, was that one of my best and almost long-lost friends, Tim, gave me a call and invited me around for drinks. Tim is good at two kinds of drinks. The first is tea. Tim did not really know this, but it was his enthusiasm for various types of tea that fostered my interest in teas in the first place. Prior to that, I had just been content with a nice cup of English Breakfast. Oh, how the world changed for the better after that - although, it is still English Breakfast that I drink the most of. The other kind of drink that Tim does is whisky. This time it was Tim who introduced me to the idea of enjoying whisky, but I who introduced him, and then his father, to whisky tastings at the Whisky Exchange in Vinopolis, near London Bridge. Again, this was an ever-fulfilling experience and a place that should be cherished for years to come.

So, I ran along to Tim's. At least this way I could benefit from getting away from river flats and up a hill. There was only one alarming moment during the otherwise very pleasant run. It was not, as had been the case during a walk along this route as a youth, the presence of cows. It was, in fact, the wetness of my *derrière*. I was running along, feeling somewhat cool, which I at first put down to the mist and dampness in the air. However, I did feel it necessary to touch my rear to confirm that it was indeed wet. It was. I thought that this must be sweat. I therefore thought that it was strange that my legs did not share my rear's enthusiasm to be so soaking wet. I then ventured my hands to the base of the rucksack, and therein lay the rub, as it were. Or, to be more specific and less pretentious, lay the water that had leaked out of my water bottle and was seeping through the bottom of my rucksack. I stopped and tightened the cap of the water bottle, making a mental note to check it regularly when in the desert; otherwise I would be in real trouble.

I ran on to Tim's, with my wet arse, and was there welcomed by his good self and his good woman. I left my trainers outside, and after concluding that I was insulting myself with my own smell, I abused his facilities and took a shower. Fortunately, I was carrying clean clothing in my rucksack, purely for the reason that it added weight. Unfortunately, my jeans were wet, but as long as Tim and Amber could stand the sight of me with wet trousers, then that was fine by me. The rest of the evening consisted of drinking tea, coffee and whisky, and a wonderful evening it was. We had one of those nostalgic evenings, which involved taking out the photo album of my trip to Nice to visit Tim when he was studying English there (as one does). Nights spent in jazz clubs, drinking beer on chairs on the beach, with the water coming up to our feet as we gazed up to a beautifully clear night's sky, talking crap and putting the world to rights, was what it was all about. Anyway, aside from its brevity, this evening's had been a good run and it finished in great company. It will be another good night to remember.

Monday, 18th December 2006

Today's run was the return journey from home to Epping. It was only about half of the distance from home to Woodford, but I had to get to work. As it was, the underground was up the creek again, and I still got in late.

Friday, January 5th 2007

My plan for training for this year is quite straightforward. I am only managing five miles a day of walking to and from Islington. It is not a distance that I want to run, and the thought of getting to the Thames and then running along the north bank and back along the south does not fill me with inspiration. I just do not like the idea of running around in a circle, especially somewhere now so devoid of inspiration. So I decided to change where I worked.

Having finished an early shift at the club in Islington, my boss drove me to the Hammersmith club on his way home, and I popped in to help out with a few operational issues that they were having. When I finished I made my way to the south side of Hammersmith Bridge, and walked along the path back to Borough. The idea was that I would be pacing it out as a route that I would then run along home from work. This was also important, because having done this route a few times already from Acton, I knew that the route leaves the river a few times and it is very easy to go too far along the front of apartment blocks, only to have to turn around and come back the same way to find a different route around. Thus, I wanted to walk it so that I could take my time to work out the best route, and then commit it to memory so that when I run the next time I will remember where to turn and not waste time and end up getting frustrated. The walk took about three hours.

Wednesday, 17th January 2007

I officially started working in Hammersmith today. Outside it was pouring with rain, and windy. On the run there from Borough, I managed to take the un-scenic route around Battersea, which added about twenty minutes to the total journey time. The last ten minutes was the only good bit, as that was the only area where the roads and pavements gave way to a more interesting path, with real dirt and everything. The rain was creating puddles the width of the path, and sometimes a few yards long as well, with a perimeter of mud. I could see people from a distance looking like they were running in circles to get around them. Thanks to my spanking new Salomon XA Pro 3D trail running shoes, I managed to run past three people in those final ten minutes of running, partly because I was genuinely running faster, and partly because I just fixed my running line and tore straight through the middle of the puddles. Granted, I did look like quite a messy boy when I eventually turned up at work, but that's the luxury of working somewhere with showers, and having a change of clothes. Unfortunately, I did forget one item of clothing, which left me walking around all day feeling much more free and well aired.

I almost screamed when the hot water from the shower hit my back, as until that point I had not realised that I had worn away the skin at the base of my back a few inches across and an inch wide. That smarted a bit. Up until recently I had also thought that nipple rub was something that only happened to other people.

I decided to walk home, and worked out a route from Hammersmith along Kensington High Street, Hyde Park, Green Park, across St. James's Park and Westminster to the South Bank, and then along the Thames back to Borough.

Friday, 19th January 2006

Having walked to and from work on Thursday, I walked in again today but with the intention of running back a nice half marathon along the South Bank. I was carrying a lighter pack this time, on account of the sores on my lower back that were still weeping and sticking my boxers to the wound. Hence, I was carrying a different rucksack that could be pulled tight and held high on my back. It took me an hour and a half to get back to Borough along the South Bank, but it was a really nice run. It was an hour and ten minutes before I began to feel a little tired in the legs, and it was all because I was starting to run out of fuel. When I reached the Anchor and came to a stop, I was not even out of breath. Granted, I could have run faster, but the goal was to run the distance, and I can work on speed over the coming weeks.

I pulled a sweatshirt on and threw a bagel in my mouth. I am not a fan of bagels, because I do not digest wheat that well, but I needed the calories and carbohydrates, and it did go down very easily. When I got back to the flat I sank the remainder of a carton of fruit smoothie and some vegetable juice, and a litre of Evian.

Saturday, 20th January

Having completed two 12-mile runs in the last week, and walked about 25 miles as well, I spent today walking to the West End, adding another 12 miles to the tally. Although my left hamstring is tight and is in need of some mobility work and stretching, there are no ill effects from the week's exercise. Today's walk did manage to break a blister on my left heel, and wore a hole in the back of my socks, smearing a small amount of blood around both the sock and my heel. I have been throwing away far too many pairs of socks lately. The plan going forward is to run a few more 12-milers each week, preferably on the way back from work rather than on the way to it, and to ensure that I am carrying sufficient kit each time. I need to patch up my back first, as it does not look as though the skin is going to harden sufficiently to stop the sores appearing. I would also like to spend a couple of days off running inland along the Thames, trying to get to a marathon distance or even further each day.

I have also been invited out to Cairo, although I gather that part of the arrangement is that I attend a presentation regarding upcoming projects for some archaeologists, most of whom would probably take great pleasure in eating me alive. Unfortunately, both for those hungry archaeologists and myself, it is unlikely that I will be able to have so much time off work when I have only just started at a new place.

At the moment I have the ability to run just shy of a half marathon without any trouble or discomfort, and I could no doubt run a lot further with the right scenery, motivation and fuel. What I need to do now is to concentrate on running distances on consecutive days, and then throwing in a longer distance when I can. I am thinking that if I can run a half marathon quite easily then I should be able to manage a full marathon if I can have access to a couple of litres of isotonic drink and some steaks along the way. It is the running on consecutive days that I need to get right first, as this will develop my ability to recover from training sessions, both in terms of cardio respiratory fitness and recovery from any physical musculoskeletal microtrauma. There are another nine weeks remaining now before a whole bunch of imbeciles from around the world all meet up in Morocco ahead of their competing in the toughest footrace on earth. I am proud to be one of them.

I also have nine weeks to refine the final stages of my training to ensure that I am physically where I want to be. I am not running to win, because for that I would have needed to spend several years training almost entirely for this event. But I do want to run as much of it as possible, and preferably all of it, although day four will be the real test of my running stamina. I can run a half marathon, which means that I can run half of what I need to on any one day in the desert. Over the next nine weeks I need to develop my fitness to ensure that I can run good distances on consecutive days. I also need to be able to complete those runs whilst carrying a rucksack of similar weight to that which I will be carrying across the desert. There is also the issue of training distances. In order to improve speed over marathon distances, it is most effective to include marathons in training, but fitness will also be improved to a significant extent by simply running good distances (Paula Radcliffe used to say that running 10 Ks were a huge help for improving time on marathons).

So I do not need to make running marathons an integral part of my training, but it would probably be good to run a marathon or two at some point over the coming few weeks, and then a few more in the build-up to the final weeks of training. The last two weeks I will taper off the distances and

221

concentrate on filling up my body with glycogen, whilst limiting glycogen losses caused by high-volume training. That means that I have eight weeks of proper training to go, followed by a week of training a bit and stuffing myself every minute that I get.

Thursday, 8th February 2007

I have managed three 12-milers this week. The result of which is that I feel good, if a little tender in the back of the knees.

During the day I find myself watching *Wild Weather* on UKTV History. The programme is covering heat, in particular in Belize and the Sahara. I have goosebumps all through the talk on the Sahara. In the 1920s the hottest temperature ever recorded was 58 degrees Celsius. The presenter states that he is practising for the toughest footrace on earth – the marathon of the sands, the *Marathon des Sables*. I have a lump in my throat. Desert heat, searing temperatures, winds. Watching the runners leave the start line fills me with a sense of excitement; seeing the expanses of desert out before them, hundreds of runners, each one out on their own amongst all that empty desert. Water loses are confirmed at a litre of water an hour and over three teaspoons of salt a day. The ground temperature is suggested to be close to boiling point, and it is fifty per cent hotter on the ground than at eye level. That makes an increase of twenty degrees of heat in less than two metres from the face to the base of the shoes.

The filming does overdo it with the dramatics to make a point. However, I know what it is like to be out there, and the thought of going through it surrounded by likeminded and determined people fills me with excitement. The thought of the runners spreading out along the marathon distances and me being on my own amongst it all, plugging away at my own pace, makes me want to be there right now. It is mentioned that an optical illusion makes the sun stay on the horizon for an extra two minutes after it has set, something that I recall but did not realise when I was making my way out of the desert near Al Faiyum last September.

Another interesting danger in the desert is a haboob. This is when the wind turns day into night, bringing forth the sands of the desert and thrusting them across the land, consuming everyone and everything in its path. Scenes of haboobs are used regularly in films featuring the desert, such as *The Mummy* and *The Scorpion King*, and 'Google Images' is worth looking at in particular. In these vast sand storms, the grains attack every part of exposed skin, and claw away at everything else trying to get within the clothes. The key is to not let it get in. Anything getting into the body will cause discomfort, and anything getting into my socks or trainers will cause blisters. Just a moment's lapse in preparing for the run could write me off for the whole race, making it an agonising ordeal with every strike of my foot onto the desert ground. If I lose the only relative comforts that I am clinging onto, then the race will turn from a challenge through adversity, into a constant living nightmare. Contrary to the opinion of most, I am not going into the desert to kill myself, but rather I am going there to truly live. I just have to rely on my having the patience and presence of mind to facilitate that, rather than be a muppet and cause myself problems by being lazy and careless.

Monday, 12th February 2007

04:00

The plan for the last week was six 12-milers. The plan was a good one. The reality was not quite so smooth. Having had to pull an all-night shift at work, I could not make my Friday run. Hence, I ran home from work on Saturday, then ran to and from work on Sunday. I made it through the front door about ten minutes ago.

The run to work was not a good one. I do not really like running there, because I know that I am running against the clock, and I enjoy the run a little less because of it. The main problem on this occasion was not the pressure of knowing that I had to make it into work in a particular time. The main problem was the pound of steak that I had eaten in the very late hours of Saturday night, together with the 1200-kcalorie breakfast, including fry-up. Whilst my body can usually handle a high calorie meal immediately before a run, I was made very much aware of the fact that I was running with a lot of undigested meat in my stomach, and although I did not feel sick or get any cramps, or even belch *that* much, I still felt a little heavy. I had to walk for a few minutes at 10 km and 15 km.

I will aim to run just three 12-milers each week for the next two weeks, and then build up again.

Monday, 26th February 2007

Well, I am recovering moderately well, still, following a nightmarish run last Wednesday. I had thought about running a full marathon, by extending my homeward run past Southwark and on to Woolwich, before turning around and running however many miles back to complete the distance. The idea was then to meet up with a friend and relax and recover for a bit before heading home.

What actually happened was that I screwed it all up. The first point that I screwed up was preparation during the day. I was particularly busy at work and I did not give myself the opportunity to eat anywhere near enough. The second point was that I was running like an idiot. I decided that to more than double my usual distance, I should calm the pace down to the slowest that I normally run (allowing for about 1:40 to reach my usual finish point, instead of the normal 1:25 to 1:30). I did this, but, as only recently mentioned, I ran like an idiot. Usually, when I felt that I needed to stride out or quicken my pace here or there, then I would. This time I resisted the urge to do so. Even more stupidly, I did not stretch out in my strides, and this altered my running pattern so that there was a significantly greater vertical component, which was not deliberate by any means, and I was barely aware of it at the time.

The third point was that I passed somewhere on the run where I had been not so long before with an absolutely beautiful woman, and that was playing very much on my mind. This was even more the case, because it was with her that I intended to recover after the run. What distracted me even further from my running was the fact that I had decided to call her, whilst *en route*, to confirm what time the run would finish. That did not help. As I had run on, I had drawn level with Canary Wharf on the other side of the river, and it had dawned on me that the next half an hour would be spent just running around it along a very dull footpath indeed.

At this point, just at Surrey Quays, the path ends and a detour is required before getting back to the river. This was coupled with the fact that I had been running too slowly; that my calves were screaming at me for being so bloody stupid as to change my running pattern; and I had no energy due to the length of the run to this point and my total lack of effective nutrition during the day. Then I considered that I was running away from a girl that would make my evening considerably better than it had been up until that point.

So, somewhat tired, fed up and annoyed with myself, I had decided to turn around early and do some speed training to get through the little glycogen that I had left. I had made it to my friend's place and spent a couple of hours there before walking back to Borough. 'Walking' was not quite the right word. 'Hobbling' was a far better one. My calves had seized up and were not happy with me.

Today, the fifth day afterwards, my walking is much improved and I have spent a lot of the day using every trick in the book (that I had available to me) to reduce the tight bands of muscle in my left lower leg. My right foot has a slight tendonitis running under the inside of the arch, meaning that I put a little more pressure through the left foot to compensate. I cannot get rid of the tendonitis before the race and still maintain or improve my cardiovascular fitness, so I will have to suffer the compromise and expect the tendonitis not to affect me so much when I am in the desert. I will probably use some ibuprofen to reduce the tendonitis a little bit further before and/or during the race, but I am reluctant because I am not any kind of fan of pharmaceuticals. I also lack the time to ice, compress, elevate and everything else that would help. So I just do what I can, when I can, to keep fit for my training.

I am doing everything that I can to help speed recovery before getting back into a few weeks of high-frequency and low-recovery training. Tendons just need a long time. The muscles in my left leg, on the other hand, were in pretty bad shape, but muscles can recover much more quickly than tendons. Self-myofascial release, massage, muscle-energy techniques, stretching, tri-planer loading, and even 'rest' have been used to relieve the issues in my left leg. Much of which took place whilst in the office at work today.

I have another three days at work this week, and I expect to manage at least four good runs. So I will run to the flat tomorrow night, again on Thursday, and then run to and from work on Friday. I am off on Saturday and I am yet to make plans for Sunday. I have three weekends left before the race, and I am working one of them. I want to use the following weekend to do a big run. I had been toying with the idea of putting in about 75 miles over a couple of days, heading west along the Thames path from Hammersmith. What would be better would be to spend a weekend somewhere with hills, as this is a component of my training that has been very much neglected. I enjoy hill training, and I need to make a concerted effort to bring this aspect of running fitness into my training. I can manage the medium distances on the flats, which has been great for making the necessary significant improvements in my cardiovascular fitness. I still need to get my legs in better shape for the inclines and the soft ground though. Realistically at this stage, the best that I will be able to manage is a good weekend somewhere, and then an evening or two out in hilly terrain after a day at work, which will not be easy. All that I need to do is find a good hill or two within an easy commute from London.

I am also into my final three weeks of training. I have not done as much as I should have to give myself a chance of running all six stages in the desert continuously. That gives me the option of either resting at the checkpoints, or else putting in a combination of running with recovery walks. What I would like to do, is to do the continuous runs between checkpoints, and just give myself the odd ten minutes to rest, re-hydrate and throw some calories down my neck. We shall see.

The point for me is that my fitness has improved tremendously, and I imagine that I could make myself into a pretty good runner if I wanted to. My changes at work have meant that I have been working a lot more than I would have liked, and my financial situation has meant that I have not been able to get out of town to train. In fact, I plan to do the shopping for the rest of my kit on Saturday, which is just after I get paid, as there is nothing but cobwebs in the account at the moment.

So, upon reflection, I could have really driven myself with the training more than I have, but I think that I can still manage some significant improvements over the next three weeks. Really, what I want to do is to walk out onto those desert sands, with my kit in the bag on my back, get myself set, and have a bloody good run.

Saturday, 3rd March 2007

Now I am trying everything. My exploits the week before last when I ran to Surrey Quays like an idiot and damaged my calf have revealed too much damage. It is not major. It is not something that will stop me running in the MdS, but it has really put the kybosh on my training. I ran last Tuesday, and made an acceptable time back to Southwark of one hour thirty-eight minutes. The run had been stilted by the fact that I could not push off from my left calf, which meant that I could not stride out, and that my pace was, therefore, restricted. But all in all, it had been a good run. Then I walked to and from work on Wednesday, and was fine. Then Thursday happened.

I had noticed that my walking was not great. I did not have the ability to run across a road. I would get pain in my calf and it would not allow for any proper movement. So that was not good. I had thought that if I started running gently, then I would warm up the tissues and be able to carry on without further issue. I had planned to run Thursday evening, then into work on Friday and back again that evening. But it was not to be. I started running from Hammersmith Bridge. I did not make it to Putney. My calf had no movement in it, meaning that my ankle had no movement, meaning that I was running like an idiot, and an idiot in pain at that.

I struggled on for barely a mile and then had to give up. I had thought that it was just a false start, but on the two occasions that I tried to run again from a walking pace, it just did not happen. This was not good. Two and a half weeks before flying out to Morocco this was *really* not good. My cardiovascular fitness is the best that it has ever been, and realistically even if I did no more training before the race, I would still not be missing out that much. The first day might be a bit tough, but that would be it. But this is not what I wanted.

I had toyed with the idea of not training in the final few days before the competition, and just concentrating on getting in the food to make up all of my glycogen stores. But since then I realised that it is much easier for me to get into a run if I have not had a lay-off beforehand. Running six days consecutively was much easier than running three days a week. So I had wanted to run six days again. Now that plan seems in ruins. I have tried everything to enhance rehab. Today I even started on ibuprofen, and I hate taking medicines. I have worked out that the problem is in the eccentric phase of soleus contraction, and even then only under heavy load.

In other words, when my heel strikes the ground during running, not walking, the stress is too great for the calf muscle to allow the ankle to flex. If it cannot flex then it cannot absorb stress, which means the stress is referred elsewhere and I cannot run properly. More importantly, the calf seizes up and I get a pain response, and it is particularly acute. Now I will run every day however far I can manage without significant pain. I will continue doing the strengthening work and rehab that I have been doing, and I will continue taking ibuprofen. I have to heal soon, because I have to crack on with my training. It is not just that I *have* to crack on with my training; I really, deeply *want* to crack on with my training.

I am looking forward to the race and I have a desire to be running. It is not just about putting in a good show in the desert, it is about putting in some good training now, and putting in some good runs for *me*. I just really do not want to let myself down. Still, it is the challenge, the adversity and the hardship that I relish. I see it as my life's history as I persist in pursuit of my goals. It will be my way and my own personal satisfaction when it is finished. No matter what happens or how well I actually do next to everybody else, I will run for me and I will run to the limits of my physical capacity. I will finish the race and run across the finish line. I will love the desert and I will love every part of the event. Good and bad does not mean anything, it is either easy or a challenge, and I must meet both with equal apprehension and due care. After all, I do live for this, and despite various trials and much turmoil over the past two years, this has been my one steady focus and goal. I have lived for this and I live to be in the desert again.

Sunday, 4th March 2007

21 Days To The MdS

Kit Day

The goal for today is to prepare all of my kit for the race. I need to check that I have everything and that it will all fit into the rucksack. Having been out during the past week to get the shopping in, I can say without fear of contradiction, that I will be representing the people that like to eat a lot during a race. I shall explain this presently, although first I shall list all of the kit prepared so far, and everything that I currently believe that I need to take with me:

Rucksack	Sleeping bag (with compression sack)
Zip-off Trousers	Shirt
Shamagh	Gaiters (from Best of Morocco – saviours!)
Shorts	T-shirt
Underwear	Pens

Paper	Camera plus spare batteries and memory card
Compass	Headlamp
2-litre Platypus water bottle	Water-Puri tablets
Mess tin	Spork
Mug	Energy-drink powder
Salt	Lighter
Lip balm	Travel toothpaste
Toothbrush	100% Deet insect-repellent
Soap	Toilet paper
Sunscreen (40 SPF)	Passport
(Blank) Medical Form	(Request for) ECG report
Penknife	Medical/Survival kit

Of the above, there were certain things that needed to be organised for travel. For example, there is no need to take an entire bar of soap, so I used a knife to cut it into a quarter. The toilet paper was arranged in 'rations' for each day, rolled up, and bagged up as two rations together and put into the food ration packs (explained later). Almost everything was put into sealed plastic bags, because I do not want to worry about sand getting in everything (and I mean *everything*). The clothing mentioned includes what I will actually be wearing during the race, so will not go into the rucksack, save for the zipped-off lower legs of the trousers. So I will be running in zipped-off trousers, a t-shirt and a shirt, along with the shamagh, sunglasses and gaiters, and my Coolmax socks. I do have a baseball-style cap with neck protection flap (French Foreign Legion-style), but from experience the shamagh feels cooler and more comfortable. It is also much more convenient if some sand gets picked up and blown across at me.

The medical and survival equipment was a tricky one to finalise. Typically, I am happy to take a field hospital with me wherever I go on my little adventures. This might include a full sterile kit, including syringes and suture kit if I am abroad, saline and everything else that I might need if I am on my own and something really inconvenient takes place. In this case, however, there will actually be field hospitals, so I do not really need to take my own. However, I have no intention of bothering matron every time I pick up a slight cut, scrape or blister. I also want to have sufficient kit if something significant happens some distance from a checkpoint. Essentially, for my own peace of mind, it is important that I can look after myself, without having to rely on the field-based medical provisions that should be available to me. Just in case the worse happens. The key to packing a good medical kit is that it should contain only the items that you know how to use, but as I have been learning about first aid and so on since I was in the Cub Scouts, that is quite a bit.

I have packed the following in my medical/survival kit:

Triangular bandage	Large dressing
Medium dressing x 2	Eye pad (as small dressing)
Zinc oxide tape (for strapping)	Scissors
Tweezers	Safety pins
Gauze pads	Assorted plasters (lots)
Gloves	Blister-repair kit
Antiseptic wipes	Survival blanket
Emergency bag	Imodium
Nifuroxazide (intestinal antiseptic)	Antihistamine
Ibuprofen (party pack)	Emergency whistle

Signalling mirror (also good for looking at wounds in awkward areas)

Aspivenin (essential kit that I am not allowed to compete without)

Many of the things that are important for a first aid kit can be improvised when necessary, but this is limited here because most kit that I will be carrying will be the bare minimum anyway, and I do not want to sacrifice one aspect of my safety or effectiveness for another. The difference between a medical kit and a first aid kit is that a first aid kit should not contain pharmaceuticals, whereas my kit has quite a few. I would take more but there are some drugs which are legal in the U.K. that are banned in other countries and it is not worth the risk. Besides, I should think that the good French doctors would have codeine and so on if things became that bad.

Generic Daily Menu

Porridge	282 kcals
Cereal	269 kcals
Powergel x 2	222 kcals
Kendal Mint Cake	350 kcals
Chicken rice	422 kcals
Mexican chilli Beanfeast	412 kcals
Custard	318 kcals
Chocolate mousse	100 kcals
Mashed potato (Bubble and squeak)	341 kcals
Chicken and vegetable soup	143 kcals
Vesta Beef Risotto	761 kcals
Total calories:	3620 kcals
Total weight:	1.112 kg

Day to day the above varies, but this gives a good general gist without me having to bore you with the plans for each particular day, which will be subject to changes in the field anyway.

The weight for the meals does not take into account the weight of the stove and fuel tablets, nor does it include the weight of water. I also need food for day seven, which is only really a breakfast, but I will make that up from whatever I have left over at the end of day six, or else I will just keep some mashed potato or custard by. At this point though, two things have become clear. Firstly, that it might be necessary to buy a chest rig for water bottles, as it will not be efficient to refill the main water carrier in the rucksack due to the amount of food that is in it. Secondly, I am a greedy bastard and will be carrying the biggest rucksack in the Sahara. Fortunately, the rucksack will become just over a kilo lighter every day, and will finish at around five kilos on the last day, plus a kilo or two for water. The first two days, therefore, will be quite tough. One good thing is that the heaviest food seems to be the breakfasts and snacks that I will be eating during the race (the Powergels and Kendal Mint Cake), which will be carried in the hip pockets of the rucksack, and will, therefore, be well balanced and soon gone.

I measured out six individually bagged portions of the porridge and oat cereal today, along with the required amount of milk powder and a pinch of salt in each. The salt should make the meals taste utterly disgusting, but it needs to go in, because I will be losing more salt in the desert than you could shake a stick at. Besides, there is always the good chance that I will hardly notice the added salt in those meals, suggesting that I will be depleted of sodium and in need of it, anyway. That, after all, is the idea behind its inclusion. It is better to have it and ingest a little too much, than to not have it and flake out into a coma in the desert. It might not be a bad idea to add some glucose come to think of it, and maybe a small amount of fructose as well. I have plenty of both in the cupboard, so I might as well throw some in there. It would be madness not to. I need to repack the rucksack, anyway, it looks ridiculous at the moment because it is so full, so the more opportunities to make it look a little more conservative the better. I have not got room for my sandals at the moment.

Monday, 5th March 2007

20 Days To The MdS

Having spent the weekend resting up, I knew that I had to test myself (and my calf) again today. I walked into work, and was reasonably okay. I could feel issues there, especially when running across roads, but on the whole I was pain-free on walking. Getting around the club where I work was also okay. I was making a point of bounding down the stairs, rather than walking, and aside from some general stiffness and resistance, everything was as good as could be expected.

I finished work after dark, and had made the decision that, for this week, I would only travel the shortest distance, that being the six miles along the royal parks, rather than along the Thames path. My kit was nice and light, as impact is still something to be limited as much as is reasonably possible. I walked along Hammersmith Road and through Kensington. Even if I had wanted to run I could not, just on the general principle that running along the street is infuriatingly mindless and dull. I reached Kensington Gardens and stopped to do some mobility work. As a man that views 'walking to the start point' as a sufficient mobility exercise, I very rarely do anything more. As I get into my pace and rhythm, everything else should fall into place. There is very little benefit from doing obscure stretches and so on that have no real crossover benefit to the movement patterns of running, anyway.

So my mobility work did have a lot to do with the movement patterns of running. I planted my left foot on the floor, and did some mobility work through the ankle, knee, hip, spine and shoulder. This was working through all three planes of movement, lots of twisting, leaning and transferring of bodyweight. It was only for a few seconds, and I was just putting more emphasis on areas where I could feel tightness, resistance and tension. I wiggled my ankle around a little bit and set off at a gentle jogging pace. The pain came from the point of the first left heel strike, along with some tightness, but all much reduced compared to my efforts of last week. It still was not good though. At this point, however, I was by no means finished with the mobility work. I changed from my gentle jog to a sideways skipping position, leading with my right leg.

After a few seconds, I faced the opposite side, and then ran backwards for a little while. I was a little surprised at how tiring the sideways and backwards running was, and so then I turned around to continue running forwards. I raised my left knee as I pushed down through my right leg and hip, and then brought my left heel hard down on the pavement. 'Yes!' The calf had been released, there was no pain and for the first time in a long time my left knee travelled forwards as the calf permitted an unlimited dorsiflexion of the ankle. As my hip extended, the knee began to straighten and I pushed hard through the ball of my left foot, my body almost bounding forwards, as I completed a full and powerful stride. I kept running for a few more metres, elated at the range of motion and reduction in pain, and then repeated the movements – side, opposite side, and backwards. As I turned to run forwards, I stooped down into a flexed-hip running position, then extended upwards to run tall, before once again returning to a normal running pattern.

I passed Prince Albert and had to break out of the run to cross the road. I reached the corner of Hyde Park and used the curb to mobilise my left calf. I walked over towards the path, and went back into a jog, then back into the mobility, this time sideways, backwards and then on the opposite side, twice through then back to running forwards. How about some transverse? I was still running forwards and then put in the necessary movements to allow me to complete a number of complete turns as I went. It left me slightly dizzy, and so I carried on forwards, then back through the mobility phases, adding in complete turns both clockwise and anti-clockwise, before getting back to running forwards again.

As I took the left across the sand to get back onto the path to Hyde Park Corner, I went through all those phases again, and then alternated striding out with sprints. I walked across the road, under the Wellington Arch, and then began running again along Green Park. This time I reduced the mobility work to just the sideways movements and then I alternated running with my feet facing forward to diagonals to each side. The injury was specifically to the musculotendinous units across the inferior medial border of soleus (or, in English, the bottom of one of my calf muscles, at the back of the lower leg, at the bottom of that muscle and on the half closest to the inside of the leg, in the region where the muscle joins onto the tendon). This meant that the specific movement that released the muscle and ankle, allowing full strides and reduced pain, was medial rotation from the hip including inversion of the ankle (twisting my left leg inwards from the hip, allowing the ankle to face a little further across still, and running slightly more than usual on the outside of my left foot). So what this turned into was something like the walking pattern of 'Verbal' Kint from *The Usual Suspects*, with just the left leg doing a compensation movement, and everything else fitting in around it.

It is quite possible, as with the final transformation of Kint's walking pattern, that compared to the utter bizarreness of my mobility work at the start of the run and along Hyde Park, by the end nobody really would have noticed anything out of place about my running. I continued on towards the Mall, introducing a frontal element, whereby I also varied foot-width from very wide to very narrow, and including varied twisting movements of the hip and ankle in this to increase the combinations. I fell into a walk at the Mall and walked across to the Jubilee Bridge and past Waterloo station. I got back into a brief run for the final part of the journey, although all of this combined contributed to a run of only a couple of miles. The distance was not good, but at least I now knew how to release the ankle and manage a good run. It was a very good result considering where I was last week.

Tuesday, 6th March 2007

19 Days To The MdS

Today's run was similar to that of yesterday. This time I walked a little more earlier on in the run, and then made my main run the section from Embankment along the north side of the river to Blackfriars. Then it was across Blackfriars, down to the South Bank, and along to the Anchor, and then continuing the run back to Borough station itself. Following on from last night's curry, I decided that the best thing to do today would be to try out some of the meals that I would be taking with me to the desert. This was a well thought-out plan. It is important that I have an idea of how to prepare the food, as well as how my body gets on with it.

One of the meals that I will be taking into the desert is a meat replacement, by Beanfeast. Now, the key to beans is that they are usually not prepared properly, which means that they induce flatulence. My guts are not on their best behaviour when running *anyway*, but today I really did feel that I should have been apologising profusely to everybody walking around that area of the Thames this evening. Not that I want to harp on about this point, but I will be eating this crap for a week, with no fresh food whatsoever, so I am going to be in a terrible state. And there is no point trying to keep any gas in.

As I used to teach my personal training students: 'If three pounds of bacteria in your lower intestine cannot deal with it, then it is best to get it out.' Well, what I actually taught was 'Better an empty house than a dirty lodger', but at least it was with sound bacteriological reasoning as well. Anyway, what with the various body odours spreading out amidst the general din of the desert tents, I can imagine our flatulence not lending anything positive to the unobtainable serenity that I might otherwise prefer.

Oh, how romantic an idea! Laying under a canvas in the quiet of the desert. Recovering from the day's heat and feeling the cool, dry air, flowing across my exposed face as I look up to the clear starry sky. The only sounds being the lightest of breezes through the tent, perhaps carrying some sand grains off the dunes, interspersed with the occasional scurrying of desert life as it goes happily about its business. No, I shall be having none of that. I shall be squashed in the middle of a tent with a bunch of other Britishers, the air stale with the smell of sweat and flatulence, and my exposed face being walked over by every scorpion, snake, spider and that bastard that had to go to the loo in the middle of the night and has bugger all night vision. The only sounds, therefore, will be the sounds of the aforementioned Britishers snoring for the homeland, farting, screaming because something landed on their face so they think they are about to die, and that bastard falling all over everybody to get out. Romantic, my arse.

Wednesday, 7th March 2007

18 Days To The MdS

The E.C.G. and Medical

Tuesday's run was similar to Monday's. That was the issue. There was no real improvement, just the fact that the injury had not become any worse. I made the decision to keep the walking going for the rest of the week, to promote recovery, and to allow myself to heal. I am not going to be able to develop my cardiovascular fitness in the last couple of weeks, as had been my intention. Instead, my plan is to recover as much as possible, and limit any reductions in cardiovascular fitness. Either way, the first day of desert running will be tough, on account of the fact that it will be the longest distance that I would have run in a good few weeks of training. By day three in the desert, I should have recovered my cardiovascular fitness to the best level that I could hope it to be. It will mean that I am less comfortable with my running when I am out there, but I would rather deal with that than risk going out there with an injury that is nowhere near adequately recovered for the event. It is not as if postponing until my next possible entry in 2009 is a realistic possibility. I have got all sorts of other silly things that I expect to be training for by then.

So, when I am not running, I am walking and doing home-based mobility and rehabilitation work. It is my field, and as my argument for doing the race in the first place was that 'if I couldn't train myself to do this event, then nobody should be able to', so likewise I am now telling myself: 'if anybody can rehab an injury like this in time for the race, then I can'.

There are two sides to that. One side is the straightforward 'this is my area of expertise' argument. I am studying this, I have been working on this for many years, and I am writing another book on the subject at the moment. Injuries happen to everyone at some point. Training is all about pushing your body beyond what it is used to in order to elicit a training effect, meaning that the body develops to prevent the same thing happening again in the future. The issue is that there is a line between the amount of damage required to elicit a training effect, and the more noticeable level of damage that can be regarded as an injury. There are various possible causes of injury. Running, in itself, is not the cause of any running-related injury. People that suffer from shin splints, knee pain, back pain, and anything else that occurs from running, are not *causing* these problems by running.

The cause of the injury is either an imbalance or a direct injury. A direct injury might be due to the sort of proprioceptive mishap that results when an ankle is twisted or somebody falls over. Running was not the cause of the twisted ankle or fall. The cause was a combination of proprioceptors in the foot and lower leg musculature that were unable to rectify the problem, and the nature of the ground to have caused the body to move into whatever unacceptable position it happened to end up in. Either way, the cause was not running. Running just happened to be what was going on at the time, and if you are out running then you are more likely to become aware of insufficiencies in the ground and in your proprioceptors, than if you happen to be sitting at home, eating pizza and watching *The Usual Suspects*.

Proprioception, as I have indicated before, refers to your body's ability to know where it is in space and time. It is effectively another sense, and one that means that you can close your eyes, wiggle your fingers and toes around, and be aware that you are wiggling your fingers and toes around. If your foot goes over a pothole when you are running, then it is the proprioceptors that send messages that this has just happened, and then the muscles have to react to correct foot position and prevent you from falling over or your ankle twisting excessively and to the point of injury.

Imbalances can be postural in nature, meaning that the way you hold yourself when sitting and standing can have an effect on the muscles of the body, which in turn can affect the way in which you walk and run. These imbalances may result in some muscles and joints receiving more stress than they would if moving 'perfectly'. In general though, most people have all sorts of little issues across the body, which lead to various compensations in the way in which they move. These compensations only become evident through injuries and/or pain if actually doing enough to cause the repetitive stress required to allow the issues to become more serious.

Similar compensations can result from another type of injury, such as an impact injury in sport, or through something like a twisted ankle. When a muscle or joint has become damaged in some way, then the body will work as a unit to displace stress to other areas, which can then become a permanent compensation pattern for a particular movement. These compensation patterns are fine until you put sufficient stress through the body to start noticing ill effects. There is also the possibility that any change from a normal joint movement may lead to greater stress through regions of that joint, in turn leading to more permanent stress and damage, such as in osteoarthritis.

A postural imbalance could also result from running with a rucksack that has not been filled evenly, or that is not carried evenly across both shoulders and hips. In my case, the damage to my left calf is probably the result of a compensation from the tendonitis that has developed under my right foot, which in turn developed as a compensation from all the uneven walking that I was doing in Snowdonia before Christmas. As tendons generally have poor circulation, injuries can take months to heal. I have been satisfied that this tendonitis is not sufficient to bother me when running, and it will not be getting better or worse during my training for the marathon. Hence, I will have to live with it and do what I can, but accept that it will not be perfectly healed until after I return from the race.

The other reason that I should still manage the recovery and rehab okay is just down to attitude. I have enough presence of mind and self-awareness to be able to push myself enough to promote recovery, and the sense to stop before I induce further injury. The goal is to complete the *Marathon des Sables*, and that will mean pushing myself, regardless of my physical state, beyond anything that my body has ever been used to before. But then, when I look back at how people regard me when I train, a word like 'nutter' comes to mind, as one of the words which regularly come up. When the discomfort of training starts to make itself known, I just zone-out and numb myself to whatever is going on whilst I concentrate on what I am doing and the end point. When the discomfort gets really high, then I just grin and bear it, because then I know that no matter how fit and strong somebody else is, I will almost certainly beat them when it comes to intensity and fighting through the pain barriers. It is just something that I can do and that I find very fulfilling. This is not the ridiculous 'No pain, no gain' maxim, nor the superb and equally wrong latest version of it: 'Pain is just weakness leaving the body' – I like it, but it is nonsense.

The pain and discomfort that I am referring to is the fitness-based, lactic acid build-up that burns and creates that excruciating feeling deep within the muscle bellies and stops most people when they are training. The key is that this is only an acid burn that goes away as soon as you start to rest, and that actual muscle failure is still a long way off. I used to train with a British natural bodybuilding competitor, who used to travel quite a way to train legs with me, because nobody in his bodybuilding gym could face his workouts. I loved them. I still think that Arnie has a lot to answer for with his whole 'training is like having an orgasm' nonsense though. Let us face it, training is satisfying, it is enjoyable, and quite frankly it can feel quite exciting and fulfilling, but it just does not quite go that far. Fortunately Arnie did eventually redeem himself by stating that 'that was before he met his wife'.

One of my colleagues recently came out with the 'machine' comment after establishing that I can run for hours every week without listening to music. I actually prefer not to because I like to be aware of what is going on around me, and when I am running at pace then I cannot even daydream. It is just all about the run. I do not think that the enjoyment really compares to the high intensity resistance training that I used to do, but it is nevertheless very satisfying, and I am enjoying it a lot more than I thought I would. Hence, I am particularly displeased that I cannot run good distances at the moment, and I even become jealous when I see other runners about. I could never have imagined that I would enjoy running as much as I do – I have been converted!

The plan for today was to get up to Cambridge, which is where my G.P.'s surgery happens to be, in order to have an E.C.G. taken and to have a 'thorough' medical. I moved down into London just over a year ago, and away from the place in Cambridge that had been my home. London was always to be a temporary arrangement, and somewhere that I could never call home, but it has done me well whilst I have been working and getting myself back onto my feet after a tough couple of years. Despite those tough couple of years, I only needed to see a G.P. during that time as the first step towards my hernia operation of January 2006. I rarely get ill, and it is even more rare for me to go to a G.P. if I am. This has been handy just of late, because every bugger I know seems to be outrageously ill. The beautiful woman that I have been seeing lately has been out of sorts for the last two weeks, so I have been quite impressed that I have managed not to catch anything.

So the people that I see at work and at play are ill, which is not a good environment at all, but so far so good. If I catch anything now I will be absolutely gutted, because, quite frankly, the buggered calf is quite enough of an embuggerance for one race. Not so handy, of course, is the fact that I now have to travel to Cambridge to get the medical certificate signed off, together with a nice printout of my E.C.G. report.

The E.C.G. and medical certificate are essentials for the race, and it is likely that anybody turning up in Morocco without these will be having a very dull week indeed. Thanks to the late-running train, I had to half run to the medical centre. The nurse was waiting for me, and maintained that my tardiness was the sole cause of her sitting around eating sweets. I lay down for the few minutes that it took to get the E.C.G. report, which was made slightly longer by the fact that another nurse had played silly buggers with the machine and caused it to not work properly. The nurse and I got on famously, having completed some respectable readings from the E.C.G., then measuring a good, and slightly low blood pressure, and then I went off to see the doctor. The 'thorough' medical examination amounting to not much more than checking my pulse, listening to my heart, and then checking lungs (by palpation and listening only, not any strength, capacity or power measurements). Two coughs later and I was all done.

The doctor spent a long time gazing over the E.C.G. report, during which time I began to wonder whether or not I would be signed off, and whether or not I would be heading out to Egypt instead to do it all on my Jack Jones, where nobody could tell me not to do it. Having been asked if I had completed marathon races before, I lied that I had, and happily took the signed off medical certificate and E.C.G. report off to the reception. The nurse was disappointed that she had to put her cake down to come and stamp the certificate, and I seemed to have spent the day either causing her to eat junk, or getting in the way of it. I headed back to London, back to the flat, and then off to work for the night. I would get some good walking done on Thursday, and then go for it with the recovery and rehab work over the weekend.

Monday, 12th March 2007

13 Days To The MdS

Since I tentatively managed a couple of miles last week, it is time for me to see how I have been recovering. Three days' worth of ibuprofen, at 1200 mg a day, combined with rehab work, massage, rest and active recovery, should have made some vast improvements. The woman in my life is currently living at Canada Water, which is about half an hour or so from where I am staying in Borough. That means it should be just over two hours of walking from my work. Knowing that I will be breaking up the walk with periods of running, I decided that I could safely estimate being at her place two hours after I was due to finish.

Whilst at work I made a point of strapping my foot and ankle, so as to relieve some pressure on the muscles that were still nagging me. This should also allow the evening's run to be a little more pain- and stress-free as well. Having finished work twenty minutes late, I headed off on the first walking phase up to Kensington Gardens. The legs were feeling okay, and I soon noticed that the strapping had shifted the stress on the calves from the inside to the outside, which was fine, as this area of muscle seems unscathed.

Some brief tri-planer mobility work, utilising a tree near where I entered the park, completed the warm-up. I started running up toward Prince Albert, and added in a few more movements to relieve pressure on the injured area of calf muscle, and to ensure that I was indeed properly warmed up. Within a couple of minutes, I began to feel that the stress was moving away from the base of the calf and up to the knee. This was reassuring, in the sense that the damaged muscle was no longer reporting any significant signs of injury. The referral of stress to the knee must just be some sign of 'weakness leaving the body…' Realistically, this was just a reflection of the fact that I have altered my running pattern to relieve tension on the injured muscle, and consequently a compensation pattern has occurred which places more stress on the connective tissue around the knee. It is acceptable as a one-off, and the strapping will be coming off after the run, so that I can resume my normal movement patterns and continue a natural course of rehab.

Having waited for the traffic to pass before continuing on my way, it soon became apparent that if I stopped running then I would indeed be late to reach my better half. I was feeling pretty comfortable with the pace, which was limited still by my restricted ankle movement, although now more as a result of the strapping than the original injury. I also realised that the route would be longer than originally planned, as it is more rewarding for me to run along the Thames path than it is to run around the backstreets of London south of the river. I ran along the Mall and around the bottom of Trafalgar Square, before taking the option right, just before Waterstone's and leading down to the embankment. I took the left on the main road under the bridge, crossed the road and continued this leg along the north bank. I crossed at Blackfriars, continuing east past the Founders' Arms, then Tate Modern, the Millennium Bridge, St. Paul's, and Shakespeare's Globe.

As I went underneath Southwark Bridge, I avoided the temptation to sprint to The Anchor, and once there continued on around the Golden Hinde, past the Mudlark, and then back to the river. This leg continues on towards and then underneath the end of Tower Bridge, before I can make my way back to the river. There is plenty of running around the place, free from the possibility of running continuously next to the Thames, but it is not by any means the worst stretch of the path. Within what seemed like only a few minutes, I found myself on the approach to Spice Island, before taking the option right, away from the Thames and to just where I needed to be.

The run amounted to approximately eight miles, and the walk back to Borough a little later in the evening made it quite clear that my state was far better than it had been a couple of weeks beforehand. Aside from the tight calf and tender knee, the walk was fine, and the tightness and tenderness of very little significance.

Thursday, 15th March 2007

10 Days To The MdS

Having spent the rest of the week after Monday walking to and from work, tonight the plan was to have another bash at the distance along the South Bank from Hammersmith to Borough. Despite various reservations about running, and in particular still being unsure as to whether or not I actually enjoy it, I can honestly say that I have been yearning to get myself back onto this particular run. I have missed it, which is certainly something unexpected.

The run itself was not really anything out of the ordinary. I was very pleased to be doing the old route again, even though I had deliberately kept the kit nice and light. The calf is still not perfect, but aside from a very slight restriction in movement, together with a barely noticeable level of discomfort around the knee, the pace simply reflected the fact that I was taking it easy. I did have to remind myself that I had been missing this, because I did not really feel aware of any particularly redeeming features on this route, but it was certainly nice to be covering familiar territory again. Knowing the route so well meant that I had a good gauge of how well I had recovered from the injury. There were times tonight when I considered whereabouts along the route I was, and all the areas along the way that I was yet to come to; and then I had to remind myself that actually this was not just a short route.

A sprint finish to The Anchor meant that the run was finished in one hour and thirty-two minutes, which is well within my average time frame for that run, although seven minutes from my personal best. Under the circumstances, I am quite happy with my progression to this point. I can now continue walking to and from work over the weekend, and will aim to perform a couple of 5 km runs on Monday and Tuesday. That should help me to maximise recovery ability, whilst keeping me trained and focussed for the MdS. I fly out to Morocco a week today to arrive just before the start of the race. Although I have not managed to develop my fitness further than the capacity to be able to run six half marathons a week, with kit, I now believe that I have not deteriorated, and the minor injury contributed nothing more than an interesting setback.

Were it not for the injury, then I would have added in two or three runs of a greater distance, but it is not a huge loss not to have managed to incorporate them. I am still concerned that the volume of work over the marathon might allow signs of the injury to resurface, but with the improvements that I have made and the knowledge that the terrain will produce far less stress, I am quietly confident that everything should be fine. My fitness levels are still a concern, as I am sure that I would have benefited from running greater distances; from getting myself running on the right sort of terrain; and from a visit to the desert in the last couple of months. But I believe that I have faired adequately with what I had available to me. Only time will tell.

Tuesday, 20th March 2007

5 Days To The MdS

I kept yesterday and today as a nice and easy start to the week. I would have liked to have managed a couple of short distances, but the amount of time that I needed to spend at work, combined with the early starts, meant that I just could not get into the right frame of mind. As a consequence, I just walked to and from work.

Wednesday, 21st March 2007

4 Days To The MdS

04:00

Another 4 am start! I really, really do not agree with early starts unless it is to catch a plane to go off on holiday. Unfortunately, the nature of my job and the industry in which I work requires me to do this. At the back of my mind I am always telling myself that it is not the best thing for my health, and that I have to focus on getting out of such long days and early starts by the end of the year. Well, as it currently stands, I am expecting to head out to Egypt on a biomedical/archaeological research project and dig at the end of the year. The real question is what will I be doing when I come back?

As I trudge my way to work, I am also very much aware of how poor the weather is at the moment. Cold and rain, even punctuated with blasts of snow, have provided my morning environment. And just to think, tomorrow night I will be by the desert in Morocco! Happy days!

15:00

Upon preparing to leave work, it was voiced that I was not in the best of health. I have worked 55 hours in the last five days, which is not unusual for me, but the long hours combined with a reasonable amount of work-related stress, the early starts and the cold, wet weather, have done well to suppress my immune system. I know that only contributes to contracting a cold *if* I happen to be exposed to cold germs as well. I am not sure about the latter, but I have spent the day blowing my nose a lot more than I would do normally. I am telling myself that it is just the effect of all of those contributing factors, rather than an actual cold, but at the back of my mind I know that there is a chance that I have contracted something. Bugger. I just hope that it passes by the time that I am home.

20:00

The lovely Bianca came around this evening so that we could see each other before I head off to Morocco tomorrow morning. The evening did not progress much further before I had to state the obvious. My "I don't feel too good" was responded to with a "You don't look too good."

I have definitely caught something, and I definitely need to get rid of it, quickly. Having a cold means an increased resting and exercising heart rate, a higher body temperature, and a reduced level of overall physical fitness. In short, I am ruined if I start running like this. My body will be trying to defeat a cold whilst I am forcing it to complete the toughest physical challenge that I have ever presented to it, in the harshest environment. This is not looking to be a good day out.

Denying a cold can work well, because it keeps the immune system ticking over and that obviously helps to keep the cold at bay. Hence, if I sneeze then I do not want someone to instinctively ask if I have a cold, because I do not want to even entertain the idea. However, once it is beyond a doubt that I have contracted a cold, the next step is to get rid of it as soon as possible. That means accepting that I have a cold, and then being proactive in limiting its effects. Realistically, I am a very fit and healthy person. I can get over the main effects of the cold within 24 hours. I have to, because whatever state I begin the race in, will remain present until the end of it. I will not be able to heal when my body is trying to recover from exercise of this nature. Nearly everybody that I know and work with has had at least one very bad cold this year, in some cases lasting for weeks. I managed to hold off getting that one. The fact that I have picked up something relatively minor is just a nuisance, arriving at the worst possible time, but at least it is of comparatively minor severity.

So, the mission for the evening is to eat as much as possible. I started on the way back to the flat, and will continue throughout the evening and tomorrow. A good amount of chilli with plenty of spices and garlic should help. Bianca also made me some tea with ginger in it. It is of comparatively little relevance whether or not there is any actual nutritional benefit in what I am eating, the point is that I believe that it is doing me some good and that alone will improve immune function. If there really are benefits in the spices, garlic and ginger, as well as the proteins, fats, carbohydrates and overall calories, then I will be all the better off for it. As well as thinking of the nutritional factors, I am also convincing myself that I am going to be free from all work- and lifestyle-related stresses until after my return. I am also going to get a good night's sleep. As long as I give myself the best possible mental and physical environment in which to improve, then I cannot ask any more of myself.

Thursday, 22nd March 2007

3 Days To The MdS

08:00

Out of bed. Priority number one: shave hair to a crew cut. Reason: I do not want to be faffing around with my hair in the desert. Hygiene will be enough of a challenge as it is. Secondly, I need a haircut and the desert will be hot enough to warrant me keeping my hair as short as possible, without allowing the sun to burn through my scalp.

Final kit check. This includes receipts for the stove and hexi fuel that I ordered from *darbaroud.com*. My tickets were definitely in an envelope somewhere…

A final check of my emails was a useful boost. I had sent a message out to all of my contacts to let them know what I was up to, and that the time had finally come around for me to head out to Morocco to do this thing. Amongst messages of support, two in particular had reigned supreme:

Bollocks to ya mate!!!! I could do that race eating nowt but Pies, Chips and having the odd Fag…here and there.

Calf strain….Shit!!! I'll tell you what you've been doing…(and) she was too much for you!!!!

Fuck off and don't come back unless you finish in the top 10. Anything less than that and yer a Girl!!!

Poof! ;o)

Stu

And my absolute favourite:

Best of British!

There will be a large Scotch of your choice on your safe return.

Colin, Matt & Chris
The Whisky Exchange
Vinopolis

The Whisky Exchange would indeed be receiving a visit from me upon my return. I had been neglecting my friends and the tastings (educational purposes only) there since my training really got going in earnest this year.

I left the flat and headed off to London Bridge station on foot. I walked up onto the platform to see another young man, short very dark hair, with a runner's rucksack and a suitcase. He looked about the right fit. We boarded the train and set ourselves up on opposite sides of the aisle. I could not resist it: 'Excuse me, mate, are you flying out to Morocco, by any chance?'

Danny was an Englishman from Bermuda, heading out to do the MdS through the American organisers. We spent the rest of the journey to Gatwick discussing our training and kit choices.

Upon arrival at Gatwick I headed off to buy a padlock for the suitcase, and then met Steve from Best of Morocco, and Rob, one of our contacts for the event. I checked in and then went off to the shops to buy some antiseptic solution and a housewife's kit. Making my way through to security into the departure lounge, I suddenly realised that the fluid limit on aircraft was still in effect. I waited until I was about ten yards from the **X**-ray machines before cracking open the full two-litre bottle of Evian and starting to neck it. I managed to empty the bottle by the time that I made it to the security guy. Well, I was not just going to bin it, was I? Fortunately, the antiseptic solution was within limits, which was handy as it was an essential part of my medical kit.

In the departure lounge I made my way over to Smith's, to see that a human equivalent of locusts had decimated the huge fridge of water bottles. That had to be the other MdS competitors. The camaraderie had already begun to build up around the departures area. It was quite easy to spot the other competitors: Looking as fit as a butcher's dog? Raidlight rucksack? Camelback? Salomon or New Balance shoes? I had already introduced myself to half the people in there. Anyway, I found a bottle of mineral water in an abandoned basket in a fridge, and then found some more water bottles in boxes near the tills. Free Evian with *The Independent*? Go on then, I might as well fill my boots.

I picked up a couple of magazines and some other bits, and then met up with Danny outside as we both raced to the boarding gate, as we were already running very late (practice, I suppose). We both realised that our promises to call the better halves whilst at the airport had also caused the significant delay leading to our current tardiness. But, as Danny put is so well: 'It takes them longer to take the luggage off the plane than it does to just let you get on late, so we don't need to worry about it.'

Fair one, and when we arrived we were still in time to begin boarding with everybody else, but I am glad that I had not promised to phone my mum as well.

12:30

I was standing up putting my things in the overhead locker and making eye contact with and greeting people as they boarded the plane. Then I saw someone looking back for just a little bit too long. Young, Indian origin at some point, jet-black hair and quite pretty. Purvi!!! She used to be a personal training client of mine a couple of years ago, along with a guy called Amar, and she had registered to compete in the event after I had told her about it. It had slipped my mind completely until she came up to me for a quick catch-up. She was looking well, and it was good to know that there would be someone out there that I knew. And just to think, all that time that I had not seen her she had been training for this as well. It was great to see her. I just hoped that she was not going to beat me. It would just be embarrassing to be beaten across the line by someone that I used to advise on fitness, someone that I was supposed to lead by example. Still, it was good to know that she had made it this far, as she was one of the few to be representing the British contingent.

I sat myself next to Rob on the plane. Middle-aged, beaming smile, oozing the sort of self-confidence one comes to expect from people of a certain position within the military, and instantly likeable. He had spent some time in Arctic and desert environments, so I was interested in gleaning as much of an insight as I possibly could from him. There is definitely an intention to head for the poles on future adventures. Rob had suffered a serious accident in the past, one that might have left him without normal function in his legs, so the MdS was very much a personal mission for him. But then, it was a personal mission for all of us, in one way or another. We all have our reasons and motivations for going in for this madness. Some just have deeper and more profound reasons than others. Rob was definitely someone that I wanted to see across the finish line, hopefully, still beaming.

The cramped seating on the plane was not as much of an immediate concern as the thought of the same conditions for the return journey. I was planning on being in traction in the centre aisle, anyway. It was one of those flights where most people preferred to be on their feet than in their seats. A trip to the toilet included a half-hour chat with whomever was about regarding their training and kit. It was a familiar theme by this point. And that was it, wasn't it? It was almost surreal to consider that every single person on this flight was heading out to Morocco for the same purpose, to compete in the toughest footrace on earth. Everybody looked pretty fit, and there were more crew cuts than you could shake a stick at. Lots of people looked Forces.

There was a lot of variability in ages though, and all in all I would have to say that it was impossible to imagine how well everybody would fair on the desert sands. All that I could tell was that everybody did look as fit as a butcher's dog, regardless of age, and that was a little daunting. But then, maybe some of them were thinking the same thing about others, including me, and then again, maybe some of them did not consider or care about that sort of thing at all.

As the flight took us over the Atlas Mountains, we looked out over the beautiful, rugged landscape. A metallic shine reflected back off the surface of the rocks. The ground eventually levelled out onto less dramatic hills and dunes. There was, nevertheless, only one word to accurately encompass and describe everything that we could see: Arid.

The queue for immigration was filled with further banter on training and kit. The Raidlight brigade had the greatest proportion of visible kit. I was standing there in my desert Magnums, with my green army rucksack over my shoulder, safe in the knowledge that people might have been jumping to all sorts of conclusions, unaware of the Salomons in the rucksack and the fully loaded Karrimor in the suitcase. A short transfer took as to the Berbere Palace Hotel in Ouarzazate. I met Mark there in the queue to get a hotel room. We all had to pair up, so Mark introduced himself as someone else without a partner at that time. At least we would not be forgetting each other's names.

Instantly likeable, Mark had flown out to Ouarzazate via his home in Italy, where he lives with his wife. Mark is also in the Forces, as nearly everybody else seems to be. Shorter stature than myself, he seemed pretty focussed on getting his kit in order in the hotel room and ensuring that everything was set for the desert. That was fine by me, as my focus and priority were the same. One thing that did become apparent very early on, however, was that Mark seemed to be the world's greatest Boy Scout. Granted, in his forties he could perhaps be better described as a very experienced Boy Scout, but this guy seemed to know everything and have everything. He is the original kit man. He could probably walk out into any wilderness on earth and turn it into his own private utopia, all with a minimum of faffing around, and all without looking further than the contents of his own rucksack. What a legend! As a rule, I always gravitate towards people who are wiser and more knowledgeable than myself, with the hope of learning something useful, and I did not have to go any further than Mark. I was very happy with this arrangement.

Having done a preliminary post-arrival kit check, I exchanged some money into Moroccan Dirhams and headed out for a stroll around town. The left turn out of the hotel took me along a sparsely populated road, with just a few shops and restaurants, and the obligatory other MdS procrastinators. I turned back and continued past the hotel in the other direction, then followed the general flow of locals, who were on their way to the town centre. I met a few other British competitors, procrastinating outside a little café, eating crêpes and drinking tea. They were ready to make a move back to the hotel, so I sat myself down and ordered a couple of crepes and a glass of tea.

I was using a mishmash of my limited Arabic and mostly forgotten French to communicate with the locals. I can be polite in Arabic, but French is the locals' second language, although most people have some grasp of English. The tea was brown, and looked like mud, which reminded me of Baldrick's special coffee in *Blackadder Goes Forth* (which utilised mud, dandruff and a cat). The tea itself was a combination of black tea with mint in it, and tasted gorgeous. It is always nice to have a good cup of tea and some good local food when in a foreign country. It just helps to make me feel that I am comfortable and at home.

I had to rush the food and then get back to the hotel to meet up with Mark, check some more particulars of the kit, collect a stove and my pre-ordered hexi fuel tablets from Rob in the reception, and then head off for the buffet dinner at 20:00. I loaded up the plate with chicken, rice, couscous, aubergines, peppers, and all the other meats and vegetables that I could mount up onto the plate. I would not be getting proper fresh food for much longer, so I wanted to make sure that I capitalised on the nutrients and flavours now whilst I had the chance. The general rule of thumb is to avoid anything that has been washed, because the flora in the water will antagonise the flora in the digestive system, and probably result in at least minor digestive discomfort (such as explosive diarrhoea). When I am in Egypt I always drink tap water and eat washed foods anyway, but I taper it up gradually to build in a tolerance. If I am away for a long time, then abstention from fresh food would lead to ill health anyway, so I tend to just crack on and get accustomed to it.

I sat down next to John for dinner, a young lad with a West Country accent. As was the theme, he had short hair, but also a short, trimmed beard, and a big smile. He was instantly likeable, and although not much was said, we were probably going to have a lot in common. For a start, he did not come across as Forces, which put both of us in the minority. I announced that I was going to head off to discover the town centre after dinner, and John announced that he would like to join me. The plan was to get a good idea of what Ouarzazate was like, and to see if I could find myself some Arabic desserts, something that I am quite partial to.

22:30

John and I returned to the hotel, and he lent me some glue so that I could fix the Velcro for my gaiters onto the sides of my Salomons. I finished and lay back in my bed, reflecting on the day so far and how I felt about the week ahead. With the majority of competitors being Forces (or ex-Forces), it probably says a lot about their mentality and drive, and generally other good things as well, except that they would probably all beat me. At a rough estimate, only about five per cent of the competitors were women, including the lovely Purvi, whose appearance on the plane had been a very welcome surprise indeed. Everybody seemed very well spoken, intelligent, and typical middle class or equivalent, no doubt having to be, in order to afford the cost of the competition, the kit to go with it, and the training required to make it all happen. And yet, everybody was their very own and special kind of nutter. Somewhere deep inside all of us, there must surely be at least one or two screws loose.

Friday, 23rd March 2007

2 Days To The MdS

06:30 Woke Up

07:00 Managed to persuade myself to get out of bed

07:30 Buffet breakfast: Lots of eggs and bacon

09:00 Onto one of three buses for a six-hour journey out into the desert

Having spent a lot of time in Egypt, visiting the deserts on both sides of Cairo as well as the Sinai Peninsula, I have seen a lot of this general type of environment before. But Morocco is still different. There are high hills and mountains, a lot of oases, and a river, surrounded on both sides by palm trees and other vegetation. The ground changes from small rocks and stones to large rocks and boulders, and then to soft sand. It is the variability in the nature of the desert here, within any given expanse of land, which makes it different. Although I am used to a changing landscape, the surface cover changes a lot more than I am used to, and the punctuated vegetation across the desert also marks a stark contrast. My desert training has given me a good grounding in what I will be up against, but Morocco is still a markedly different beast indeed.

After a few hours, the coaches pull over so that the lunches could be distributed and we could have a break outside to get through them. What we did first, however, very much set the tone for the rest of the MdS. What happened can best and most accurately be described as 'The One Hundred Man Piss', as all the men filtered out of the coaches and lined up in three ranks facing the desert, arses towards the coaches, and we all relieved ourselves into the sand. The women, all in a similar dilemma, made their way around the other side of the coaches, across the road and behind a mound. It is so easy being a man sometimes. The sight of us was worthy of a photograph, and the order of the day seemed to be:

1. Relieve yourself
2. Take a photo of everybody else still relieving themselves (not included)
3. Have lunch

Back on the coach after lunch we continued on for another couple of hours. We saw a campsite off to our left, comprising a number of small, new tents, which we initially took to be our own. 'Fucking Pykies' was the comment that sent us up laughing. 'I *hate* fucking Pykies,' continued the lines from *Snatch*. The coaches continued on, and we pulled up a few miles further down the road by a row of four-tonne military trucks. Everything was fitting in place now with what I had seen on previous television coverage.

Nobody was standing on ceremony. When we saw the trucks we threw our kit in the backs and climbed on board, before being driven out into the desert. If anybody was in charge I failed to notice them.

We threw our kit onto the trucks and were driven out away from the roads to the bivouac camp. We dutifully arranged ourselves into tent groups, and headed off to our home for the next couple of days. For me this would be 'Tent 99'. We dumped our kit down and went back to collect our water ration of 4.5 litres. The bivouacs housed eight people each, and so far we had managed to keep ours to the far more manageable and civilised six. Tent 99 comprised myself, the Last Boy Scout (Mark), John, someone John had met up with in the U.K. beforehand called Selwyn, and chums Richard and Carl.

The bivouacs soon had the sides pinned down with rocks to help keep out the wind and the sand.

We made a start of going through our kit again, comparing who had what 'Gucci' kit, and sharing out bits and pieces when we found what was missing. Mark basically kitted everybody out with at least something for the race, and there was never a time when we heard him say anything along the lines of 'No, actually I don't have anything like that going spare'. We were also sorting out our food rations. Our food was going to be checked, along with our survival and medical equipment, and we needed to make sure that it was all in good order. For me, that included throwing a bag together with a breakfast in for the morning of the last day, stage six, which was the seventh day of the competition.

It is always important to lay down ground rules when sharing a limited amount of space with other people, especially when you do not really know each other and everyone's idiosyncrasies, on any real level. Richard proclaimed the first house rule: 'No knocking one out in the tent.' Never mind.

Mark, as well as being the one-man outdoor adventure shop, was also a man of initiative and ingenuity. That was the reason that he carried so many condoms with him. Now for me, condoms mean only one thing. They mean an excellent means of carrying up to one litre of water in any survival situation, spermicide notwithstanding. But to Mark they mean something else. To Mark, a condom is the perfect camping pillow, inflated and placed within a stuff sack. Genius! Carl was quick off the mark to blag himself a couple of Mark's necessary spares. I have always been content to make use of the base of my rucksack as a pillow.

The rest of the guys also had mats, such as thermorests, or even just the basic polystyrene versions. I had not brought one, partly because of space, and partly because I only really use them for insulation, and the ground was not likely to get cold enough to justify their use in the desert. What was becoming apparent, however, was the collection of stones underneath the bivouac's rug that suggested a mat would indeed be useful. Naturally, Mark did have a spare, but as it was a balloon version, and frankly because I could not be arsed, I decided to leave it.

Carl started up a conversation about the little personality-driven things that people should always bring with them on these sorts of exercises. It is true that when you are away from your creature comforts, and especially when in difficult and challenging circumstances, that it is important that you have something with you to make you feel more in control and at home. Carl was, therefore, impressed at the bottle of Tabasco that I had brought with me. He almost fell over when I started offering out the contents of the half-kilo box of desserts, which I had bought the night before in Ouarzazate with John. They were a sort of shortbread held together with coconut oil, which I believed would be just the thing for stocking up my carbohydrate stores before the race, as well as giving myself the experience of an Arabic dessert that I very much enjoy. I bought those simply because they were the only things available. I was hoping for Baklava and so on as well.

Carl then began wrapping his wife's sarong around his head, and then asked how it was that I made my shamagh look so good. The lesson began. I had learnt from my Egyptian friends, but was wearing an army-issue version rather than a traditional Bedouin one. I wanted to look as though I was familiar with this sort of territory, but not *that* familiar. Somehow, no matter how perfectly the sarong was tied around his head, it still just looked to me like he was finding ways to dress himself up in women's clothing.

We all then, very wisely, followed the example set by a few others, and began collecting large rocks to weigh down the sides of the bivouac to protect us from the wind. We kicked back for a while, before going off to have our dinner, along with the 750 other people all with the same time slot. As the evening closed in, it became acutely apparent that it was not going to be a warm night. The wind was blowing and it was carrying a chill with it. We all had our fleeces with us, because at this point we still had our suitcases with us in the bivouacs, but we were starting to have second thoughts about what we would be taking with us into the race. This even concerned us more than the proximity of people standing close to the bivouac and relieving themselves. The bivouacs were arranged in two rows, making up a circle, with people walking to the outside of the circle and then choosing what they believed to be a reasonable distance, and then standing there urinating. As one of us might have put it: 'You just wait, by tomorrow there'll be someone, about ten yards from the tent, probably French, taking a shit.'

One must presume that he was referring to the French as they had the farthest to walk to get there…

Someone then passed the tent carrying a bunch of twigs.

John: 'We demand a shrubbery!'

Me: '…with a two level effect…'

John: '…and a little stream running down the middle.'

Others: 'WHAT?'

John and me: 'WE ARE THE KNIGHTS WHO SAY…NEE!!!'

Brilliant. Another Python fan. We would be getting on like a house on fire. Carl's general contribution to tent entertainment, up to this point, primarily comprised humming a couple of Queen songs, which he later seemed to deny, and the perpetual sound of the *Star Wars* theme. The consensus was that the landscape looked precisely like that used in some parts of the films. Which was fair, considering that a lot of it was filmed not that far away in Tunisia.

By this point the decision had been made; sod the weight and added bulk, it is cold enough, and we need to be taking warm clothing out with us on this race. As Richard then put it to us, if we had known how cold it could get at night then we would have packed completely differently. I agreed entirely, as I had not really prepared for the nights to get quite as cold as it was getting to be. I also believed that in contrast to my usual diet, I had consumed far too much wheat over the past couple of days, with which I emitted a particularly strong and full-bodied release, which echoed around the tent.

It had to be said as well, that Richard and Carl had come up trumps with their choice of bivouac. They had selected the best bivouac, in terms of its condition, and there we lay, under a clear and beautiful night, before the silhouette of a wonderful landscape. It was just such a shame that the landscape was persistently punctuated with people standing around relieving themselves.

Saturday, 24th March 2007

1 Day to The MdS

Having survived the night, there was a general agreement that it was indeed, absolutely freezing cold. Well, a general agreement, with the abstention of Selwyn, who was apparently perfectly warm in his sleeping bag. It was also true that the quality of flatulence during the night, primarily resulting from the internal workings of Mark, John and myself, was absolutely superb. Not pleasant, by any means, but superb by its sheer quantity and exuberance. The three of us, all positioned on the same side of the tent, would henceforth be regarded as being on the flatulent side of the bivouac.

The night had also seen Carl burst his condom, having over-inflated it. This would have been less of an issue if the fact had not been announced to everybody within earshot. There are some things that a tent full of men do not want shared, and the misadventures of one of its occupants with a condom would be one such thing. The looks were almost enough to make us feel that an explanation to the others was warranted. None was given, obviously, as it was far more amusing to consider what was going through everybody else's minds.

I also passed some of the morning considering how much more confident I would be if I had a full set of Helly Henson's base layers, including long johns, a nice RAB windproof jacket like Mark's, and a good lightweight fleece. I was sure that I would now be taking the lighter of my two fleeces with me, but it was still heavy, bulky, and not that warm. I brought it with me for walking around Ouarzazate, not for taking out on the race. I did have a very warm and very thick RAB fleece, but that was far too bulky to take with me in the rucksack. I would have to compromise on being a lot warmer than if I left the fleece behind, and a bit cooler than if I took the RAB with me.

The main thing happening today was the check of medical and survival kit, and the food check. We had to have certain items, such as a penknife, signalling mirror, antiseptic solution and Aspivenin pump, as well as a minimum of 2000 kcals per day. It was not made clear precisely what was expected for the seventh day of the event, which was really just a breakfast and whatever we needed to get across the final, short stage of the event. There was a lot of concern about how we proved how many calories we would be carrying, as most of us had decanted and repackaged everything in favour of reduced bulk and weight. Consequently, we did not have the original food labels. We were also informed that the medical and survival equipment would be weighed separately to the food, so we separated everything accordingly.

We queued up according to our race numbers for a particular time slot, and had our E.C.G. and medical forms scrutinised. We were then issued with a signal flare and salt tablets. We also now had a 'Road Book', detailing all the stages of the race, including maps and distances between checkpoints. All of these had to remain with us throughout the duration of the race. The doctors quizzed us on our health and fitness for the race, and then let us get on our way back to the bivouacs. What happened to the kit checks? I weighed my rucksack, but only because I saw where I could do so; most people had missed it. There was no check of the kit or the food that we had all spent the morning sorting out and organising. How frustrating!

Back at the bivouac, I dumped my kit down, and tended to some personal hygiene. I cut my nails and gave myself a wash as best I could.

We all went to get our lunch in. The queues were annoying, and we were looking forward to going self-sufficient, purely because we would be able to work at our own pace instead of theirs. Selwyn and I had lunch together away from the others in a separate big tent. I did not want to be sitting on the floor, all cramped up around the little tables, and Selwyn did not want to be sitting on the floor either. Selwyn is a 55-year-old joiner from Wales. He is the mature one of the group, and his motives for doing the event are possibly the hardest to fathom out of all of us. There was something very deliberate, determined and strong about Selwyn. I could not work him out, not that I wanted to, but he was very different and very focussed.

He explained that training for this event allowed him to have real personal time to himself, some time just for him to do something for 'him', aside from the usual responsibilities and habits of his everyday life. Selwyn is a legend, instantly likeable, and one of the nicest guys you could ever hope to meet. He just emanated kindness and strength.

As the evening drew on, the Great Clothing Debate continued, with our favourite Carlos wondering whether or not his Helly Hensons, his T-shirt, long-sleeved shirt and shirt would be sufficient, or whether or not a fleece would be required as well. Guys are usually pretty good at packing the minimum required for any trip, but this time we were really trying to ensure that we would be taking absolutely everything that would be essential for us. There are a lot of things that we would *like* to take, but very few that we will actually need, and everything is qualified in terms of its contribution to the bulk and weight within the rucksack. I had decided to take a second set of underwear, which I announced was 'Just in case I brown myself, so then I can wear them whilst I wash the originals.'

I could have come up with any reason, but that was the one that gave the most amusement to the others, and it was, therefore, the best. The guys wearing Lycra shorts were not going to be taking any, so as to prevent chaffing. Their main concern was whether or not the thin layer of material would allow the sun to burn their anus. These are issues that one simply never gets to discuss in any normal situation. But, put a bunch of us in the desert, and all sorts of otherwise bizarre things suddenly become normal debate and areas for concern. On a brighter note, some of the guys were vocalising their concerns that they had no real understanding of precisely what it is that I do. They put me down as a 'Man of Mystery', although that changed to an *International* Man of Mystery, when they accepted that we were indeed in Morocco. At least it changed the subject.

We had a briefing in the centre of the camp, during which Patrick Bauer (the founder of the race) and Alison (an interpreter and journalist) introduced themselves, and we were given a demonstration of how to use our signal flares, and the arm movements for attracting helicopter attention. There were times in the past when people would wave their arms to the helicopter, and the people in the helicopter took it that they were just waving at them, which must have seemed reasonable under the circumstances. So we were shown how to stand to form a 'Y', already well rehearsed from years of youth dancing to The Village People, although now one can never rationalise why. We were informed that we should also be prepared to use our flare if somebody else needed help.

We collected our water ration in the evening. This would be sufficient for us to get through the night, cook our breakfasts in the morning, and then we would collect some more before the start of the race for our Camelbacks,

Platypus, and/or water bottles. We had been issued with two cards, to be carried on a lanyard around our necks throughout the event. One was a medical card, which would be used to record any visits for medical aid, and the second was to record our collection of water from the checkpoints. Time penalties would be awarded for anybody that did not collect water from a particular checkpoint, including the morning and evening checkpoints at the bivouac sites, and for anybody that did not dispose of their water bottles in the bins provided. Looking after the environment, methane emissions aside, was taken very seriously. We were required simply to attend the water checkpoints, as we did not *have* to collect the full quota of water from each point if we did not wish, but physically going there was the important part.

The Competition Phase

Sunday, 25th March 2007

Stage One: 29.3 Km

06:00

This is the first day of being self-sufficient for the race. So, at 6 am we start going through our kit and preparing breakfast. For me that involves heating some water, some of which I pour into a cup to make some soup, and the remainder I use for my porridge. The porridge is in a food bag with milk powder, cinnamon and some salt, and tastes lovely.

07:30

The workers appear, amidst shouts of 'Y'allah! Y'allah!' They descend onto the camp and start demolishing it so that it can be moved on to the next site. I collect the 1.5 litres of water from the mandatory checkpoint, and decant it into my Platypus, along with my homebrew carbohydrate and electrolyte mix. I sort out the rest of my kit, unaware of just how relaxed the vibe was that I was giving off, until Carlos pointed out that 'You look like you're out for a stroll!'
I am really not good at getting my head into gear in the mornings. At least Carl refrained from calling me Voldemort, Lawrence or Ralph, this time.

Each bivouac has a black bin liner attached to it, for disposing of general rubbish as well as the empty water bottles. Carlos, during the evening's activities, had disposed of his burst condom in the bin. This would have gone unnoticed if, in keeping with the recent history of the condom, the bin had not also gained one hole too many, thus spilling its contents out over the ground. This would still have remained relatively unnoticed, if our dear Carlos had not once again verbalised what he had seen, thus earning us some very concerned and perplexed looks from our fellow competitors.

Now that the whole camp had been alerted to the presence of a condom amongst our rubbish, we changed the subject and agreed that last night had not been as bad as the night before. This did make us question our kit, again, but the general consensus was that if we had experienced it get cold, then it could get cold again.

When all of my kit was away, I took off my shirt and zipped off the legs of my North Face trousers, and then covered myself in 40 SPF suntan lotion. I took out my second breakfast, the oat-based cereal with fruit, milk powder and salt, added some water, and polished that off. I received a few brownie points from the guys for the second breakfast idea.

08:30

As instructed, we made our way over to the start line for photographs and a visibility check of our race numbers. We made a point of shaking hands and wishing each other 'The best of British luck' and so on for the day ahead. There was an atmosphere of just wanting to crack on – a typical pre-race energy, but not necessarily the excitement that I have seen at other races. We just wanted to start getting through it, and the end was nowhere in sight.

From left to right; Selwyn, Carl, Richard, Mark, yours truly, and John.

As we walked over to the start area, I asked John if he was familiar with the African poem, 'The Lion and the Gazelle'. He was not, which was great, because it meant that I could tell him whilst reciting it to myself, and it is always better to say a mantra out loud rather than just inside your own mind:

> '**When a gazelle wakes up in Africa,**
>
> **It knows it must run faster than the swiftest lion, or it will be killed.**
>
> **When a lion wakes up in Africa,**
>
> **He knows he must run faster than the slowest gazelle, or else he will starve.**
>
> **In Africa, it does not matter if you are the lion or the gazelle.**
>
> **What matters is, when the Sun comes up, you'd better be running.**'

There were camera crews around from various countries, focussing on certain groups. They had been around since we arrived in the desert, and we had mainly been ignoring them. I was in the start area, facing the guys, when I saw an oriental guy off to my right-hand side. I was just doing a very subtle tri-planer calf stretch and ankle mobility exercise, and I would not have thought that even the guys in front of me would have noticed that I was actually doing an exercise. But this guy did. I pretended not to notice him, but was aware that the camera was on me and that he was making a circular path behind me. There was no way that I was going to pass this opportunity up. To the guys in general, and at a little more than a whisper: 'Is he still recording me?'

'Yes!'

With that, my arms and legs straight, I quickly bent forwards from the hips to touch my toes, bouncing up and down a few inches in the most unhelpful stretch that I could think of. But it was 'Old School', and these guys were not accustomed to anything else. I stood up, my arms stretching up above my head as I leant backwards, bounced a few times, and then went forwards again. My motivation was the fact that I was wearing a rucksack, and that every time I bent forwards I revealed my arse to the camera, which must have looked very special indeed. All that stretch actually does is cause the muscles to fire quicker and tighten, which can be really useful if you are about to do something requiring explosive power, but which, therefore, had no relevance to what we were about to do whatsoever. I kept it going for a bit, and then went into some outrageous chest stretches, taking my straight arms out to the sides of my body, level with my shoulders, and then forcing my elbows back.

At this point I decided to stop, but it was too late; the cameraman had moved around next to me and wanted me to continue. I informed him that I was, in fact, done, and that I am not comfortable with requests. He then proceeded to give me the worst interview that I have ever had. It featured such vague questions as 'What do you think of the desert?' 'What do you think of the race?' and 'What do you expect to earn from this event?' The pointlessness of the questions was matched by the contempt and sarcasm in my responses, the cringe-worthiness of the whole thing causing the rest of the guys to take a deliberate step back away from me with every answer. Well, at least I managed to amuse myself, although 'Parky' was clearly struggling a bit.

09:35

Following a briefing from Patrick Bauer (in French), and Alison (translating into English), including birthday announcements, a three-minute countdown with some very questionable pop music, the race was underway. We poured out over the line as a helicopter flew around us and directly overhead, mainly sideways, whilst a cameraman sat on the side to record the action. There was the predictable chaos of too many people trying to get through the start area, made annoyingly worse by a number of people intending only to walk, who had positioned themselves towards the front and therefore, in the way of those of us intending to run.

The first thing that I noticed was that my running posture was tilted forwards more than I am used to, as a result of the weight of the 14 kg (31 lb) rucksack, and my intention only to get into a moderate (rather than fast) running pace. This meant that I was putting less stress through my calf, a consequence of which should be that I can manage better and get further without it seizing up. I would know tomorrow, but for now the plan is to just get to the first checkpoint and then get through the day. I checked my watch to see that I had been running for a few minutes. I always give myself ten minutes to get into my running pace and to start to feel comfortable with what I am doing. So far, so good. The field was spreading out as well, with some people already finishing their running, and slowing to a walk. However bad things became, I would have to give myself the full ten minutes to work out whether or not I could keep the pace (as well as the British end) up. The weight was definitely significant on my back, and the running pattern was limited (which was a good thing for the 'long run'), but I was feeling comfortable. I was feeling even more comfortable for getting past other runners, although I was very much aware that this could well be a temporary arrangement.

As I approached the first hill, I decided that I would keep to my pace, and just get up and over it. That worked out okay, but I knew that I had expended a lot of energy in keeping to a run, and the majority of people around me had all slowed to a walk to get to the top. By the time the second hill came around, I realised that I was expending far too much energy for far too little gain, and it would be more efficient to walk up one side, get my breath back in doing so, and then run down the other. I still managed to run most of this one, but I slowed to a walk when I was near the top. The other side of the hill was sand dunes. I modified my strategy further. I would generally aim to run the entire distance between checkpoints, but slow to a walk for steep and long uphills, and soft, sandy ground. Just how steep and long the uphills, and just how soft and sandy the ground needed to be to warrant a walk, I would decide at the time.

This strategy seemed to work well for me. I felt comfortable. I could get my breath back and relax a little when walking for those short periods, and the saving in energy would translate into a quicker and more comfortable running pace when on better ground. This strategy seemed to be what everybody else around me was using as well; and it was something that had been recommended to me before leaving for Morocco. I just needed to be here to see that it made sense.

I knew that the Moroccan brothers, along with the other elite athletes, would be running regardless. But that was their thing. That was what they had trained for, and as a consequence, their bodies would be much more efficient at running up those long and steep inclines, and over the difficult soft sand, than ours. My plan was to run this race as best as I could, and that was precisely what I was doing. So far, I was feeling good, working hard, and enjoying taking in the sights. Walking also gave me the opportunity to take photographs, and a more preferable opportunity to stop altogether, if briefly, in order to check my hydration.

As the route took us into the hills many of us slowed to push a walking pace
and save ourselves for running again on the flats and downhills.

As in keeping with Monty Python's race for the incontinent, we were all taking regular opportunities to check how hydrated we were. If our urine was clear, and we were urinating frequently for the amount of fluid that we were consuming, then that was a good sign that we were well hydrated.

We rounded a hill to see a few Land Rovers and some locals out to greet us as we ran past. Great – the first checkpoint! I put my hand out to meet the hands of the local farm children that were congratulating us in French, English or Arabic. I thanked them in whichever of the three felt right at the time. We ran across a small bridge and passed a couple of photographers and race officials. We then ran past the Land Rovers and around the next hill. Where was the checkpoint? Where was the water? Bugger – it wasn't the checkpoint! I had even accelerated because I thought that I was about to have a rest. What an arse. Oh well, onwards I go; the checkpoint must be somewhere near here.

Half an hour later, when I finally arrived at the first checkpoint, twelve kilometres from the start line and an hour and a half after starting, I collected my water bottle and had my card stamped. I found some shade around the back of a 'Landy' and dumped my rucksack on the ground, whilst I helped myself to a Powergel, half a Kendal Mint Cake, and a litre or so of the water that I had just collected. I had the pleasure of meeting fellow Britishers Graham, Tom and Owen, all three from Scotland and all training partners who were currently doing well and working to a plan. They came across as well disciplined with their plan for the race and their approach, well-trained and very much with youth on their side. Just like me (hah!?). What did impress me was that they were also making good progress with regards to the rest of the field, despite also carrying heavy rucksacks, all around the twelve to fourteen kilo marks.

I took a fifteen-minute break at the checkpoint, whilst I got through the food and water, and got an impression of the next leg to the second checkpoint. I left the checkpoint, quickly getting back to my running pace, and almost immediately found myself on soft sand. This was tolerable for a few minutes, but then the futility of it all meant that I had to get back to a walking pace again. The dunes were low and shallow, but they still involved climbing up a couple of metres here and there, and they seemed to go on for a long time. Once I ran out of the dunes, the ground hardened and it was time to crack on, even though that meant running some long uphill sections. When the line of people in front of me were all at a walking pace, I fell in behind them along the track, and we all walked to the top of a steep hill. The second checkpoint became visible when we reached the summit for the second time, but there was still another 'summit' to go before we actually reached the checkpoint.

I repeated the drill from the previous checkpoint, although this time I had been issued with twice the amount of water. I topped up the Platypus and drank my way through a litre and a half of water. The remaining water was tipped away and the bottles disposed of at the collection point. I treated myself to just over twenty minutes of rest before moving on. The three Scots had been in and left during this time, but I had to keep to my own plan. The next leg was a long one, and I had felt tired at points during the previous section, so I wanted to know that I was in the best position to start off on the final leg to the new bivouac camp. When I started to walk out of the checkpoint, I gave myself a mental slap, stopped and threw the rucksack to the ground. I had been out in the sun for a long time, and I would do well to apply a second lot of sun lotion. After a brief pause, I was back on my way.

Because the checkpoint was high on a hilltop, it meant that we would start out of it running downhill. The downhill itself was steady and along a single track. The surface was hard but made up of small to moderately sized rocks. That meant that although it was possible to run fast, it was equally possible to fall over or at least inadvertently kick a rock and damage some toes. So, it was fast but careful. On the plus side, the front of the Salomons were reinforced with a thick layer that limited any forces meeting the front of the shoe, which must have saved my toes several times over during this section alone. The stretch as a whole made for a pleasant run, but led onto sand dunes. By comparison these were horrid. They sapped so much energy. This was compounded by the fact that, as it was 1 pm, the sun was feeling considerably hotter than a few hours before. I started out on the sand dunes, running, which then changed to walking up, running down and running the flat to the next incline. After a few dunes, I was walking up, running down, and walking the flat to aid recovery. After not too long, I was walking the lot.

I walked out of the dunes and after a slight delay to allow my heart rate to calm down, I got back into the running. It was flat, stony ground again, meaning that a moderate pace was quite appropriate to get me where I wanted to go, without allowing me to become excessively tired or trip over every stone along the way. The flat ended and an uphill section over a similar nature of surface took us within sight of the bivouac camp. The camp was a couple of miles away, beyond what looked like another nice flat. As I got onto the 'flat', I realised that there was still actually a slight incline; a slight sting in the tail of that final leg, but it was still one last run to the camp. I plugged away, continuing to suck my isotonic homebrew through the Platypus (keeping to my plan).

There was no use forgetting about the environment, or about what I was doing. Just because I would be resting soon, I would still be running for a little while yet, and I did not want to create a snowball effect by crossing the line dehydrated on the first day. A few long minutes later, I crossed the line, a relatively unemotional affair, at 14:15; four hours and forty minutes after the start. I collected the three 1.5 litre bottles of water from the checkpoint and headed off to find the bivouac.

I dropped the water bottles at the entrance of the bivouac and threw the rucksack in, roughly to the position where I had been on the previous nights in the other bivouac. I was the first man home from 'Tent 99', and I arranged the rucksack at the end of the rug, and lay back and relaxed. I then negotiated myself back onto my feet and went off to relieve my bowels. Well, following the pleasure of finishing the day's run, it made sense to reward myself with another of life's pleasures (one assumes that someone might be interested in my movements, so I will keep you updated). I returned to the bivouac and lay back, using the rucksack as a pillow. Allison passed and greeted me, and then came back and asked for an interview. Bless her, I was showing no intention of sitting up, so she had to negotiate herself into a position next to me so that we could share the microphone.

'It's nice to be back in the bivouac is the first impression. It was a *great* day today. We were very anxious to get going this morning. We knew that we would be out for the midday sun as well. And it was very good! I am used to doing a bit of training in the desert. I have done a lot of work out in Egypt before, but that meant that I was used to the heat, and I was used to a lot of the terrain, but the nature of the sand dunes and the size of the hills was something that we weren't used to. So that was certainly interesting, and it gave us the opportunity to try to gauge how much we could actually run, and how much we would be walking

And, yes, essentially there were two good checkpoints. It was quite manageable to run most of the first, then discipline to give ourselves a ten-minute break and then carry on and slightly less far to the next one, and again good to get some water in and a good rest after that. Things that were perhaps a little different and (that we) weren't expecting was the breeze; quite a pleasant breeze but then once it died down you really feel the full force of the heat, and just how much the sand dunes and the hills can take out of you. So managing to get back here and managing to have run most of it; yes it's quite nice to be able to lie down and then looking forward to sorting out my feet and then getting everything ready for tomorrow. Tonight is just sorting everything out, getting through the food and recovering.'

I am not entirely sure why I was using the royal 'We', seeing as I was talking about myself and had not even spoken to another competitor since finishing, but I am sure that it made sense to me at the time. The verbal diarrhoea was also inexcusable.

As I said in the interview, my priorities were recovery, food and feet. I knew that one of my toes, the third on the right foot, was not doing well. I took off my Salomons and socks, and had a good look. A blood blister had formed at the end of the toe, and was pushing the nail away from the skin. I decided that it would look better for some air, and so made a start on getting my food ready. From a physiological perspective, the sooner the food goes in the better. There is a window of opportunity over the first forty-five minutes and then up to the first hour and a half after exercise, in which the body is very efficient at taking in carbohydrates and using them to replenish glycogen stores. The longer that it takes to get carbohydrates in, the slower and less efficient that process becomes, meaning that stores might not be replenished for the next day, and in an event such as this it can trigger another snowball effect. Depleted glycogen stores would lead to feelings of hunger and premature fatigue, as well as headaches and diminished levels of concentration.

Before I started tending to either food or feet, Richard and Carl returned together, at 15:07. I was very happy to see them both, and they had both finished the race in an excellent time. Apparently they had walked the lot, which I considered even more impressive for the time that it had taken them to finish. I asked whether or not they had seen any of the others, but they had not since the first checkpoint. I stripped down and stood outside the bivouac, washing myself with my eighth of a bar of soap and a quarter of a bottle of water. I took longer than usual cleaning certain areas, as personal hygiene really does mean leaving nothing unattended, much to Carl's disapproval.

I made a start on the food, but distracted myself with attending to the blister. The blister was still growing so I had to deal with it before I risked increasing the likelihood of losing the nail. Thanks to a sterilised safety pin and the T-shirt that I used for gauze, I patched up the toe and left it to the air before putting a plaster on it. I then got back to preparing, cooking and eating my food, an activity that I continued through the rest of the evening.

Mark was the next back. He had suffered a bit, having started off a little too fast, but had then taken stock and sorted himself out. He was concerned about his hydration, and, in fact, we were all concerned about his hydration, as he told us about the various signs that things had not gone according to plan. It was not too long before he was in good order again, a relief for us as well as for him. John was the next man home. He had started off at a run and found that it was not working for him. He also sorted himself out, thanks to some good awareness and management, and was looking very comfortable in no time.

Selwyn came in a bit later, and it was great to see him. Tent 99 was as it should be, all men home, and all cracking on with personal admin and preparing food. The preparing food aspect of it all was something that I may have been doing more than others - as Carlos put it so well: 'You're great; you run and then you just eat. It's all you do!' Fair one.

That was certainly the plan. To run and then to recover, which meant resting and eating. I ate all evening. Sometimes you plan to do something and although you think you are doing it, you are not doing it to the extent that you intended. If somebody notices that you are, then you are probably doing well. So that boosted my self-confidence. The key other thing Carl pointed out to me that evening was his general displeasure with me 'lathering myself' outside the tent. Fair one again, probably.

Richard commented on my rucksack sores, which were across my shoulders and waist, and I accepted that I would have to deal with them before starting out in the morning. I had voiced my plan not to email home at any point during the race, as I intended to spend all of my time focussed on what I was doing, and resting and eating whenever I had the chance. Carl acknowledged this point of view and assured me that I was a miserable bastard for not emailing my girlfriend. I knew he was right, but I just did not want to get into missing her and then feeling distracted from what I was doing. I just wanted to live the race for a week and forget about home. That was not going to happen, and young Carlos was spot on.

Another concern of the day had been the 'rim sores' experienced by some of the guys, due to either chaffing or the intensity of the sunlight through their Lycra shorts. Nothing can really prepare one for the despair and agony that shroud one's outlook on life like a dense fog - like the outlook across the bivouac on Carl's arse, or indeed on Richard's arse and certainly no less on John's arse. An abundance of cracks was certainly not mentioned on any waiver form that I might have signed; although 'shock and awe' was certainly something that I had heard mentioned pertaining to the Gulf. It must be a desert thing.

19:00

Having recovered from the abundance of cracks and rims, Sarah, one of the Best of Morocco representatives, appeared at the bivouac with some printouts of emails for us. Because I was a miserable bastard, I had decided that I did not want any contact from home. I had not known that emails would be printed out and brought around to us. I had been concerned that people would get fed up with me for not emailing them back, which I was especially disinclined to do if it meant finishing a day's run and then standing in a queue to use a computer. I use computers enough at work and at home and I really did not want to be using one when I was in the middle of the desert. Had I known that printed versions would be brought around to us, then I would have emailed everybody before leaving and asked them to send something via the *darbaroud.com* website.

As it happened, a friend, Mark Hibbitts, managing director of www.newbornfitness.co.uk had taken the time to look at the various websites, and found out how to send me a message. That was really good initiative on his part, and something that meant a lot to me because he had gone to some trouble and taken the time to do it. In short, I was very grateful.

Tente N° 99

Dossard N° 685 : Hines

De: mark hibbitts … - le : 25/03/2007 12:22:02

keep going you mad f%*£er. Hi Matey..Dunno if you'll get this but if you do I'm thinking about you and wishing you luck. Now if it's ok with you I'm off to soak my feet in the bath and have a cold beer...Mark…

It is exactly the sort of thing that you need in the desert, just to confirm that normality does exist in the world, but it is a world a long way from where I happened to be. It was definitely appreciated.

We were all getting into our sleeping bags pretty early, as once we had eaten, there was not much else that we could do, and the sun was on its way down after 18:30. It was never really a question as to whether or not Carl was asleep. As much as I may have made a significant contribution to the flatulent half of the tent, Carl was in a league of his own when it came to snoring.

Monday, 26th March 2007

Stage Two: 35 Km

00:00

Sandstorm

The wind was up. I looked out across and towards the other side of the camp and I could not make out the tents there. The wind was blowing through the bivouac, and sand was getting everywhere. It was in the sleeping bag, in my clothing and the gritty feeling when I brought my teeth together told me that it was in my mouth.

I woke up next to find my world was made up primarily of canvas. I could not tell if the bivouac had just come down on my part of the tent or if it had completely fallen down. At least I was not getting any more sand blasted across my face. Ten seconds later I was up, following on from Richard and

Carl, who were also out of their sleeping bags and getting the poles shifted back into position.

Once we were back in the comfort of a properly erect bivouac, the wind carried on howling through and trying its best to make the canvas into a sail. One of the ten-inch iron pegs was wrenched out of the ground and, because it was still attached to the canvas, was being chucked down around me with the force of the wind and a metallic clanging against the rocks. Sand was one annoyance, but having to pull an iron peg out of my face would really put the lid on it. I made a grab for the dancing peg and untied it from the line to the canvas. I gave a shout out to the others, because it looked as if some more were working their way free on the other side of the tent.

01:00

I was just lying there. The wind was still howling and I was not managing to stay relaxed. My body was just tensed up waiting to see if the canvas was going to work its way free and make for freedom across the camp. I was just ready to have to leap out after it. I was then very much aware that this could go on all night, and that if it did then I would be knackered by the morning. Even if I was asleep, if the canvas took flight then I would be awake in seconds and we would all still be able to chase it down. Besides, it was unlikely that the whole thing would get free. I tried to think about my better half and relax a bit. I fell asleep again soon after.

01:30

I heard the workers around the other side of the tent, near to Mark, banging in the pegs.

06:00

I woke up to find that the shower peg from *Psycho* had been reinstated in its correct position. A quick word around the tent confirmed that I had started snoring just before they finished banging the peg into the ground.

By eight o'clock it was morning as usual. John helped patch up my back and shoulder sores, so as to help prevent them from worsening.

08:30

The briefing took place by the start line. Patrick and Alison were stood atop a Land Rover at the side. There were still 756 people starting today, so everybody had safely made it through the first day. We had a few minutes of music to listen to, the ridiculous Ketchup song amongst others, and then the countdown in French.

We poured out across the line again, the usual minor pushing and shoving to get into some space, and got moving as the helicopter flew along to our right and then towards us, sideways, overhead. It was a good start. I got into some space quickly and got up to the Saharan shuffle pace of the day before. Some competitors are moving up the field, and some are moving down. Some are already by the side of the track and checking their hydration. The ones that baffle me the most are those that must have started at a running pace but reduce it to a walk within the first two minutes. That just does not make any sense to me. As I have said before, the toughest part of the run is probably the first ten minutes. The body is still trying to work out what is going on and trying to physiologically catch up with the demands. Once I am through those first ten minutes, then my breathing rate has levelled out and I am into a comfortable running pace. I have to push myself through this period, and then I am set for the rest of the run. The only time that it gets difficult later on is if I run out of fuel (effects of temperature, hydration and external factors notwithstanding).

The run starts off over a flat that leads into a pass. I am heading south by south-east, into the sun, although at this time of day that just means that it is bright in a clear blue sky. It will be another couple of hours before it really starts to heat up. After a couple of kilometres, the ground becomes more stony, slightly undulating, and with the mountains ahead of us. Continuing south, the route bears south-west once I reach the start of the pass.

Some parts of the stage took us high up into the rocky hills, but once at the top is was still good running ground.

The front of my Salomons had enough protective rubber on them to save my
toes from feeling the impact as my feet managed to find
every rock in the Sahara.

The undulating ground gives way to a more dramatic landscape, and
everybody ahead of me has reduced to a walking pace to get up the steeper
climbs. I always leave it as late as possible, hoping that I have made a few
extra yards on the person in front of me, but make sure that I am walking
before I start using up too much energy.

The other side of the climb takes us down into a valley for just less than
a kilometre. The second climb is quite imposing. The ground is much rockier

and there are at least a couple of hundred yards of climbing to reach the summit. At least there is a cool breeze that whips around the side of the mountain. It is usually good practice to turn around when feeling a little out of breath, because by that stage I am always most of the way to the top, and the scenery behind me makes it a worthwhile climb so far, and the sight of hundreds of other competitors snaking their way down the side of the previous mountain and out across the valley is also a good boost. If they are behind me then I want them to stay there, but they are all hot on my heels.

The surface around the summit does not strike me as the safest, with a steep and deadly drop a few feet to my left. Because I have increased my pace and I am trying to get past some people, or else reduce the amount of faffing around required to get to the next part of the path, at times I am only inches from the edge, but it is all calculated and safe in my own mind. I am more than a little concerned though that anybody suffering from a dehydration-associated reduction in co-ordination and concentration might not fair so well. I have a little run down, then along, and then up a bit, along, and then it is the start of the main descent. A sandy flat at the base of the descent leads us into the first checkpoint, where I am happy to find Owen. I take a good quarter of an hour rest to take on a third of a Kendal mint cake and a Powergel, along with a litre of water, and then I am off and on my way again.

Exiting the checkpoint, I walk for a minute or so then get up to my running pace. The sand hampers progress, but that eventually gives way to a more sturdy ground, and I am moving at pace again. There is a slight uphill, but as it is not too steep, and the ground is relatively hard, it makes sense to carry on running. The slight uphills and undulating ground makes way for a proper, grown-up climb, that requires much greater effort, and reluctantly a bit of a walk. A footpath leads around a hilly area, across a stony ground, but the frustrations of having to walk allow the risks to be moved to the back of my mind as I pick up my pace on the flats and descents. I walk when it is treacherous, and for anything less I am moving as fast as I can, slipping and sliding as if on a bank of scree. The second checkpoint comes into view and I do my best to hold back. I am always concerned that I will view the checkpoint as the finish line, and use up too much energy in getting there, not appreciating the fact that I will use up too much fuel, increase the risk of dehydration, and just tire myself when I need to stay focussed for later on. I just want to stay consistent for the duration of the race. That is the game plan anyway, but various factors, including a mild elation, mean that pace increases a little anyway, but I at least limit it to just striding out and then taking on more fluid through the Platypus.

I am greeted at the second checkpoint by the beaming smile of a lovely French *controlleur*, one of the volunteers proud to be here on 'the toughest footrace on earth'. I smile back, fully aware that I must look as if I have been suspended in a sack for two days with the crap beaten out of me, but I try to be friendly and charming, anyway. I am friendly partly because I am a friendly person, but also because these people are standing around all day, and if I can do something to make them smile or to help them remember me, then that might work in my favour if I need anything later on. Plus I am out here for a week; so making friends is one of those things that will help me to get through the event.

I leave the checkpoint after twenty minutes or so, continuing along some stony ground, with the route then leading across a dried-out riverbed and track. I find myself amongst competitors with whom I was at a similar point yesterday. In particular, I recognise a woman who must be at least in her late forties, and although she is not a fast runner, she manages a pace somewhere between a fast walk and a slow run, and just has the sort of consistency that means that if you let up your guard for a moment then she is a mile in front of you. I appreciate that I am not really here to beat anyone, and I am trying to run my own race, but there is something about someone moving slower than me that really makes me want to beat him or her across the finish line. The reason that she ends up ahead of me is because she is consistently fast, even on the uphill sections, and she does not rest much, if at all, at the checkpoints.

It is a good strategy, but not the one that I would be happy with myself, and that is probably why I want to beat her. But, in absolute fairness and truth, I have a lot of respect for the competitors that just go straight through the checkpoints, even if managing a slower pace than me. They are just challenging themselves in a different way, and playing a slightly different game, but it is just as tough. The benefit of my way is that I have the edge with speed, and if I have the right ground then I can make a lot of distance in front of them very easily, but the ground beyond that can be very unpredictable.

The track comes away from the hills and riverbed, and I find myself heading out across a plain. The plains are deceptive because the mountains on the other side never seem to get any closer. I can really feel the sun now. It is beating down hard and there are still no clouds in the sky and no shade anywhere to be seen. It is not that I want the sun to go behind a cloud, or that I want to find shelter and hide until later on, but it is just knowing that there is no respite here. It is knowing that I am running with kit across a sun-baked, white and stony plain, with no option but to get to the other side, and that other side is just not getting any closer. Granted, if it became too hot, then I could save some energy by walking, but then I would be under that hot sun for twice as long. I really do not care for my options. I only really have one that is acceptable to me, and that is keeping my head down, keeping my 'consistent' steady pace, and getting to the checkpoint at the other side of the plain.

The mountains on the other side of the plain never seem to get any closer, and whilst it is solid ground for running over, there is no respite from the midday sun and the monotony of the unchanging landscape.

The checkpoint is in view for a long time. Across a flat plain I can easily see where I am going, but although it is easy ground to run, the midday desert sun seems to sap all of the available energy out of me. With some relief, the checkpoint does eventually start to grow on the horizon, and after a while longer I run into the checkpoint and collect my water. I meet the usual checkpoint procrastinators around the back of the Landy, partially protected by the sheet of canvas held up by a couple of poles, presenting the only source of shade. I do not take the rucksack off, I just start drinking the water and finishing off the last of the day's Kendal mint cake. I rationed myself to two Powergels a day, something that I would change if doing this again. I should have allowed myself one Powergel for each checkpoint, so an average of three a day would have been better for me. It is just nice to have those extra calories, extra carbohydrates, and extra electrolytes to go down with the litre of water.

I comment to other guys that I just feel like cracking on and getting the final leg done and dusted. Owen asks me if I am ready to get going, because he could use a wingman for the next part. Fair one; what we were all looking at from six kilometres away was the biggest climb in the whole race, a mountain consisting primarily of a face of soft sand. I have never seen sand reach that height before, and it had been a daunting prospect to me ever since it came into view just under an hour ago. If Owen could use a wingman then so could I. Up until this point in the race I was happy to just do my own thing, but I could imagine that if the going got really tough, then it would be nice to have somebody else there forcing the pace. I asked for a couple of minutes to polish off the Kendal mint cake and most of the water, and then we were good to go. I was not really that tired from the last leg, as it had been flat and quite easygoing. The heat had been the only reason that I had been feeling it for the past hour, and as the next section would start with a walking climb, I would be finding it quite comfortable by comparison to another run across a flat.

We left the checkpoint together and were onto the soft sand almost immediately. Sand dunes are about a third air, and with the extra weight of the pack, each foot sinks a long way into the ground. When it is steep and you are

The sand reaches all the way to the top of the climb, as Owen (centre of photo) and myself, prepare to begin our ascent.

walking as if climbing the stairs, then it does not help to have the foot sink a foot or so into the ground between steps. We had a tiring climb up the sand before it levelled out onto a ridge, although still only a third of the way up. We looked back to see the checkpoint a long way off behind and beneath us, with a line of competitors making their way across the plain, whilst others in front made their way up the rest of the sand. We plunged onwards along the ridge,

316

towards an area where the sand met the rocky side of the mountain face itself. Competitors were on the rock face next to the sand, making their way up a single track towards the top. One guy thought that he should try to stick with the sand, and climb up and around the rocky section, but he should not have. He scrambled up about ten metres before losing his footing in the super-soft sand and sliding down past where he had started out on his one-man mission. The clever fellow decided to get back into the line and climb up with everybody else.

I stuck close in behind Owen, almost matching him step for step, and he was putting in a lot of effort, meaning that it was not easy going to keep up with him. But that was what we both wanted, to push ourselves and get it over with. I was grateful to reach the rocks, because they represented solid ground, and I was happy to climb up the rocks and be generally more efficient than I was when floundering around in the sand. The rocks were typical of what you might expect; large rocks presenting the main source of support for climbing, with smaller rocks giving away under foot and heading towards the person underneath. The key is to take your time, to let the person above move, and wait for any dislodged rocks to either stop moving or fall past you before moving yourself.

Owen was consistently apologising for sending half the mountain in my general direction, but he was being careful and it was not as if he was kicking his feet back and trying to create problems for me. I told him not to worry about it. We were all hot and tired anyway, so accidents would happen regardless. What did annoy us was a small group of Frenchmen who decided to stop and take photographs of each other. Granted, it was a spectacular view and they were probably great photographs, but down below there were people hanging on by the skin of their fingernails and waiting to move into a safer and more stable position; just because David Bailey was alright it did not mean that everybody else was. It was just inconsiderate and that sort of thing really annoys me. We made our disapproval clear at the time.

We climbed up along the rocky path and were soon back on sand, sticking close to the rocky side of the mountain, whilst up ahead we would soon be traversing the top of the sand, using a rope that had been secured into the rocks. It was then that a shout went up from behind us: 'Doctor!' I looked back and someone shouted up that a doctor was needed and to send the call up to the top (expecting that on a mountain such as this, a doctor or other member of the support team would be on hand). I continued the call up to the top, but Owen was already on the case: 'I'm a doctor. I'll go.' He stepped out onto the sand as he took his rucksack off. I told him I would take the rucksack and continue up to the top, and wait for him there. Owen ran down the sand away from the rest of us. Just as he neared a rock that obscured our view of the casualty, a flare went up to alert the support crew and helicopter. One of the support crew, apparently another doctor, came running past us and would be reaching the casualty soon after Owen.

I turned back to the climb ahead and made a start. The guy ahead of me, another Englishman, offered to help with the rucksack. I carried it for the first part of the climb, he carried it for a huge section of the climb after that, as well as the traverse, and then we both shared the load for the remaining climb to the top of the ridge by the summit. We fell forwards into the sand, the rucksack between us, and turned around to watch the others making their way up. Blake introduced himself, and I thanked him for his massive help with the rucksack, and let him know that he could carry on and that I would wait for Owen to come back up. Before he did, he informed me that the Brits were hoping to commandeer the megaphone at the finish line of the last day, and sing 'Jerusalem' to the other Brits coming in over the dunes. That sounded good to me, and I offered to write out the second verse, as he told me that none of the rest of them knew it. I was not sure quite how the other non-Brits might take it though.

I was actually glad about all that had happened. I had wondered how I would react if somebody had an accident and needed help. I wondered if I would stop and help or if I would do the minimum possible and carry on with the race. Morally I had done the right thing, but I had not known that this would be the case until now.

I had some pretty strong reservations regarding the inclusion of this mountain in the race. I enjoyed it, and I love climbing, but I thought that it might take a few people out of the race because they were not good at scrambling up - or just through accidents. Most of us came here for a run, so to me this came across as a section that was just a little too dangerous for some of the competitors, and I failed to see any relevance in including it in the course.

Owen came into view less than ten minutes later, thanked me for lugging up his rucksack for him, and we set off on the descent. I explained Blake's help, and that he was as much to thank as me for his part in taking up the extra pack. It had reminded me of that expedition to the Pyrenees when I was 15, amongst a group of 18 year olds, and a couple of instructors. On the first day, on the first climb of that midsummer's day, one of the instructors had collapsed and thrown up. A little later, after lunch (siesta, and wanton [mighty] walking stick damage), one of the 18 year olds collapsed through heat stress, and the rest of us pulled together as a team to get him recovering and then put in a med-evac plan to get him out of the mountains. The casualty was put onto a stretcher, and later walked, whilst the remaining team had to double-up with his rucksack and the rucksacks carried by the instructor and myself who went off to raise the alarm and get help. The legend of the evacuation, whilst carrying 'Not one, but *two*' rucksacks, is something that will probably stay in my mind for a while. This time it was my turn to carry 'Not one, but *two*'

The view down from the summit as I awaited Owen. The previous checkpoint is just visible in the middle of the photo, with the plain out on the other side having taken an hour to cross.

rucksacks, if for substantially less time and distance than those guys had had to.

The descent was rocky and along a twisted route down the side of the mountain. We managed to get down with a controlled pace, not allowing ourselves to get carried away with momentum, and kept some banter going

320

with the Britishers behind us. Owen explained that the casualty had just collapsed due to the effects of heat and dehydration, but had already regained consciousness by the time that he arrived. As we neared the bottom of the mountain, we could see the bivouac camp off in the distance, a little way along a fairly flat plain. It was a welcome sight, even if still a little way off. Owen and I continued to run, but soon the flat plain became sand dunes and we were restricted to a walk. We could use the recovery time, anyway. The Velcro around my gaiters had mostly fallen away from my Salomons the day before, so I had not put the gaiters on today. I wanted to save them for a more sandy stage later on. As a result, the sand from the dunes was not having to struggle to find its way into my Salomons, but it was not really bothering me.

As we finished scrambling over the last few dunes, with the bivouac camp close to our front, I had to suggest that we get back to a run to the line. It is just not cricket to get through a day like today and then walk across the finish line. Besides, all of that recovery time in the short dunes meant that we had plenty of energy left to make a go for it. Owen agreed that it would be rude not to, and we crossed the finish line a few minutes later, in 270th place, just over six hours after we started this morning.

We collected our water from the checkpoint just after the finish line, and staggered off to find our bivouacs. It is the only thing to look forward to after the day's run; collapsing into the bivouac, getting the feet out, cooling down and then getting the food on the go. So it was a complete pain in the arse to find that the bivouac was yet to be erected by the workers. That was really annoying for both of us. We staggered on and found another bivouac, and we both sat down there whilst waiting for ours to be put up.

My right foot was not feeling good, or more specifically, the toe was not feeling good where the blood blister had been the day before. It just made it more of an embuggerance to have to wait to be able to sort it out. When the bivouac was up I collapsed inside and stripped off. I tended to the toe, and found a couple of other blisters that had come up. My shoulders were pretty sore as well, and the skin on the left shoulder looked as if it had been moistened, torn, and turned through 90 degrees. It was just a couple of layers of skin, and I was not going to dress the shoulders or feet tonight, as I wanted the air to do its thing. I would cover them up at the last possible moment before tomorrow's run. The body heals itself much better in the presence of air than if covered up. A dressing is often much more useful for preventing foreign bodies from entering the wound. As long as I kept it clean, then I could cover it up at the latest opportunity. Tomorrow would be a shorter run, anyway.

One of the other British competitors is a fantastic guy called Ed (we never introduced ourselves, so I checked the name from the competitors' list by race numbers. If I have made a mistake then please accept my sincerest apologies and let me know!). He is a genuinely sincere character, and always interested in, and positive about, other people's progress. I met up with him whilst walking around the camp and had a brief chat. He had been next to the casualty when he went down. It was one of the 'continentals' that made a grab for the signal flare and let it off. Meanwhile, Ed was giving the casualty a well-deserved slap and treating him to some water, which brought him back from the edge in no time.

It is the presence of mind that someone like Ed has that you really want in this sort of event, and in Ed's mind, there was no need to set off the flare. In fairness, all that the casualty needed was some fluids and a rest, then for help with his rucksack to get him the rest of the way to the bivouac camp, a few kilometres away on the other side of the mountain. Granted, if it had been more serious, then full medical equipment and some sort of evacuation may have been necessary. In the circumstances as they were, a few sensible people could have looked after him. As it was, somebody panicked and called for the cavalry. It was not necessary, but in those circumstances you just have to do what you believe is right, and it certainly did the casualty no harm. We were all just a little concerned that he might be losing his security deposit, because somebody did not have Ed's presence of mind to assess the situation fully and act accordingly.

Carl and Richard arrived back soon after I had settled down. We had some banter about Owen's rescue. To Carlos, Owen had to be a young doctor, as answering the call to help is something done less and less by more mature doctors. The truth is that there is little that a doctor can do in most medical emergencies in the field, which could not be accomplished equally as well by someone with a good knowledge of basic first aid. It is all about preventing the condition from worsening, and promoting recovery. You do not need five or more years of medical training for that. You just need to be able to slap someone in the face a few times and get some fluid down their neck. I would still take my hat off to Owen for being good enough to go and help, and even more so in the knowledge that he really would be limited in what he could do.

Carl and I went off to collect some rocks to hold down the sides of the tent. I was barefoot, as I did not have any flip-flops or sandals, and I was reluctant to put my Salomons back on. That was a bit of a mistake, because there were horrid spiny things that had been blown off some of the plants in the area. Although it was not too much trouble to pull the penny-sized things out of my feet, I discovered soon afterwards that they left parts of the spines as a memento. I did not want to risk infection, and John was gracious enough to use my tweezers to pull out the many splinters. I have a lot of time for someone that will tend to the feet of someone that has not changed his socks for a few days, and has been spending his days running around the Sahara. At least my feet were dry because I had left them out in the air. John did also ask the inhabitants of the bivouac if they had noticed that he had become my bitch, and it was generally accepted that they had. Everybody needs a 'buddy' out here, or a couple of people that you can ask for help. You would tend to say yes, even if you were not happy to, just because you might have to ask them for help later on. Anyway, I was happy that John was my new 'special' friend.

John had been studying the road book for a little while. He then announced that we were not taking part in the 150-mile race that we thought that we were. The actual distance was much closer to 140 miles. I was not a happy bunny.

Me: 'I paid two and a half grand to run *150* miles across the desert!'

John: 'Yeah, bloody fun run!'

After our little laugh at the idea that we had been hard done by, a more insightful and intelligent member of the team (that would be Richard, then) pointed out that the distance varies according to the terrain. I was sure that the elevation of the day's mountain had not been taken into account for the total distance of the day. To me, it seemed that the distances were 'as the crow flies', rather than the total distance travelled. That at least made sense. I was concerned that the huge number of dropouts the previous year might have meant that things were made easier for this year. I really hoped not, because that made no sense to me at all. It was enough in my mind that our water rations had been increased. As I understood it, the huge number of dropouts was due to the English coming along unprepared. We certainly came across as the most 'have a go' contingent, by comparison with some of the more die-hard competitors from other nations.

I had a wander over to one of the comms tents. There are two, one for telephones and faxes, and the other for emailing. I stood in the queue to get into the tent to send an email, and started chatting with Suzi, from Peckham, who was in the queue in front of me. She had been shuffling quite a bit, and her feet were not in the best shape. But, most importantly, she was enjoying herself. Like me, she also currently lives and works in London, and comes across as someone very ambitious in her work and plans for the future. I saw Graham as well, and his feet had just been treated in one of the medical tents. I was just hoping that he would make a good recovery for the morning. Not that it made a huge difference; he would be getting himself through the next day whatever happened, but I would like him to be able to put in the pace that he wants to.

I was in my sleeping bag by 19:30, with everybody back in the bivouac that should be. Selwyn was last in again, but he was a strong man and managing his own pace well. He had been suffering a bit, but that was nothing that some good food, and the experience of the day, would not fix for tomorrow. He was certainly in better shape than a lot of the people in the camp. The sight of the 'walking wounded' was horrendous. It is never nice to see people in pain, and on day two to see people hobbling around and clearly in all sorts of agony, was not a good thing. I was wondering if they would be dropping out, or if they would carry on regardless the next morning, knowing that the latter would be the case for most of them. It was just that mentality. This is such a tough event, and I can imagine that it becomes hell if you are injured and in pain. You then lose so much of your sense of comfort and enjoyment, and then the event becomes a real mission. This is day two, and it will just get harder and harder over the coming days. I could not help but feel sorry for some of them, and incredibly grateful that it was them and not me.

Two days in, my focus was to get through the next, shorter day. That would leave me in a strong position for the long fourth stage. When I am through stage four, I can hopefully have a day off to recover, with 'just' a marathon and a fun run left. To get through stage four well, I would need to start it in as optimal a condition as possible, and that meant one more relatively straightforward and injury-free day. After that, I would drag myself the rest if I had to. What I did know, was that everyone of those walking wounded would be working a lot harder than me, and in need of much greater mental focus and discipline. Again, I took my hat off to them.

My only change to the game plan for tomorrow was to take in more salt tablets. I was pretty happy with my hydration strategy so far, so I did not really consider myself in need of any more. But, realistically, a little more salt would probably be better for me. I would rather take in a little more and see how I get on, especially as I am taking in plenty of water, than risk not taking enough and becoming dehydrated.

Tuesday, 27th March 2007

Stage Three: 32.5 Km

The morning routine was the same as before; deny that it is morning, get out of the sleeping bag at the last possible moment, get my first and then second breakfasts on the go, tend to my injuries, put on the suntan lotion, and ensure that all of the kit is packed accordingly. Once I have collected my water from the checkpoint then I fill up the Platypus.

The morning's briefing carried with it the news that there would be eight fewer competitors starting the race today. There would also be a solar pump at the first checkpoint, for those of us that wanted to use some warm water for a wash. The ridiculous music came over the loudspeakers again, just before the countdown to the start of the race. Weirdly, and indeed annoyingly, that ridiculous music was now already synonymous with the build-up to the day's race. Hence, the music came on and the goosebumps went up. I was getting goosebumps to this nonsense? I have never felt so deeply disappointed in myself in all my life, I am sure. Still, the desert changes a man…

One of the interesting little features of the MdS is that the finish line and start line for the next day's race are one and the same. So, we ran in from one direction to the camp, and this morning we all went back under the finish line so that we could start the day's run in the same direction as we had finished the last. We had already commented on the long open plain that would take us to the first checkpoint. It was going to be another first leg of running towards the rising sun, out across a wide-open plain, and with the mountains off in the distance. The route would be due south, around some hills, with the first checkpoint just at the front of the pass. What is not mentioned in the road book, of course, is that in running across the remains of the previous night's camp, we would also be running across the site of the recently filled-in latrines. In fact, running across the site of the camp introduces all sorts of problems, knowing as we do that most of us went alfresco, at some point in the last twelve or so hours.

I seem to be getting into my running pace a little quicker than before. That might be partially a training effect, and partially a result of the slightly lighter pack. I am also more familiar with the routine now, so I just want to crack on and get into a good position where I will feel comfortable. So, sooner than usual, I am up to my running pace and just settling in nice and comfortably. Today is a shorter day than yesterday, although only by about 2.5 K, but it is longer than the first day and with the same number of checkpoints. The first 5 Ks are nice and flat, with hills then appearing over to our left-hand side. The going is pretty fast, with the ground nice and firm, consisting of small rocks and vegetation. I am used to my timings now as well. 10 Ks can take anything from an hour and a quarter to over two hours, depending on the terrain and hills. But, on an average ground in this race, I can expect 10 K to last between an hour and a quarter and an hour and a half. With the checkpoints varying between 10 K and 12 K, I work out guestimates in my head as to when I can expect to either reach the next checkpoint, or at least to have my first sighting of it.

I pass an old wall with a couple of locals sitting down outside it, and realise that I am running on something equivalent to a main road into a small settlement around an oasis. As I run past the wall, I see the checkpoint, looking stunning, and I run in about an hour and twenty minutes after the day's race started. I notice a few competitors just collecting their water and going straight through, but I am happy to use the opportunity to rest and go through my usual routine. Owen is already there, and Graham comes in shortly after me. Some of the *controlleurs* have taken to drawing pictures on some of our water bottles, which is really quite sweet. Some have also started calling me by my first name from memory, rather than by having to check the race number against their list first. It all just adds to making the checkpoints something to look forward to.

Another habit at the checkpoints is to discuss what we have ahead of us before reaching the next one. Someone has always just studied the road book, and gives the rest of us a run-through of what we have got coming up. We are always seeing the same people, and everything is always positive. Nearly every discussion about the leg we have just finished will have a positive spin on it, and the same about the section ahead. When we ask each other how we are doing, we are always looking to find ways to give each other encouragement and support, which, considering our mental attitudes regarding our own expectations towards ourselves, is a very good thing. We could choose to shut up and just think about ourselves, but most of us choose to take an interest in everybody else. Granted, we might look at people that are suffering and get some relief out of knowing that we are doing better, but I still want those people to make it across the line, and there is then a lot of mutual respect amongst those of us that are really trying hard to push ourselves.

Owen's brother, Tom, is suffering from ITB syndrome, which is putting a lot of stress on the outside of his knee and slowing him down. Whoever is at the checkpoint first, whether it is Owen or Graham, asks the next when the last time was that they saw Tom and how he was doing. As I know the three of them now, I am included in that, and, in fact, Tom is one hell of a strong man. I know how debilitating that injury can be, and even when he is restricted to a walk, he can walk a lot faster than I can. He is also visibly gutted that he cannot move at the pace that he wants to, when some might like the excuse and take it easy, and he just pushes himself to move as fast as he can and give it everything that he has got. He still reaches the checkpoints soon after us on most sections, and quite often I see him ahead of me, even though he should hardly be able to move. It is people like that who give us all a mental slapping. If his body can be under that amount of stress, and if he can just push that to the back of his mind and keep putting one foot in front of the other, then the rest of us have no choice but to do the same. The fact that he can do it at a million miles per hour gets us focussed as well. He is just a really strong character, an absolute animal when it comes down to it, and he will also make it across that finishing line if he has to drag himself across it.

I leave the checkpoint at a walking pace, keeping to the track, and having to squeeze myself past a lorry coming in the opposite direction. I can only imagine what these locals must think when on one day, over seven hundred absolute nutters suddenly start appearing out of the desert, and run through their little oasis, pissing everywhere.

Past the truck, I am back to a running pace for the next 6 Ks. The occasional Landy, or similar, appears along the side of the track, checking up on our general condition. The open plain seems to allow the sun to be focussed in on us, with the dry air trying to leach all of the moisture from my throat. Thanks to the Platypus, there is no danger of that happening, although I do make a point of checking the base of the rucksack every now and again to satisfy myself that the Platypus has not started leaking.

The plain is a salt flat, with the ground having an almost honeycomb appearance, with the cracks seemingly descending through the parched earth forever. There is certainly no question of my being in the desert. There was apparently rainfall shortly before we arrived in Morocco, which allowed a lot of vegetation to appear. The ground is solid now, but there are also rugged plants scratching at us as we run through sections of them. After 6 Ks, the flats end and the incline starts. I had been running towards the competitors ahead, noticing early on how they were walking a snaking route up into the hills, and wondering how far I would get before I too would be walking. I reached the back of the snake and fell into a walking pace along with the others. This is still recovery time for me, so I enjoy it, and it also gives me a chance to look back at where I have been running, check my hydration if necessary, and take a few photos of the surroundings and other competitors.

The salt flat gave way to stony ground, making up the carpet of the hill, and after a slight climb, I find myself struggling along with the others to move up a steep wall of sand. There are times when the going gets really challenging, when some competitors naturally slow down and take it easy, so that they do not work too hard. In my view this is the same principle as walking the MdS instead of running it. It might be a workable strategy that is right for you, but I would rather just crack on and finish the game. Hence, I find myself digging deep and even becoming inefficient, just for the sake of moving past some of these procrastinators. I am not going to finish this race and tell myself that my timing was the result of the other competitors. It can only be the result of how I tackled the race, and that means doing it my way from beginning to end, even if some people might think that I am an arse for tearing past them only to get a few yards ahead.

I reach the top and take a couple of photographs before continuing along and then beginning the descent. I run down from the hills and across the stony ground. There is an open plain to run across, and then a valley through to the second checkpoint. The checkpoints are divided up, four routes in for the first checkpoint, and two routes in for the remaining checkpoints. By 'route', I mean a Land Rover with a flag outside it, and then a small section about three metres long and less than a metre wide, with a sign to indicate which race numbers should be received there. One *controlleur* is sitting under a canvas shade by the Landy and records our number and time; another clips our water card; and another issues one or two water bottles accordingly. I run into the second checkpoint as my new best friend runs to the end of the checkpoint and shouts to me, 'You are a lion!' which was nice. I was out of French witticisms, so I just give her a beaming smile, thank her, then go to see who is sitting around the back of the Land Rover.

Having managed the first two sections of the day quite comfortably, it stands to reason that there is a sting in the tail. There is a significant climb prior to reaching the second checkpoint; it is a big sandy climb and then a lot of hills and sand dunes before reaching the camp. There is a quick run across a riverbed and then straight into it. One climb is about 18 degrees, and full of sand. After the descent, there is still plenty of climbing to be accomplished, although this time on a much harder and rockier surface. Granted, it is the ground that I would usually prefer to walk along, but I am rarely doing what I would 'prefer' to do in this event. Whenever possible I throw caution to the wind and run when I can, walking when I have to. I leave the area of the hills after a big climb and very long descent, and can see the camp in the distance. Before I get there I have got a few Ks of hilly dunes to negotiate - and no gaiters. At least there will be less sand left over for everybody behind me to run through.

Earlier on, when I was pounding the floor of the salt flats, I really felt that I was in an open oven. The sun was beating down on me and the white ground was reflecting it back up. Now I am past that midday heat, but I still feel like I could be in a film, struggling to move, and lost amongst sand dunes, in the middle of nowhere. Then I suck on the mouthpiece of my Platypus, giggle to myself, and start tearing along the dunes. Granted, they sap my energy and I am walking up one side and sliding down the other, but I am moving and enjoying myself. There are other competitors some distance behind me, and a couple of lunatics manage to get past me, but they do not get far ahead. I leave the area of the dunes and pick up my pace along the couple of kilometres of stony ground to the bivouacs.

The bivouacs are up this time, and I collapse in and lay back. It is such a wonderful feeling, just lying there out of the sun, my upper back and head resting against the rucksack, and just cooling down and contemplating the day that has just happened. I am quite content that I have managed to get through the first three days with nothing more than some minor blisters to non-weight-bearing areas of my feet. That means that I am in as good a condition as I could have hoped to make my attempt on the fourth stage of the event. I remove my Salomons, and spend a few minutes evicting sand from above and beneath my Sorbothanes. I then do the same with my socks, taking a moment to appreciate that they really are impressively crusty and solid now. They feel like cardboard.

Carl and Richard are first back again, followed by John. In the spirit of taking an interest in each other's efforts, John asked me if I was off like a gazelle again. I conceded that I had indeed taken off like a gazelle today, albeit a gazelle with four broken legs and a lion hanging on its' back, but I was still having a good stab at it. As the emails were handed out the sad truth was that nobody sent me any messages this evening, which was still, of course, down to me not asking them to, but I still felt that it was a shameful lack of initiative on their part.

The quote of the day very much belonged to Carlos. It went 'Brace, brace, brace, they're going down.' What followed cannot be written, nor really thought of, without a tear coming to my eye and a chilling moment of pure, distilled fear. When the lid went back on the Vaseline, we all exhaled as one.

While I was lounging around this evening, clad in my long-sleeved shirt and North Face beige trousers, Carlos informed me that I looked as if I had just been out hunting big game. Not a bad idea that. I would be quite happy to be out in a hunting lodge somewhere further south on the continent, relaxing after a day on safari. I am not sure how it is that I manage to convey whatever image it is that Carl has of me, but, as I am generally perceived as being comfy and very well at ease, then that has to be a really good and positive thing. I am comfy and I am relaxed. Granted, I would like a nice warm Radox bath, some

338

good food, and a night in with the girlie, but considering where I am, I think that I am feeling as good as can be hoped for.

That really has to be the next biggest thing. If you can get all of your preparation and training in order, and if you can complete the day's runs as you see fit, then the next most important thing is to be really comfortable when your body needs you to recover. I think that I am like that anywhere. I always try to work out what I need to do to make myself feel at home, and most of the time the right clothing, a shelter, somewhere to lie down, and a full belly, are all that I need. I tend to my personal administration first, and then the rest of the day after the race is just about recovering and relaxing. I have got friends all around me as well, which is a huge help. The surroundings are beautiful, and I feel more at home here than I do in London, anyway. Take me anywhere away from a town or city and towards somewhere of real natural beauty and I am happy and at ease. Carl still has not come to terms with me 'lathering myself' outside the tent though. The part when I was cleaning my parts seems to be particularly disagreeable to him.

Wednesday, 28th March 2007

Stage Four: 70.5 km

The key difference this morning was that shortly after the canvas was taken aside, John asked me if the creature behind our heads was indeed a camel spider. Indeed it was. It would seem that it had made itself at home about a foot from our heads during the course of the night. We leapt into action, or rather leapt for our cameras, and chased the poor thing around whilst attempting to get the perfect shot.

Another change for today's run is that, because it is the long stage, the elite runners begin three hours after the rest of us (presumably they then run past us about three and a half hours later). The elite runners are those that finish in the top fifty, and the benefit for us is that it is good to see them run past us, giving us an idea of just how it is that they finish so well.

Today's run is 70.5 Ks (42.2 miles), with the cut-off time being tomorrow evening at 19:00. Hopefully everybody would be safely back long before then. The plan for many of us is to make sure that we get the distance covered before tomorrow, so that we can have a full day off. It would be nice to get it finished before dark, but with it getting dark shortly after 18:30, that is disappointingly unlikely. It is hard to know for sure anyway, because the

Et voila! The humble Camel Spider.

distance itself is not the issue. The issue is the terrain, and any terrain in the desert seems to take at least twice as long to cover as an equivalent distance elsewhere.

Another key difference for today's run was at the start line. The main song at the start was AC/DC's 'Highway to Hell'. It seemed fair, considering. To me though, this day is going to be similar to the last three, just running between checkpoints. The difference is that there are more of them. That is not so bad. I had rearranged my meals for the next few days, as I would not need any Powergels or Kendal mint cake on the last 11.7 km day, so I could use them today. I would also be foregoing second breakfasts for the following days of the race, as they were in a position in the rucksack ready for me to retrieve at the latter checkpoints. Fuel is actually my biggest concern, because I am going to be using a lot of energy getting through today. My rucksack is lighter, and is close to, if not slightly below, 10 kgs (22 lbs) for the first time. My calf is going to be taking a lot of pounding today, but I just need to get through. I imagine that at the end of it, I will be in a far worse state than I am in now, but it is just two more days of exercise after this; a marathon and a fun run, and I will be getting through those.

The countdown in French came to an end and we were across the line. I jostled for position and got into my run. Every day so far had been along a flat to begin with, which gave me the opportunity to warm up and to mobilise my calf, prior to any tough terrain and climbs later on. Today started on a sandy hill, the worst possible ground for me to start running on. This was also 'walking' ground for me historically, but I plugged away. After five or so minutes, I realised that my calf was not playing the game, and I was becoming knackered, however much I wanted to be running. This hill seemed to go on forever, and it was too sandy to run efficiently. Highway to hell? It's in the wrong direction! Well, it was certainly an embuggerance. I could think of nothing better to do than to get into a walk and carry on up the hill. I was being overtaken by lots of other walking competitors. Whenever I change from a running to a walking pace, it always takes me a little while to build up to a respectable speed, and there are just some really strong walkers out here.

I took a pause at the side of the route and checked my hydration. A shout came up from a little way down the slope: 'I see you!' I looked back to see Lee, another fantastic character and a familiar face from the checkpoints, storming up the hill at a fast and strong walk. Satisfied with another successful result from my field test, I started walking with him, chewing the fat and so on. After a couple of minutes of pleasantries, it was time for him to plug back into U2, as he wished to employ their help to get him up the hill. He then proceeded to storm on up ahead of me. Ipod Nano really should sponsor this race. All I had in my mind was the recollection from the Pyrenees - that time when Ross would look at the rest of us and echo that line 'Let's take this fucking hill!'

And off we went.

The hill levelled out and I tried to get to a good shuffle. It was still sand, but I had been walking for far too long. Today is the first day that I have been bothered by my calf, and the toe that had the blood blister also feels particularly sore. During the previous evening's personal administration, I had used a safety pin to try to remove some signs of infection from around the toenail, and it had just felt a bit too unfriendly and uncooperative. I had lost a lot of places in that first climb, and I was in quite a bit of pain. Both were things that I did not appreciate, or want to accept. I told myself that it had probably been like this for the last couple of days, but because I had been running then, I had not had the chance to notice the pain. 'Pain is temporary'... and I *must* run!

So, after a 3-km climb up the highway to hell, I managed to half-shuffle, half-stagger across the plateau, before starting the descent on the other side. The ground was quite stony, and the sort of ground that I would usually go across quite carefully, but that was not on the agenda anymore. I picked up my pace, becoming aware of my now much lighter rucksack, and started running hell for leather down and across the stones. As the ground became sandier, I still managed a reasonable running pace, again pushing myself that little bit harder than I would usually over this sort of terrain. I reached the first checkpoint and gave myself a fifteen-minute break before cracking on. I needed the rest, as usual, to take on the food and water, but I also needed to assess my situation. I had lost a lot of places and would need to pick up the pace to the next checkpoint. I was also amongst people that I do not usually see. The running brought me a fair distance up the field, but I still needed to compensate for all of those places that I lost. Accepted, I am not necessarily racing these other people, but I know in myself where I should be ending up, and it is further up the field than this.

I left the checkpoint and after a minimal walk I was back into my running. The ground was far more favourable than in the first leg, and the sandy areas were not too soft to run on, so I continued to run the shorter and shallower uphill sections, and kept my head down. So down was my head, in fact, that I barely noticed Mark over to my half-right as we neared the summit of a small hill. I kept my head facing him as I ran past, a beaming smile across my face, and we gave each other some friendly encouragement. Deep down, of course, I was thinking 'bugger'; Mark is never usually this far ahead of me, so I must be losing my touch.

The route to the second checkpoint was quite straightforward. Just some slight inclines here and there and generally the same stony ground. We were running to the end of the valley, and this nature of surroundings - the stony ground with hills around us - was becoming very familiar. The route into the second checkpoint took us up a sandy pass between the hills, and I gave myself another fifteen-minute break. On the first day, two checkpoints was the total that we had, after which it was on to the bivouac camp. It was a bit of a concern to think that I had four more to go before that final leg. Still, I was not going to wait around any longer than the fifteen minutes, so off I went.

I ran off the sand of checkpoint two and was soon running across an *oued* (a dried-up riverbed). The ground looks amazing here, like the parched patchwork or honeycomb ground that you often see in films set in the desert, usually shown to demonstrate just how incredibly hot and moisture-sapping it is. A lot of people seem to perceive this image as a sign that it is too hot to run,because I cannot think of any other reason as to why they walk. We are getting towards midday now, and it is hot, and the ground makes it feel hotter, but running on this dry ground is like running on a pavement. There might be

The ground in the *oueds* is almost pure white. Here, the run is taking us towards the dunes and mountains in the distance.

a little more stress going through the joints and connective tissue, but you can run fast on this ground, which is precisely what I am trying to do. The riverbed is not completely flat, as there are small bumps in a wavelike pattern across the ground, together with brush that scratches at the legs. I make my way across it and into short sandy 'hills' on the other side. They are barely significant enough to call hills, but they *feel* significant enough to mention as such.

I make it out of this small area and I am then on flatter ground leading across a plain to sand dunes. Those are proper sand dunes up ahead. They look beautiful, but they also look like great big sand dunes that I will not be able to run through, so I just have to keep my head down again now and run until I get over to them. Again, it is the same thought going through my mind as I approach; at what point are people starting to walk, and can I make it a few more yards, before I have to? It also seems like quite a long way across the plain, and with the heat, it is not necessarily that easy to keep moving at a run, but I have to and I do. I would hate to be walking on sand for a long time, thinking that I should have run further before I got there.

The sand dunes were beautiful. The sand was soft and I was once again in another part of the same film, floundering away as I clambered up the side of the first one. It is great fun in a way, to be struggling up one side of a vast sand dune and then plummeting down the other. I am not quite sure of a better verb to describe how one manages the descent down the side of a steep dune. The shallow ones can just be walked down, but the long steep ones are quite a bit different. If you launch yourself out then you fall quite a long way, as your foot then connects with the sand again and you sink down even further. As you do that you are throwing the other leg out as well. A controlled plummet really is the most efficient way of doing it, although there is a high likelihood that your footwear will get filled in with sand in the process. There is probably no benefit in having your arms outstretched and shouting 'Wheeeeeee', but I seem to find myself doing it sometimes anyway, just in case.

I manage to find some long sections between dunes where I can run a bit, and pass a familiar face, with which I have never spoken before. I greet him and am met with a response of concern, because 'I usually pass him a long time before this'. The cheek of it! I explain that I had passed a lot of people that I would usually be passing in the final leg, so actually it was he that was doing particularly well, rather than me that was doing particularly badly. I did mention the bad start, but he really was the one making the difference. Sean and I walk up and along some dunes together, before I see some good running ground, and wish him luck before I start heading off again. The checkpoint flags are sticking up out of the top of a ridge of sand, and as I clamber up the sand between the flags, I see that the checkpoint itself is just a few yards further on and on some flat ground. I run in, collect my water and glow stick (for the night phase), and sit myself down in the shade behind the Landy.

It is always good to be met by some familiar faces at the checkpoints, and even more so when they are dishing out compliments like 'Here he is, the great man,' and 'Hi there, big fella'. This time a guy comes in laughing and shakes my hand, by way of introduction. He looked as though he was in two minds as to whether or not to shake my hand or if to just have a stab at knocking me out. It seemed that we were constantly passing each other over the last few kilometres, and last few days for that matter. I think that he was either going to introduce himself and be friendly, or else slap me for the sheer annoyance. It is very easy to take it personally when you put in a lot of effort to get past someone, only to have them pick up the pace and run past you. We had been doing this to each other a lot, and it was just down to us doing better on different terrain, so fortunately he decided not to take it personally. I had been doing the same with Ed as well, but he had got some wind in his sail and disappeared ahead of me some time ago.

Lee was at the checkpoint, and had been struggling with his guts a bit, as had I, and I shared out what little toilet paper rations I had left with him. He was also going a bit slow today because of his feet, which were in absolute agony, but other than that and his guts he had no problems at all. We walked

out of the checkpoint together and made our way out of the dunes. Lee had done this race once before, but after a sympathy head start on the last day, due to injury, he was back to make a proper and dignified second attempt. So far, so good. We reached the top of another *oued*, and I let Lee go on ahead as I needed to check my hydration. I then ran out across the *oued*, and left Lee behind, as he needed to check my toilet paper.

The ground on the other side of the riverbed was equally parched, and covered with tamarisk trees. I made my way through, although it was hard to run due to constantly having to pick my way around the trees and brush, and was then on my way up a steep climb. It was another aggressive-looking hill, although nowhere near as high as some of the ones covered so far, but we were all down to a brisk walking pace as we negotiated our way up.

The descent was far more challenging than the climb. It seemed to go on forever as we worked our way down through a narrow, rocky and unstable passage. It is at times like this that you just want to get to the bottom. You might have been struggling to get to the top, but the way down can take an age as you pick your way across the rocks and down along the narrow channel. Also, if the person in front is going slightly slower than you, and there are people charging down behind, then it tends to get a bit tense as we all wait to reach open ground so that we can get into our desired pace. We get there, eventually, and we all spread out as we get to our running speeds. The ground is hard and stony, so aside from the extra care required to prevent one from tripping over, it is relatively good running ground. It continues on, and a few Ks out to the front we have got an area of sand dunes, not as high as the lot before the last checkpoint, but they are still looking quite high and daunting enough.

At 15:10 the first of the elite runners overtook me. I made out the short stature of Lahcen Ahansal over to my left. I looked across at him and started clapping and cheering him on. His pace was fast and consistent. Most annoyingly, of course, it looked 'easy'. He was not struggling, so he was simply fit enough to run at this pace all day long. I was looking forward to seeing him reach the sand dunes, because I knew that he would still be running, but it would be good to see what happened to his pace. Whilst this was going on, I was still running myself, and there were a couple of Brits up ahead of me. I knew what was coming as I prepared to overtake them. Yep, there was no way they would let this opportunity slide. They started looking around, a look on their faces like they were not expecting to recognise me, as they were hoping for the next of the elites. As soon as they clocked that it was me their expression changed and became far more cheerful: 'Come on, mate! Great going! Second place, go on; nip in behind him!!!'

Bastards.

Lahcen's brother, Mohamad, passed next, again to the cheers and claps of the rest of us. It seemed that it did not matter how knackered we were, we still found something to cheer these guys on, probably because we thought that it was important to them. Lahcen reached the sand dunes up ahead and just carried on running. Granted, he did slow down a touch, but then he was running uphill as well, and he was still flying. It all looked impressive, and his training certainly put mine to shame. He was out in this environment all year. He could choose the highest peaks, the softest sand, and the hottest days, and he could run as far as he wanted to. He had access to the exact terrain and exact climate in which he would be competing. You cannot ask for more than that in training.

That is not to play down any of it, because his training would, therefore, have been tougher than ours; and the point is that he gave himself the environment to adapt to in order to become the best athlete in the world, in this race. If I moved out to Morocco and trained every day for a year, then I still would not be close to him, because he has been winning this race for a decade now by training harder than anyone else. But that level of training would put me into the elites, at least. But that is not why I signed up to do this race. I signed up to finish it, and then decided that I would finish it having run as much as I could; and I have ended up coming out here and running all but the toughest ground. And I am loving every minute of it.

I know in my head that once I reach the fourth checkpoint that I will have broken the back of this fourth stage and the race as a whole. I get to the sand and run up the first part of the dune before I am forced back to a reluctant walk. I run down the other side and keep plugging away, trying to keep ticking over at more than a walking pace. It is then during that slow run that the third man of the elites passes me. This one is gracious enough to thank me, and he looks a little more like he needs it. The fourth guy actually applauds me, on the basis that we are all doing well, even if we are only racing ourselves. Or maybe I just look a little bit more ready for the knacker's yard than him.

The fourth checkpoint comes into view and I continue my running pace into the checkpoint. I pick up my water and head over and sit down behind the Landy to my right, as per usual. Having seen that the only guys I know are over by the other Landy, I pick up my water and rucksack and go and sit down on the ground with them. This is team Helmut, an awesome group of guys, out here raising money for Great Ormond Street. The first time I noticed them was the first day at the camp, when I asked Mark about their 'Pain is temporary' slogan across the back of their shirts. Mark then continued the Lance Armstrong quote 'Pain is temporary. It may last a minute, or an hour, or a day, or a year, but eventually it will subside and something else will take its place. If I quit, however, it lasts forever.'

That quote has been with me throughout this race. Whenever I was in pain, I thought about it. Whenever I needed to run a bit faster or was tempted to take an easy route, I thought about it. I thought about what he had been through and it put everything else into perspective. You do not have to be world-class to get something out of it, because it does not really matter; we are all pushing ourselves, and world-class athletes have pushed themselves harder and with greater consistency than the rest of us. But it is all the same sport, in a manner of speaking.

We all greeted each other. Alison was preparing to interview one of them. I had decided that this would be a long break for me. I had matters of personal administration to attend to, namely my feet, so I got them out and let them dry out whilst I made a start on my food ration for that checkpoint. This would be the last of the Kendal mint cake and Powergels for the day. For the next two checkpoints I would have some of my otherwise 'second breakfasts'; the oat-based cereal with milk powder and salt that I just needed to add water to. Oceane, the French *controlleur* who was my new best friend, came around the back of the Landy to see what I was up to and to introduce herself.

We established quite early on that, aside from general pleasantries, we could not really communicate with each other. Her English was rubbish and my French was worse. I probably could have made the effort, but I was more concerned about my feet, and I had much more in common with the people around me than the support crew. 'Team Helmut' were so-called because they had spent a lot of time on detachment in Germany, and one of the guys was so amused by the name Helmut that people started calling him that after a while. This was the first checkpoint where the whole team had been together during the race.

Team Helmut moved on and I finished up attending to my feet. I made a start out of the checkpoint, aware that I was feeling a little less than perfect, but there was still enough fuel in the tank. The ground was flat as I rounded a hill to my right, and I could see the sun making its way towards the horizon to my left. I had spent forty minutes at the checkpoint, which was roughly what I was expecting, although half an hour would have been better. I made my way down a slope, and my feet screamed at me a bit, and I had to go carefully until I was on the flat again. I walked for another couple of minutes and then got into my run again.

The ground was predominantly flat and stony, although at times it would be undulating and sandy, but I would endeavour just to keep to no less than a Saharan shuffle. As the ground evened and hardened out, I was back to my favourite game of drifting past people. The elite runners were still passing us, which made me slightly anxious about overtaking. A group of Scandinavians started shouting at me to cheer me on. As I approached an American who started turning to see who the shouting was for, I beat him to it; 'No mate; I don't know what they're cheering me for either.'

The flat ground was going to give way to hilly ground in a couple of minutes, but I was going at a slow enough run that I would be able to just keep it going regardless. I passed a couple of English competitors, and a woman started cheering me on. I confessed that they should not cheer me as I had started at the same time as them, but I thanked them, anyway. The woman said that they were cheering anyone that was still running at this point, and the guy with her told me that I must be 'very strong'. No, I thought, just very bloody-minded, and the only people that I considered 'very strong' were the elite runners and people like Selwyn. The rest of us were just managing to get through doing whatever we were putting our minds to. And I was too knackered to thank him for being kind.

After the baby hills, the terrain remained much the same all the way to the fifth checkpoint. The only thing that changed for me today was that I was out running as the sun went down. I had left the fourth checkpoint at 16:40, at which time it was starting to get cool. For the first time the sun created shadows across the landscape, the shapes of the hills being stretched and distorted across the ground in front of me. By now it was close to dusk, and the temperature had dropped significantly and in no time at all. It made it easier to work hard, but the coolness against the skin did not feel as pleasant as I thought it would. It just made me feel concerned that the temperature would be dropping further and that when the sun disappeared completely, I would need to get my glow stick in place (which meant another stop, so I hoped that I could tie it into a checkpoint). I could eventually make out the fifth checkpoint in the distance. It was a long and flat track before I reached it, and I was still racing against the falling sun and cooling air. The landscape had become a moonscape. The cold added to that perception.

I ran into the checkpoint to see Team Helmut again and a few other familiar faces, but on the whole there was nobody there, and it was like a 'ghost checkpoint', rather than like the earlier checkpoints where we were greeted with warm smiles and an abundance of procrastinators. By now the mood had definitely changed. It was time to just get the food and water in and get cracking. As one of the Helmut boys put it: 'Just a cheeky half marathon now and we're done.'

A cheeky half marathon. I had done plenty of those in my training, and I knew that on good ground that would only take me around an hour and a half. Whatever was up ahead, however cheeky it became, that was the total horizontal distance left to go. I finished my food and took out the glow stick. I played around with it and managed to tie it into the strapping of my rucksack as best I could, although I was not confident that it was going to stay put.

I left the checkpoint as soon as I could and started running again. The support crews had driven past; attaching glow sticks to the tops of the red-stained route markers, so that we could see our way through the night. It was dark enough that I was straining my eyes to keep a check on the stony ground as I made my way up a slight incline and then past a couple of continentals. I made it about fifty yards past them and then stopped and dumped my rucksack on the ground. I had screwed up a bit. There was no way that I was going to get far without my head-torch on. I started feeling in the top pocket of my rucksack, and the two guys I had just run past were soon next to me shining their torches in to help me out. I did not need them to, because I had always ensured that everything in my rucksack was packed in such a way that I could access it whenever I would need it, with the minimal of messing about. I must have seemed like an idiot to have run past these guys without a torch on in the first place though, so I was grateful for the camaraderie. I put the torch on and continued running, slowly.

I could see the glow sticks of about twenty competitors up ahead, moving steadily along the track. I knew that Team Helmut was amongst them, and I was hoping that I would be able to catch them up, but I also knew that they were moving at a good pace towards the next checkpoint and I would have my work cut out to reach them. As the time went by, the sun disappeared and the stars came out. The sky looked beautiful and as I found myself in a walking pace to get up a particularly long uphill, I gazed up at the constellations. The glow-worm was still up ahead of me and I was chasing after it, although it seemed that my chances of catching up were becoming slimmer and slimmer. There were still elite runners passing, although by this stage it was hard to know if they were only elite runners or a combination of elite runners and nutters like I had been. But I did not have that in me anymore. I had noticed that my feet had swollen a lot.

Most people had mentioned that they had brought footwear one or two sizes up to allow for their feet to swell, but I could not because I have big feet and a size up was not available. Now I was starting to struggle. My toes were squashed and the slight impact of running was really starting to hurt. As I came down the other side of the hill, the wind starting howling across the moonscape and the sand was tearing at my skin and eyes. I remembered Richard's comments about the number of soldiers in Iraq with corneal damage from the sand, and I felt that there was nothing that I could do but hope that I would not be affected.

This was starting to become horrible now. The wind carried a chill. I remembered my first visit to Egypt, for the Millennium, and an Egyptian friend warning me of how the cold feels different in the desert. It is a different kind of cold. It chills the bones. It had never made sense to me at the time that I was told, but I had duly taken my fleece along with me that night by the pyramids. I think that it is because of the dry air that the cold feels different, and I was beginning to really notice that cold now. I had tried to hold my sunglasses against my face to protect my eyes from the sand, but even with the head-torch on there was not enough light to make out the details of the ground. The wind was blowing at my shirt and I buttoned up the front and the cuffs.

I half-staggered across an area of sand before I was out on the stony ground again. I managed a Saharan shuffle past one guy, who had annoyed me by not returning my greeting as I passed him, but before long I was back to a walk again. My feet were throbbing and I was not having a good day out. I looked up at the sky, trying to derive some pleasure out of something, and I started thinking of home and my girlfriend. I recalled that every time that I had gone out somewhere on my own, whether it was the overnight walk in the Peak district, the couple of days in Snowdonia, or my mad day out across the Egyptian Sahara, I had always known where I was, how far I had to go; and I had my contingencies for when it was time to call it a day. None of that was available to me now. I was playing at somebody else's game, to somebody else's rules, and all that I could do was to keep putting one foot in front of the other. Pain is temporary.

The guy I had just passed came striding past me and headed up the next hill. I was feeling pathetic and annoyed with myself. I needed to be running, but I just believed that if I ruined myself tonight then I would not make it through the next marathon stage. I still needed to leave something for that, even if it was just the last layer of skin on my toes. I reached the top of the hill to find the guy that had just passed me standing there. He looked at me and asked me if I knew where we were supposed to go. We could not see any markers, and there was nothing to give us a clear indication of direction. We could just work off a bearing, but there is a danger that if you start slightly off course, then you might miss the checkpoint by a few hundred, or even just tens of yards, and then just walk on lost through the night. I switched off my head-torch and scanned the horizon. My instinct was to carry on along that original bearing, and sure enough I could make out the faintest of glows against the night sky, just below the horizon. I pointed it out and explained that it was the glow of the group up ahead, and with that I switched my torch back on and started running, pounding the ground to make up the distance.

It was clear by now that I did not stand any chance of catching up that group ahead, but I still wanted to be working as hard as I could, even if just for myself. I got to the bottom of the hill and started my way up the next one. By now this guy was hot on my heels. Either out of respect or out of embarrassment for getting lost, he was not going to overtake me. I was walking fast now, probably the fastest I have ever walked, and either he could not get past me or else he had resolved not to. There is always the concern that ego will take you past someone, and then you will not be able to keep that pace, and then you lose pride when you find yourself behind them again.

I was near the top of the next hill. This guy was still there, a couple of paces behind me, and somebody else had caught up as well. I was chin-strapped. I was plugging away, and I was a million miles from giving up, but I was just not having any fun anymore. It was one of those times when you just need someone to press on with, something to act as your wingman to share some of the crapness with so that you can help get each other through. I stepped off to the side and turned to face him, trying not to blind him with the light of my head-torch. 'Alright, mate? How are you doing?'

He was also feeling friendlier this time around, and we introduced ourselves. I had to confess to Scott that I had a severe case of the munchies for a Mars bar. The big slabs of chocolate that I had bought at W. H. Smith's at Gatwick were sitting in my suitcase, and I would dearly love for those to be with me right now. I could almost taste the chocolate in my mouth. A curry would have gone down quite nicely as well. Scott and I kept the banter going. At the back of my mind I was sure that the 12 Ks to the final checkpoint were the longest 12 Ks I would ever travel. It was as if every K wanted to make a point to me.

Scott and I walked into checkpoint six, and I took off my rucksack to get my fleece out. I also took off my race number from my T-shirt, did up all the buttons on my shirt, tucked it all in, then put the fleece on over the top, and attached my race number to the front. Another competitor came in, a young woman whom I had seen a lot of on the race, always doing well and pushing a good pace. She asked us if we were ready to go on, but I said that I still wanted to get sorted first, and Scott kindly asked if he could crack on then. As those two left, Graham and Lee arrived. Ye Gods, it was good to see them! Graham dished out the morphine, but I was fine as I was. The pain was a nightmare inside my Salomons, but I would rather not be without it. Pain is a good indicator of what is going on in the body, and as much as it can be an annoyance, I would rather put up with it than be numb. But then, as I explained earlier, I came off painkillers the morning after my hernia operation, and lived in pain for a week, because I did not want to risk damaging my liver by taking unnecessary pharmaceuticals. However, I am a bit weird, I suppose.

Lee headed off straightaway, having reminded me that he still owes me some toilet paper, whilst Graham sat himself down and started getting himself sorted. I suggested that we could rest in a bivouac that had been put up, if he wanted, just to get out of the gale for a couple of minutes, but the back of the Landy was fine for Graham. I finished my food and we were both set to continue. It was cold but I was still taking in the water and salt, because it is very easy to neglect hydration when it is cold, and I was making a habit of drinking whenever I could, especially when I did not feel that I needed it. The thirst response is useless. One or two gulps of water can quench thirst, but by the time you are thirsty you are already a half a pint of water for the worse. Hence, you can begin a snowball effect by which the body becomes more and more dehydrated, but you do not realise because you are continually taking in pathetic quantities of fluid.

Graham and I left the checkpoint together. His feet were far more screwed than mine, but at least his morphine would kick in soon and he would be floating into the camp. It was just 6 Ks left now. That was half of what we had just done, but then that had seemed to take forever, and I did not want to go through any of that again. Still, it was the last leg of the stage, after which I was set to climb into my sleeping bag, prepare some food, and then get my head down for a good night's sleep. I was also on track as regards getting the sleep in today, and giving myself a full day off tomorrow. Those thoughts were going to make these last 6 Ks a lot easier to pass. The most comfort I had though was having Graham with me. He had been a familiar face from day one, and it was good to actually chat with someone about what they do when they are not running around in the desert, about work and about home.

As the ground became more undulating, eventually changing into sand dunes, we were having to check the compass to make sure that we were still on track. The markers were very difficult to see because they were so far apart. The glow of the sticks would also be lost in the hills, because if you were in a trough, then it was hard to distinguish a glow stick on the crest from all the stars behind it. We also saw other competitors struggling with the same problem. On a couple of occasions there would be a couple of people in different areas of the horizon, searching for the way on, and we would either work out which way was the most likely route, or else just head straight between them and work it out from the top. We saw one guy off to our right who seemed way off course, but as he was heading generally in the right direction, I was confident that he would be okay. The bivouac camp came into sight after a few kilometres, which made me feel a million times better. It was not a straight line there though, and we still needed to get out of the hills. The bivouacs and tents came and went from view, and it almost felt as if we were not getting any closer, but we *were* getting closer, and at some point acceptably soon we would be marching into camp.

There was one last climb up a sand bank before we reached the camp, but it was close enough now to touch and there were people from the camp that had wandered out in our direction. We staggered up the sand bank and crossed the line together. We were not going to hold hands or anything, and we were relatively reluctant to be the first one to put our foot across the line, but I was knackered and if I did not walk over the line then I would fall over it. Our times were recorded equally though, and our placings the same. We had just made it into the top three hundred again, but it had been my worst day in terms of where I came overall. Still, considering the pain and amount that I had walked over the last two legs of the stage, it would have to do.

We crossed the line at 22:40, collected our water, thanked each other for the help in getting through that last leg, and headed off to our respective bivouacs. Once again I was first man home, and I dumped my kit before heading off for a final hydration check. The buggers had put the camp in an area surrounded by a sand bank, so I had to stagger up all eight foot of it, there and back, in order to go to the toilet. That was very unfair considering what we had all just been through. I got back to the bivouac, removed my Salomons and socks, and climbed into my sleeping bag. My feet were no doubt a disaster, but I would have a whole day to fix them tomorrow. I was tired enough that I could have just closed my eyes and fallen asleep, but I was disciplined enough to get my hexi-stove on the go and cook up some dinner.

I lay there with my arm outstretched to stir the glop, occasionally leaning closer to feel the warmth of the fuel tablets and to try to concentrate on stirring enough to keep myself awake. I got through the mountain of food and moved the stove and other cooking kit off to the side. I thought about the day just past, and my relief at having finished it, and was impressed for a moment that I had managed to cook my food before settling down to sleep. It had been superb to see the elite runners pass us, although I had not seen one of the Brits whom I had been looking out for amongst them. It had been great crossing the line with Graham. I would have had a really tough night out if it had not been for him and Scott. I wondered about who would be the next back to the bivouac, and whether any of the guys would sleep out at one of the checkpoints, which a lot of them had discussed. Nothing could have made me want to trade staying out on the course with being sorted out at the camp and knowing that I have a full day off tomorrow. I rested my head on the rucksack and quickly, peacefully, fell asleep.

Thursday, 29th March 2007

Stage Four: 70.5 Km (Continued)

01:40

Richard and Carlos arrived back at the bivouac. I think that John also came in at this time, but, as I am never fully conscious until the afternoon, I did not stand much chance of getting any clarity of thought for some time yet. I stirred from my slumber and awoke to greet them and check that they were doing well. It was good to know they were back and safe. I checked up on the others, but they had not been seen since much earlier on in the day. Safe in the knowledge that they would not be spending the night out on a checkpoint, and had indeed completed the longest stage of the race (just a marathon and a fun run left!), I went back to sleep.

08:00

Mark arrived back. Again, he had been quite happy with his completion of the fourth stage, and made himself comfortable whilst I, true to form, continued to do bugger all until it was warm enough to emerge from my sleeping bag an hour later.

The morning routine would obviously be a bit different today, as we would be staying at the bivouac camp, and I was very much planning on an easy day. I hobbled over to Doc Trotter's first tent. There were two medical tents. If you could administer your own treatment, then they would give you the tools to do so (a scalpel, gauze, iodine, plasters, elastoplasts, and paper sheet for cutting your feet open on were all the rage at this tent). If you were in a slightly worse state, then you would be directed to the local butcher's (the second medical tent), where they had a simple means of dealing with problem areas, which was essentially to cut them off. Either way, whatever was left of you would be thrust into some blue sterile foot coverings, and you would be sent on your way.

This was usually quite a slow process, especially if retreating from the second tent. The lovely Sophie had a play around with my toes and then brought me the kit. I had managed to find a rickety stool to sit myself on, and in a couple of minutes I had become Zorro of the Silver Scalpel, and was giving an Australian tips on how to administer treatment to his own feet. Curiously, he had never treated a blister before in his entire life, which just suggests to me neglect during his upbringing. He had this 'lost sheep' look about him as he just sat there with his paper sheet, holding onto his scalpel blade, then looking across at me to see how I was getting on (waving the blade around in the air and trying my best not to decorate the interior of the tent). I calmed down and helped him out, until Sophie arrived and told him what he should be doing, and to ignore the homicidal Englishman in the corner.

I made my way back to the bivouac, greeting the others on the way. It was unusual, and a little disconcerting, to realise that the camp was nowhere near full yet, and so many people were still out on the course. I did not feel sorry for them at all, they were just doing their own thing, but I was silently wishing them all the best, and hoping that they would be making it back in soon.

Just after 11 o'clock we were all called out to the area in the centre of the bivouac camp for an announcement. Tent 99 stayed put, partly on the grounds that we were perfectly positioned to see and hear everything from where we were, and partly because the miserable bugger that *told* us to go there had been so impolite. I also refused to move because I did not want to aggravate my feet by moving around on them any more than I had to. Whilst we waited for everybody to arrange themselves in the centre of the square, we pondered what the reason for the announcement could be. Not everybody was back yet, so it made no sense for a general briefing.

Patrick and Alison climbed on top of a Landy and started off with the sad news. One of the competitors, a Frenchman from Brittany called Bernard, had passed away. There was a lot of detail about his health checks and how everything seemed to be fine, which later bothered us a bit because it sounded more like a 'CYA' announcement rather than one whose mood should have been nothing other than sympathetic. Bernard was 49 years old, only a few days short of his 50th birthday, and had arrived back at the camp in 45th position. He awoke at 3 am to greet his friends across the line, and then having returned to sleep, he could not be woken. It made sense to suppose that he had died of an M.I., but despite what Patrick had told us about his E.C.G., we knew nothing of any aspect of his health or lifestyle, and it was ridiculous to speculate as to how it had happened.

Whatever the actual cause, it was likely that it would have led to his death at some point in the future, if it had not been triggered earlier by his incredible performance in the race yesterday. It was a shame, in the sense that it was so impressive to have finished in such a high position, which meant he had put so much training into his preparation. It was also a shame that he was leaving his family behind him and that they were not with him when he died. I doubt that anybody could complain about anything for the rest of the race now. A minute's silence followed the announcement, and I was sure that thoughts would be spared for Bernard before the run tomorrow.

We all sat back for a bit and had a chat about the news, just trying to get our own perspectives clear in our minds. With so many people in the tent having a medical background, or working closely in medicine or being with people that worked in medicine, the concept of death being a part of life was one that did not require any emotional adjustment. It was sad that it had happened, although it would have happened, anyway. I felt that it was a sad reflection on the race, because with only a little over 700 competitors now left in it, everybody seemed to recognise everybody else. When a number of competitors died during the Great North Run in 2005, it was sad that it had happened, but amongst so many thousands of competitors, it is likely that very few people would have known them from the field. In a race like this, I knew that the guy had run past me four days in a row and I would have noticed him.

Anyway, before long the subject had changed and we were back to the normal banter. Films, medicine, Monty Python and penis jokes prevailed. I decided to wash myself using a clean sock that I had been carrying around with

THE MARATHON DES SABLES

me. I put some water in a clean and empty food bag, rubbed some soap in, and then used the sock as a flannel. As per usual, Carlos ('of the Platinum Scalpel and Golden Hands') strongly disapproved of the attention paid to my nether regions, more on principle now than general displeasure (although that was still significant). I finished cleaning myself and then proceeded to clean the socks that I had been wearing for the past week. I hung them on one of the bivouac's guy lines and went off to collect my water ration for the day. The lovely Oceane felt compelled to comment on the fact that I was still so pale, which my compatriots put down to simply good admin. The T-shirt and shirt that I had been wearing every day but today had also done well to stop my chest seeing any sun until this point, and as I was spending most of today in the tent, nothing much would change today either.

Selwyn made it in at 15:30. He had got some sleep in on the course, and arriving back he seemed more concerned about some sores on my shoulders than anything to do with himself. He really was a good man. He seemed completely nonchalant about the whole affair, and once again he looked how he sounded, which was absolutely fine. He told us that one lad had been told to quit the race or else he would lose a couple of toes (one can only hope that he meánt through injury). From his perspective, he had certainly seen people in more trouble than me. He had also managed to get himself slightly lost, which was not at all difficult on the night phase of that course. The last person came in around 16:00.

The emails were dished out at 16:15. I received only one, although a very welcome one it was:

Tente N° 99

Dossard N° 685 : Hines

De: bianca … … - le : 27/03/07 22:09:06

how are you?. hey sweety!! Hope you are good!!! I don't think that you will check your mail, but I will just send you one anyway. Good luck, you are almost finished!..mwha xxx

---

Almost finished my arse. Well, it was nice to hear from her. That was my only message, which was entirely my fault as I had not let people know about the system. We were also restricted to one email per night, of no more than 1000 characters, to take no more than fifteen minutes to type and send, on a French laptop with quite confusing characters if you are not used to them. I think that the French keyboard is more difficult to use than the Turkish keyboard, and that is saying something. We also do not have Internet access, so we cannot check our emails, nor can we check the email addresses of our friends. Some people are making calls with their mobiles, which is quite impressive, and I only hope that it is not to work. I am not planning to use my mobile in any case, partly because I disagree with the concept of using one out here, and partly because of the fear of receiving messages from work. John only received fifteen messages from his friends - who were sending him messages every night - so that was nice for him. Git.

In point of fact, I had managed to read my message twice over, which I then read to everybody in the tent, read to myself again, wrote some notes on how devastated I was on receiving only one, whilst John was still very much reading through all fifteen of his for the first time. He did feel it necessary to share with me the fact that he had received fifteen messages, which was kind of him. I did think that I should at least have told my mother about the communications set-up here. It would have been nice to hear from home.

On a brighter note, my Salomons were doing quite well. John certainly seemed to think so. The others just seemed a little more than concerned that we did have this tendency to smell each other's footwear. It can be very monotonous in the desert sometimes. Trying to ascertain and qualify the sensory enigma of shoes that have covered over a hundred miles in the desert can be quite exciting, in a way, fraught with danger as it might be.

I decided to mix things up a little today by going to a latrine, rather than going alfresco, although it did reaffirm my belief that the open air is the only way of truly appreciating a quality bowel release. On the way back, and possibly without sharing my thoughts on that subject, I helped Suzi up the sand bank so that she too could go and take delight in the 'facilities'. Before doing so we exchanged some banter on the previous day's adventure. As ever, it was always pleasant, positive and encouraging. There was lots of mutual interest in how we were doing, and lots of encouragement. Suzi was in very good spirits as well, which I had come to expect from her, even though my reason for helping her up the sand bank was that her feet were so shot she would have been crawling otherwise.

Today was a great day for lying around and talking to the guys in the tent. Richard is a fantastic character. Anyone can tell at once that he is clearly a man of distinguished good taste, a man of class and style that is duly worthy of respect and admiration. These exact same qualities can also be thought of when in the company of Carl, although in this case it is by contrast Carl's carefree absence of any of them. Carl (very much the Zorro of the surgical world) is the thinking man's best friend, provided that the thinking man in question is generous with his own sense of humour and does not object to conversations based entirely on his fascination with feet. They are both easily recognised for their contrasts, and either of them would be a prime candidate for the position of being the world's most wanted 'Best Man'. Both have the sort of contagious positive outlook that presents everything as being beneath them (because *it is*). However I do have to consider, that even amongst Carl's incessant jokes on the colour of Richard's hair, that Richard knows Carl is far enough beneath him for it not to be worthy of concern. Carl, by contrast, knows that Richard can think whatever he likes, because at least Carl will never be ginger.

After a brief respite at the bivouac, I made my way back over the sand bank and found an area that was relatively devoid of rocks and stones. I really wanted to have a good crack at the marathon stage tomorrow, but my legs were getting tight and I was not running fast enough. I needed to teach myself how to run properly again. Up until now my running had been in a pattern that compensated for the heavy rucksack. When I start running tomorrow, my rucksack will be comparatively very light indeed, and I should attempt a much faster and more upright posture.

I threw my top on the ground to my side, and used it as a marker along with a bush up ahead, and started doing some sprints, followed by some mobility work and then some stretching. It dawned on me that it was not particularly normal to be out in the heat and doing this sort of thing, certainly nobody else was, but I knew that for me this was the best thing to do. I felt much improved afterwards - especially my calf - although I realised that I would have to do more to release the tension again in the morning. Realistically, my muscles were tight, my feet were passable although not brilliant, but my pack was so much lighter. I really want to get a good place tomorrow, but then I expect that a lot of people will be after the same thing.

What looked like a checkpoint was set up in the square in the middle of the camp. We were informed that we needed to collect new race numbers for the marathon stage, because that was going to be 'press day', and apparently brand spanking new race numbers would make all the difference. What was a nice touch was that we were also issued with a cold can of cola. I hate cola. I really, really, derive no pleasure whatsoever from cola. I do not like the taste, and I do not like how nasty it is for the teeth and pancreas. The point that I am trying to make here, and I fear that it may be getting lost, is that I just do not like cola. But it was cold. It was the only cold thing that I had touched in the heat of the day, and that made it feel like the nectar of the gods. It was for that very reason that I actually drank it, just for the principle of the thing and the gratitude towards the guys, who thought it would be a nice touch. And it was a nice touch, in fairness, because it was so unexpected.

The rest of the day followed the usual pattern. I ate, and when I finished eating I went to sleep. That is a good end to any day for me. All that was left was a marathon and a fun run.

Friday, 30th March 2007

Stage Six

Marathon Stage: 42.2 km

So, this is going to be it. The last day of running before the fun run to the finish line. As a full marathon, it will be the longest, except for the fourth stage, with three checkpoints before the last bivouac camp. There are a lot of unknowns today. I did my movement work yesterday because I want to have a good run, and my fastest run of the whole race. My kit is a lot lighter, and I binned the last of my Beanfeasts, much to the rejoicing of my tent mates (and my guts, which would have written a 'thank you' card if they could). I collected the water ration and put two litres into my Platypus, along with some of my homebrew energy and electrolyte drink.

The plan for today is to run the checkpoints, as usual, but to limit the time at each one as much as possible. One of today's key unknowns is what everybody else will be doing. The course today is a fast one, save for some sand dunes, so whilst some people will put in the same effort as usual, some, like me, will be really going for it. Some, unfortunately, would be fairing a lot worse than they would like, on account of injuries and so on.

There was a good atmosphere as we made our way to the start line. We had broken the back of the race now. Just this marathon and that fun run left and then it would all be over. We had the usual briefing, and the thanks were given to the competitors who had placed stones at the site where Bernard had passed away the day before. The guys that had shared a tent with Bernard were asked to lead everyone out at the start of the race, to which, understandably, nobody objected. The birthday announcements were made and then the ridiculous songs blared out, before the penultimate countdown of the event.

As we spilled out again over the start line, I found myself back in my usual pace and making progress along the first few hundred yards of the course. I concentrated on extending my stride and getting out of the usual semi-shuffle that I was starting off in. This was why I did the work yesterday, but four stages of running with kit were forcing me into my former running pattern. I put my mind to it and managed to extend my stride and run with a more upright posture, at the same time increasing my pace. So far, so good.

We reached an *oued*, with the sand-coloured ground giving way to the whiter, more compressed ground. We were barely into it and there was a bottleneck. A steep bank of a few metres led down into a trough, and people were almost queuing to take the easiest route. I spotted a couple of others that had picked their way through the bushes and had found a steeper, but otherwise clear, section of the bank. *Controleurs* were rushing to get ropes attached, but we were not going to wait for them. I have slid off a glacier in the Pyrenees before, lying back on my rucksack like an inverted tortoise, and flying off the ice onto a gravel surface further down below. So, a couple of yards here was not likely to be an issue. So we slid down one side and then ran across and

372

charged up the other. My mind drifted to thoughts of wildebeest managing their impressive river crossings further south, possibly with a touch more grace than us lot.

The *oued*s created some excitement like that. Even if it is just the gently undulating, wave-like riverbeds, punctuated with brush, that irritate the skin, it gives you something to think about and concentrate on. With alternatives such as 10 Ks of open plain, the *oued*s made a welcome change. In this particular case, it was trying to slow us down, but it was the start of the race so we all seemed to rise to the challenge and charge on. The wildebeest could have learnt something from us.

We left the riverbed proper and made our way out across a salt flat, the only indication of a lake that had once been here. Once at the other side, we ran across a track and followed another branch of a riverbed further on. The route then led across sandy ground between hills, and I took the opportunity to note that there were a lot of runners around me whom I have not noticed before. There are plenty whom I do recognise, some of whom I have passed far earlier today than on previous stages, and it all shows that today is a very different beast to that to which we have become accustomed. In my mind I just try to control my quicker pace, not allowing myself the pleasure of moving past runners that are already running at a good pace themselves. I have four legs to get through today, so there is no point ruining myself before the first checkpoint. I check the time and try to work out when I should expect to see that first set of flags and Landies. The leg has been pretty fast so far, and I am running at a faster pace over ground where I might usually take it a little easier.

I am feeling the heat and I let my mind switch off from what is going on around me. The runner in front is going at a good speed, which seems identical to mine, so I just allow myself to keep with his pace, and then let my mind wander to other things. I think about getting over the finish line tomorrow, and start singing to myself and going off into my own little dream world. My gaze is fixed on the guy in front, so as I start to switch off from it all and start daydreaming, everything stays just fine.

I round a hill to my left and there is a long open plain before a short climb to the checkpoint. I get to the CP and go through the usual procedure, although it is restricted to well within five minutes, and then I am off again. The next 8 Ks are pretty flat, with good ground, so I just keep the pace going. I question myself about not taking a rest at the checkpoint, but I feel good and I just keep going. I am still taking in my isotonic fluids through the Platypus, and I am not feeling unusually hot or tired. But then that is the old quandary. I feel 'alright', but if I felt like this at work then I would have the day off, but considering I am in the fifth day of racing and managing myself towards the halfway point of a marathon in the Sahara desert, 'alright' seems perfectly appropriate and accurate.

I head across another *oued* and into the sand dunes. They are not much in terms of height, but they still slow the pace right down again. I get out the other side of the dunes and head across a flat punctuated with yet more dunes. The second checkpoint comes into sight further into yet another area of sapping dunes. I use the same strategy as before, pausing for only a few minutes whilst I take in some water, Powergel and Kendal mint cake, and then I carry on, making use of the minimum of rest.

The ground today was generally much flatter and consistently easier terrain to run across. John and Selwyn (above) were doing their bit, in their own way, to keep the British end up and put in a good effort on the last 'proper' run.

I leave the checkpoint and am back into the dunes. I am at a walking speed, although trying to move as quickly as I can, but it is always a sluggish pace compared to what I would like. These dunes do not compare with some of the others that we have been through in terms of height, but we are still climbing up and running down the other side, still sinking deep in and having to work hard to get anywhere. I am just recovering from a climb and descent, in the middle of a trough between shallow ridges, when a shout goes up right behind me: 'Oi! Cunt face! I wish you'd get the bloody hell out of my fucking way.'

I turn around, bemused, to see Carlos right by my left shoulder. I am absolutely delighted to see him, sharing a moment as Richard comes down from the last ridge directly behind him. I comment that it is good to see that they have discovered running, and following a brief catch-up, they carry on ahead of me. Although perhaps I should be a little disheartened to have them overtake me, I am not at all, and am simply very happy that they are pushing such a strong pace. I have been putting in my biggest effort today, and with them walking every day up until now, I find myself happier to see them doing well than I am disappointed to have them pass me. Which is awfully jolly of me, considering.

I get out of the dunes and pick up my pace across harder ground. Once again, the ground becomes punctuated with dunes, but they are not enough to slow me down, and I reach the third checkpoint to see Richard and Carlos waving as they leave. Oceane greets me in and seems impressed with my progress, and I see a few of the other regulars at the checkpoint as I arrive. Lee is amongst them, and dutifully hands me some toilet roll and apologises for not getting it to me the previous night. It had not been an issue because Selwyn was carrying around a whole roll with him, and he had been quite happy to let me take some of his.

Meanwhile, back at the checkpoint, it is once again down to a few minutes as I take in some water, some salt tablets, and the last third of my Kendal mint cake. I consider refilling my Platypus, as it must be getting low, but I decide that I can work around it. Instead of taking in two or three gulps of fluid every time that my mouth is dry, I will ration myself to just one at a time, although I will not restrict how often that will be. Having just consumed a litre of water, along with some salt, and apparently being perfectly well hydrated, I believe that I can cross the line with something left in the Platypus, and even if I drain the bag a kilometre or two away from the finish line, I will still be in a good state of hydration and will have nothing worse than a dry mouth. Today is the last proper day, and I need to keep light, so I believe that I can do this without any significant compromise on hydration.

That decision only took a few seconds to arrive at, and I have been giving it thought from when I first analysed the road book for this stage the day before. As I leave the checkpoint, I am thinking about the strategy. I need to keep a light pack to be able to run fast, but if I become dehydrated by even one per cent, then my performance will decline, and I will be running slower. I have to get it just right, but I think that I have and will. The checkpoints have been coming up thick and fast today, because I have been running faster

between them, and it will be about an hour to the finish line, just a cheeky 11 kilometres further on ('cheeky' this time because most stages are made up predominantly of 10.5 K sections).

The ground is firm and even, and so far I have not drained the Platypus, although it is still a slight concern. Over to my half-left I see a range of beautiful, almost mountainous sand dunes rising up out of the ground. They are beautiful. They are stunning. They are the bastard sand dunes that I will be running across for 6 km to the finish line tomorrow. Fun run? Bloody hell. I run down from the plateau, with the bivouac camp about 5 kilometres off to the front. The ground is still firm, although slightly undulating, but with the occasional gulp of isotonic drink still keeping me going, I feel good to get there in fine form. I keep the speed consistent for the first few kilometres and then pick up my pace a little for the last two. As I approach the line I see a few competitors sitting around the area by the finish line, which is a first, and then I start hearing them cheering me on. Today is just that sort of day; people are putting in their best efforts, and then the others are giving that extra support in acknowledgement of it. As I begin to wonder if Richard and Carlos are there, I hear my name shouted out and make it a dignified sprint finish across the line.

I check my position and find that I have come in 260th place, which is not that great, but is the result of so many people having a different run today than they have done before. A lot of people save themselves for the marathon stage, rather than risk burning themselves out beforehand and then having a terrible day out. I met Owen at the finish line, and thanked him for giving me the encouragement to get across the line. After some brief banter, I head around to the area where a few other competitors are cheering the others on. Richard and Carlos are not there, so it was only Owen who was calling my name, which made me appreciate his efforts there even more. I go over and have a chat with one of the *controlleurs* who made some eye contact with me and whom I had not seen before, and then congratulate an English woman who came in over the line. She had been walking every stage up until now, and had then pulled this fantastic performance out of the bag today. I finish socialising and head off to find the bivouac. Richard and Carlos were indeed sitting on their arses doing nothing much when I arrive: 'Wankers!'

Richard begs my pardon but I am quickly excused, when I point out that it was my understanding that it was indeed an accurate comment, particularly in light of our discussions and tent rules that had followed. It transpired that their superb effort today was the result of them realising that they reach the checkpoints much quicker if they run. It does concern me sometimes that people's very lives are in their hands. In kind, Carlos briefly apologised for his onslaught of abuse, simply claiming that it was the most abusive thing he could think of at the time. And it is the effort that he therefore put into it that makes it mean all the more to me.

I had finished the race at about a quarter to three, and now I have a nice long evening to recover, although the feeling that it was all over was already beginning to dawn on me. There really was not very much left to do. The sand dunes look horrendous, but there are about five and a half Ks of flat ground before we get to them, and one way or another I am going to be making it across that finish line tomorrow. I take off the Salomons and have a look at my feet. There are some impressive blisters, but all restricted to non-weight-bearing areas of my toes, and all due to me not being able to buy a pair of Salomons a size up. I am impressed that they have done so well. Over a thousand miles of running covered in training, as well as the MdS, and I only really had problems of any significance after a hundred miles of the race.

Having cleaned my feet, I decided not to do anything to treat them, and just left them to the air. Tomorrow I will be having a proper wash. A wash! The very idea seems almost alien, like a beautiful dream becoming a reality. The need for a shower is higher on my list of priorities than proper food, which is really saying something, especially considering how much I long to get proper food in. I am happy with today's run. It had been good from the start, and I had run over ground that I typically would not have over the first few days. My feet were not great, but they did not really bother me, and my normally restricted pace extended quite favourably after the first few hundred yards. It was all good.

We were informed that there would be a concert at the camp in the evening, care of a Paris orchestra. I welcomed that news very happily. My concern was that Selwyn might not be back in time for it. I went through my usual routine of getting the food in, and had a good chat with the guys. It was a nice and relaxed atmosphere now, and there were no concerns about the next stage. It became apparent that I would have to drain the fluid out of a blister on the side of my big toe, as there was a lot of it there, and I would be struggling to get my feet into my Salomons tomorrow if I left it like this.

As the evening drew on, it was four and a half hours after I finished the run, and I still could not bend any of the toes on my right foot, save for the big toe. My third toe had become swollen, most probably due to the culmination of small amounts of impact to the heads of the bones, now that my feet had swollen to be squashed against the front of my shoes, and somewhere along the line the inflammation was such that they had all decided to have the hump with me. I kept trying to move them, but it was not happening. It was a concern, but I would still be getting through tomorrow, and after that all that I have left to do is heal.

It was around eight o'clock that the concert started. Richard and Carlos made their way over there, but Mark and John had resolved to stay put. I was going to give that tactic a go as well, as my feet were still a little sore, but when it became apparent that I would not be able to hear the concert from the bivouac, I decided to make a move over there. I greeted Richard and Carl and stood and watched the performance. The Paris orchestra played a number of short pieces, and we had performances from soloists as well. When one refused an encore on the grounds that 'they had travelled a long way and were tired', we jeered back and generally had a good giggle at the very idea. That could easily be written down on any list of things not to say to people that had got this far in the *Marathon des Sables*. Dutifully, the band played on. We enjoyed Brahms, Bach and Handel, amongst others, but those are three of my personal favourites.

I hobbled back to the tent afterwards, and met up with Selwyn, who had indeed managed to get back in time to enjoy the performance. It was a very nice touch to have put the concert on. I made some more food and settled in for another cold night, thinking about how much kit I would bin from my rucksack before starting the run tomorrow, and thinking about a proper wash and a proper dinner tomorrow night. That buffet will be carnage when we get to it.

Saturday, 31st March 2007

Stage Seven

Final Stage: 11.7 km

Breakfast this morning was the winning combination of custard followed by mashed potato. After that, I binned the mess tin, the hexi stove, the remaining fuel tablets, and the few remaining items of food. I had spent the night knowing that this would be the last night sleeping in the field on this event, the last night of being dirty, of having to cook dehydrated food, of having to take a dump outside, and of being cold and having to sleep fully-clothed and retreating from the wind in my sleeping bag.

I packed away all of my kit, every now and again looking over to the sand dunes. The bivouacs had been left up today, as there was no rush to get them anywhere else to erect again. All I can do is get myself to those dunes as quickly as possible, because I will be walking the last six kilometres across the sand once I reach them. I hobbled over to the line with the others. I was a little concerned that Selwyn overtook me on the way. I really had stiffened up quite considerably. We had a briefing once again, and once again we just wanted them to hurry up so that we could get this final leg done and dusted. The atmosphere now suggests the idea that we have already completed the race; and we knew that everybody stood there at the line would be making it to the finish.

The race started and I crossed the line and tried to at least get myself up to a shuffle. The rucksack weighed next to nothing, but I was so tight that my speed was pathetic. It always took a little while to get into my pace, but today I only had a few kilometres before I would be slowed by the dunes, so I needed to be running fast now, and that was just not happening. I had gone from a shuffle to a good striding run yesterday, but now there was just nothing going on in my legs. I watched as some of the field extended their lead off towards the dunes, and were clearly managing far better than I was. Mark and John made their way past me to my right, which I was made aware of as Mark demonstrated his more caring and sympathetic nature: 'May I offer you a wheelchair?'

He probably had one in his bag.

With that, and using nothing but aggression (because physically I was in bits), I managed to gather a little more pace and moved past John, and then past Mark a little later. I saw Richard and Carlos on the other side of the field up ahead, but knew that they would be moving too fast for me to catch up with. I continued moving up the field, with some of the field not liking that very much and moving back past me, but on the whole I was making progress. Mark flew past me over to my right, and I could see that he was pulling out all of the stops for today. Nothing was going to slow him down on this one.

I reached the end of the plain and then we were running in lines through brush and tamarisk trees. Not long after that we reached the base of the dunes. For the first few dunes we were getting into the habit of passing each other again and again, according to which part of the dunes we found the easiest and which part we found the most difficult. I was walking fast, and some people were still up for going faster. Mainly, people with walking poles were flying, although on any other terrain they had generally been slower. Today did not really matter much for overall placing. With over a hundred and thirty miles behind us, the one to two hours to get through today were not going to add much to the overall ranking. I was contemplating checking hydration, and then waiting to see if John would catch up with me, when a familiar voice shouted out from behind: 'You lucky, lucky bastard!'

Excellent, he was here, doing well with his poles. It was great to see him, and I explained that I was tempted to wait to see if he was about. We evened out our pace and carried on through the dunes together. We probably did not need to wave our arms around as much as we did when we ran down the sides of the dunes, and shouting 'Wheeeeeee' was definitely unnecessary, but aside from annoying some continentals I think that it helped. After a while, we could see the next plain around the outskirts of the dunes, with indications of upcoming Merzouga, such as roads and small buildings, dotted about in those areas. After that, we saw people coming in the opposite direction, and a few people on dune buggies, all of whom had come in from Merzouga, either to explore the dunes or to see us heading towards the finish line. It could not be that much further along now.

We came up over a ridge and saw the small town ahead of us, and with each subsequent ridge, we found ourselves getting closer and closer as we kept a good and strong pace across the sand. Children had come out into the dunes to give us encouragement, and soon we could see supporters and families of some of the competitors, lining the top of a ridge a little further on. A couple of photographers at the top of the penultimate ridge were privileged to the sound of John and I whistling Monty Python's 'Always Look on the Bright Side of Life'.

John helped me to get my Union Jack off my rucksack, and we came over the last of the sand dunes to the cheers of other British supporters. We had agreed that it would be rude not to run the last dune, so off we went, cheered to the finish line by all the supporters around us. We arrived at the line to join the back of a queue of other competitors. We had to hand in our medical cards and then collect a packed lunch and a card with a bus number and time. So much for Jerusalem. We shook Patrick Bauer's hand and smiled for a photo. Then it was a stroll through the little town, one that would be expected in any such town in that part of the world, in which every child with something to sell tries to sell it to you, and everyone without asks if they can relieve you of your kit to sell it to somebody else. It was nice to think that there were no more runs to complete tomorrow, and that we had now reached the end of the 22nd *Marathon des Sables*. I dumped my kit in the luggage area under the coach, got on board, got comfy, and made a start on the lunch.

After six hours of the most dangerous coach driving I have ever witnessed, we made it back to Ouarzazate and walked on to the hotel. The lovely Oceane had informed us that we could take a Landy, but it was only a couple of minutes to the hotel from where the coach had stopped, so John and I decided to walk. I could not walk particularly fast, because I was carrying my Salomons in my hands, but still managed to run across the road, much to the dismay of the others hobbling along. In fact, they had been annoyed by our comparatively fast walking pace as well, but it was entirely due to the fact that I needed to get to the toilet. A real toilet at that.

I met Mark at the room. He had flown all the way to the finish line and had got in a little while before. I took my kit straight through to the bathroom, and began stripping off and putting everything into my rucksack. To pass the time, John and I had removed most of the strips of plaster covering our sores whilst on the coach, but there was still some left. Having removed a particular length of plaster on the coach, I had opened up a sore on my hips, and as I then peeled my boxers away from the skin in the hotel bathroom it started to bleed. Each time another length of Elastoplast or a plaster came off, I ran out to Mark to share my bemusement with him. My ankles had also swollen a lot from the coach journey, so they looked hilarious as well. I still could not bend the toes on my right foot. I climbed into the shower and managed, in only about ten minutes, to thoroughly rid myself of every grain of sand on or in my body. The only things left were remnants of the adhesive from the Elastoplast, but I could not scrub that away without opening up more cuts, so I decided to leave that for now.

I cleaned up and then put the rucksack into my suitcase. I would not open it or touch it until I was back in the U.K. I made a start on my chocolate, and shared some food with Mark as well, and washed it all down with a coke. And, contrary to all expectations, it actually tasted pretty good. I dressed myself in some clean clothes, and headed off for a walk around the shops outside the hotel. I was not able to find anything that grabbed me, aside from the staff, and so went back. I met up with the others in the restaurant, and made a start of clearing out the buffet. The fresh food, the meats and vegetables were like *manna from heaven*. The sight of the walking wounded had persisted to the hotel, and by now we were rating ourselves on how impressed we were with each other's walks. I had put on a stunning one which any Igor would have been proud of, but had to stop after I greeted someone coming towards me with genuinely the same tragic walk.

We ate, had a couple of drinks, and then headed back for a relatively early night. Climbing into one of the beds at this place was never an easy experience. They had been made up in such a way as to ensure that you could not actually get into them. Your first step before climbing in was to strip back all the sheets so that they lay loose over the bed. What was special about tonight was that I also had to gather the sheets and blanket above the level of my feet, as the pressure of any weight against them was uncomfortable. I could have thrown a pillow under them to aid their recovery, but as I have size 13s, I tend to think that just sleeping with my feet pointing up is sufficient for the toes to be raised. Every moment of getting comfortable in that bed was a pleasure. A clean sheet in place of a sleeping bag with sand in it was the first difference. A warm blanket, four walls and a ceiling was a pleasant second. A couple of soft, clean pillows in place of my rucksack was third. Carlos not snoring within earshot was fourth. As a show of solidarity, the flatulent half of tent 99 was very much represented in its entirety in this room though, but you cannot have everything. There was nothing that could stop this from being a beautiful night's sleep.

Recovery Phase

Sunday, 1st April 2007

Following a beautiful night's sleep, I got out of bed at 07:15. I had woken up earlier, but had stayed in bed for longer, primarily because *I could*. I went off to have breakfast, and met up with Richard and Carlos, along with some chaps from the RAF, and we discussed the possibilities for the 'next big thing'. The staff helping to prepare and serve the buffet were happy to see all of us competitors. They were also happy to help us pile the food up as high as we could. When I returned to the table there were comments that I had beaten one of the other lads in bringing the most back to the table. I explained that I tried getting some sausages on there as well, but they had kept rolling off the top. It took a couple of trips before I was satisfied. Again, the pleasure of fresh food was incomparable, save for yesterday's first shower. Everything just tasted better than I would have expected it to otherwise.

The main plan for today was to return the flares. You could not do this in England. 750 people could not walk around a town and into a hotel carrying signal flares. The things were lethal, as Carlos was attempting to show, and it was another one of those race oddities that you had to consider in the right perspective. Queuing to return the flares took a couple of hours, which did not make much sense at the time, and even when they were handed in I could not see the cause of the delay. One pleasure of the queue was that I was given an interview by a French journalist, much to the amusement of the some of the others, and I attempted to bring some sense of dignity to the occasion by adding that 'Carlos had been missing his daughter Lotti and sends his love'. Well, I thought that it was more meaningful than 'Running through the desert was hard work, funnily enough, but at least we all managed to relax in the evenings and tell nob gags'. We returned the flares in what was, in fact, a shop run by the organisers, selling various items of desert kit, running kit, and a CD of the music from the start of the stages. The CDs were surprisingly popular. I decided that I could live without the Ketchup song, and bought a desert jacket, a hip belt for water bottles, a shirt, and a long-sleeved T-shirt because according to Oceane, 'It matched my eyes' (I am so weak).

I checked the race results before leaving, to see that I had come in 277th overall, having run for thirty-six hours, forty-eight minutes and eleven seconds. The winner had come in at seventeen hours, twenty-five minutes and six seconds, so I was close. My quickest pace had been during the marathon stage, when I was running at just shy of 5 mph. My slowest was the fourth stage, at just over 3 mph. Those speeds do not take into account rest periods, and they were measured over horizontal ground 'as the crow flies', rather than taking into account changes in elevation and so on. Lahcen Ahansal had an average pace of about 8 mph for the entire race, which was phenomenal. 8 mph is a good running pace on any terrain, but this was his average over a course that included mountains and sand dunes, and this was his tenth consecutive win. I wonder if he will ever be gracious enough to let his brother win one year.

I was escorted back to the hotel by a group of French *controlleurs*, who told me about their reasons for coming out and volunteering to help in an event such as this. Amélie was from Paris, and saw the event as something awe-inspiring that it is just an amazing thing to be a part of. I think that was a key difference. As a competitor, I was feeling a little deflated now that it was over, and I was looking for the next big thing to focus on, but Amélie felt that it was enough just to be involved in something like this. I could imagine volunteering as part of training, or to learn something about the event prior to competing in it myself, but I doubt that I would ever want to tell my grandkids that 'I dished out water in the toughest footrace on earth'. It just seems to be lacking something. I think that there must be something in the fact that the vast majority of *controlleurs* were women. There was to be a presentation and various speeches back at the other hotel later that afternoon, and they invited me over, but as a Brit, I had been put off because it was reputedly boring, although we felt there might be other reasons for keeping the Brits away from the other competitors.

I met up with John and Selwyn and we spent the afternoon by the pool, drinking, eating and playing dice. I put my feet up and let the air get to them, and hoped that having them raised on a chair would help reduce the swelling and drain the blister on the side of my big toe. My feet were by no means aesthetically pleasing, but at least they were ready to heal. John took the opportunity to take a few photos; something nice for the album.

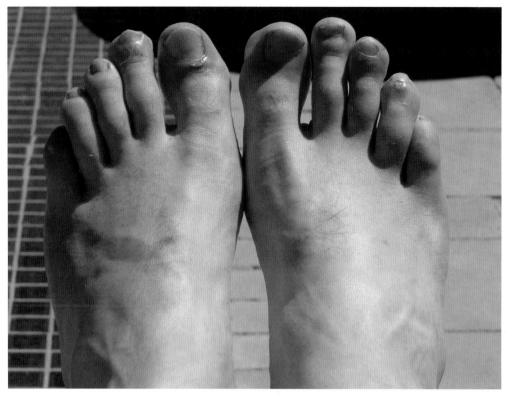

Well, slightly swollen, a tad more yellow in some parts than I would ordinarily like, and one or two blisters here and there, but otherwise; Perfik.

There were still plenty of walking wounded hobbling around the grounds. Suzi was fairing particularly badly, although a night of drinking and dancing had apparently been the primary antagonist for her current state, accepting that she must only have been able to dance having first anaesthetised herself with alcohol. We were later joined by Richard and Carlos, and later still by Mark. Having been nothing but supportive of each other across the desert, it all fell apart during a friendly game of dice. As the evening drew in and became cooler, we continued drinking in the bar until dinner, and would have stopped playing dice completely but for the fact that Carlos was 'playing for my soul', although there was no mention of what I would win if he lost. We all turned in for the night shortly after dinner. As far as recovery goes, we were doing very well for ourselves, and none of us were particularly worse for wear.

Monday, 2nd April 2007

I get up, shower and rush to get some breakfast in before heading to the coach. We leave shortly after 6 am to go to the airport. We were dreading the flight back since the flight out. It was so cramped that we could not imagine any comfort whatsoever since we were in bits after the race. But, contrary to earlier fears, the flight was as tolerable as it ever can be for someone over six feet tall. Well, I did manage to stub my blistered big toe under the seat, which cut into the nail and caused quite a bit of blood to make a mess of the place, but other than that it was fine, and at least it sorted out the blister.

Having arrived back at Gatwick, I picked up my luggage and said my goodbyes to the others, before jumping on a train back to London. It felt strange, because I had spent over a week surrounded by people all involved in the same event, and now with every step, the surrounding population was becoming more and more diluted. There were three of us on the same train. I walked from London Bridge to the flat, dropped off my kit and then headed off by foot to see the other half. That is it. I have now finished the race and made it back safely. It is all back to normal now. I see the people around me and know that they do not have a clue about the 'Marathon des Sables Finisher' T-shirt that I am wearing, nor why my feet look in relatively bad shape in my Karrimor sandals. I wonder if I will ever randomly bump into anyone from the race, or if I will ever see anyone that I recognise from the race again.

Wednesday, 2nd May 2007

It is now one month on since I returned to England following the race. I am able to run again properly, and I enjoy doing it, although I am not yet seriously training for that 'next big thing'. Three toenails came off after a couple of weeks, and there are a couple of others that will fall off soon enough. I met up with John and his missus for drinks in London, and we will be meeting up some more in the future; and I have been in email contact with Richard and Carl. Having been working before the race, to the point that my immune system was knackered and I really stopped enjoying what I was doing, I have since resigned. I will now work three days a week, whilst also working on my M.Phil. and Ph.D., and I will concentrate more on writing and developing my own business interests. I will also use the extra time to get back into doing the amount of training that I want to do. It was madness to put my work first, before my own health and happiness, and now I am prioritising things accordingly.

When my own business takes off, I will be working just as many hours, if not more, and that will be the same with my academic studies. The point, however, is that all of that will work around my own lifestyle, and it will be work that I truly enjoy doing and find rewarding. I think that it took that race to demonstrate to me how much I value doing my own thing and living the life that I want to. Perhaps next year I will have had little joy with my own business and I will be back to working for another company full-time, but I have to give this a try for now. Besides, next year I will be competing in another ultra-endurance event, and who knows what profound effect that will have on me?

The *Marathon des Sables* was an incredible experience and it is one that will live with me forever. I will remember the horrible food, the stones under my sleeping bag, and the wind blowing through the tent and clawing at my face in stage four. But mostly I will remember five awesome guys: Selwyn, Mark, Richard, Carl and John, the great laughs we had and the incredible camaraderie amongst all of the competitors in the camp. I will remember Ed, Graham, Owen, Tom, Lee, and Team Helmut, and various other guys whom I saw out on the course. I will remember climbing that nasty hill with Owen and Blake, walking the final leg of stage four with Graham, and crossing the finishing line with John. I will remember the landscapes, the moonscapes, and the searing open plains. And I will remember that deep down I loved every minute of it.

And at least I refrained from mentioning Speed Rimming or Dogging International (far less interesting than you might imagine).

Fact Sheet

The Legend of the Screaming Camel Spider

- The camel spider is not really a spider, it is a type of scorpion.

- The camel spider can run at 10 mph.

- It loves the shade, and will therefore run at 10 mph towards people that offer it, such as by standing around in the desert or putting up tents.

- If you try to take its shade away, such as by running, then it will chase after you.

- You will not be able to outrun it.

- It screams when it runs.

- The camel spider will suck your face off whilst you are asleep.

- The camel spider has a very nasty bite.

- It can grow to the size of a dustbin lid.

- They are called camel spiders because the large ones often hang under the bellies of camels and can only be seen when they lean back to look around for new shade.

- However large, the camel spider is often very difficult to spot, and its whereabouts is often only given away by its screaming as it runs.